# CREATING DATABASE-BACKED
## LIBRARY WEB PAGES
### Using Open Source Tools

STEPHEN R. WESTMAN

American Library Association

Chicago    2006

**Stephen Westman** is the Digital Information Services librarian at the University of North Carolina at Charlotte, where he has been since 2003. In that capacity, he is extensively involved in creating databases to organize and provide access to information on the Web. He has held similar positions at Georgia College and State University, the University of Texas at San Antonio, and the Ohio State University. Throughout his career, Westman has been very interested in information retrieval issues. He has worked extensively with databases for almost eighteen years, focusing for the last ten years on using relational databases to create Web pages and applications. In addition to his work in library technology, Stephen is also a trained musician, having studied at Michigan State University, the University of Michigan, Louisiana State University, and the University of Illinois at Urbana-Champaign, where he also earned his MS in Library and Information Science in 1990.

---

The paper used in this publication meets the minimum requirements of American National Standard for Information Sciences—Permanence of Paper for Printed Library Materials, ANSI Z39.48-1992. ∞

**Library of Congress Cataloging-in-Publication Data**

Westman, Stephen R.
   Creating database-backed library Web pages : using open source tools /
Stephen R. Westman. *150-8732*
      p.  cm.
   Includes bibliographical references and index.
   ISBN 0-8389-0910-8
   1. Library Web sites—Design.  2. Web databases.  3. Web site development.
   4. Open source software.  I. Title.
   Z674.75.W67 W47 2006
   006.7'6—dc22                                          2005022408

Printed in the United States of America

10   09   08   07   06        5   4   3   2   1

# Contents

To Phillip, who taught me how to listen to myself

# Foreword

Libraries are full of lists. Lists of books. Lists of magazines and journals. Videos. People. Internet resources. And so on. It can be a monumental task trying to manage all of them.

That's where the relational database comes in. In a digital environment, the relational database is the most efficient way to manage large lists of information, limiting the number of places you need to store data to one place. Make an edit there and the change ripples through your Web site, eliminating the need for you to touch every page. With their efficiencies in maintaining data, relational databases are well suited to the highly structured data of libraries.

The purpose of this book is to teach you about these databases and how they can be used to create database-driven Web sites. Written by a librarian for librarians, the methods and examples of this book should strike a chord with readers, making the learning process easier. The process is not easy, but it is no more difficult than learning the intricacies of the MARC record or the nuances of a particular bibliographic index.

In today's globally networked computer environment, people increasingly expect to interact with a library's collections and services through a Web browser. This means that libraries must maintain a Web presence, if not Web servers. Creating and maintaining small sets of static HTML files (perhaps a hundred) is not too difficult. On the other hand, when you start maintaining sets of thousands of pages, the process gets old pretty quickly. Moreover, the implementation of relational databases forces you to think very critically about the data being stored and reported upon. Thinking critically about data, information, and knowledge is a core characteristic of librarianship. It seems as if relational databases were made expressly for libraries and librarians.

This book will provide solutions to the challenges of maintaining lists of data in an era of globally networked computers. First, it describes in great detail what it means to design and maintain a relational database. Second, it demonstrates how to write computer programs, in the open source language PHP, against the relational database for the purposes of generating HTML pages and searching the database's content.

By exploiting these two techniques it is possible for a minimum of people, with an albeit diverse set of skills, to maintain large sets of data and distribute that data immediately and accurately on the Web. If you take advantage of the techniques described in this book, you likely will be able to drastically reduce the amount of time your team spends writing HTML. You and your library will be able to work more efficiently. Content specialists will be able to focus more on content, and infrastructure providers will be able to focus on access.

If there were two higher-level computer skills I could teach every librarian, the first would be designing and maintaining relational databases, and the second would be indexing. Each technology represents two sides of the same information retrieval coin. On one side is data maintenance, and on the other is searching and finding. This book fills a particular niche in Libraryland. Specifically, it provides a structured method for learning relational databases and applying them to the problem of maintaining large sets of HTML pages for a library Web site. In turn, this book empowers you to put into practice the principles of librarianship in a "webbed" environment.

The subtitle of this book, "Using Open Source Tools," represents a topic near and dear to my heart. Open source software is just as much about freedom as it is about computer technology. In fact, it uses computer technology to express freedom. These principles are not too far from the principles of modern librarianship, and therefore, the use of open source software is a natural fit for librarians. Information has never been free. As information professionals we understand this better than most people. There are real costs to collecting, organizing, archiving, and disseminating data, information, and knowledge. Despite these costs, you don't need your checkbook when visiting a library. The reasoning behind this is based on the belief that free access to the world's data and information will enlarge the sphere of knowledge and understanding. These same principles form the basis of open source software. It allows the individual or group to take control over hardware and software instead of the other way around. Open source software provides you with more choice and more opportunity. Just as we believe free access to data and information will expand the sphere of knowledge and better humanity, the free access to computer programs will enable us to expand our ability to use computers as tools to improve our lives, not become slaves to them.

As you read this book, Stephen Westman will make these themes more apparent. First, you will learn how to collect, organize, and disseminate your data, information, and knowledge in a digital, globally networked environment. Second, you will learn how to do this in an open source environment. A powerful combination. Read on and become empowered.

—Eric Lease Morgan

# Acknowledgments

For any large project to be successful a number of people need to be involved. This book is no exception. Many people have provided inspiration, support, helpful criticism, and encouragement.

First, I want to thank Judy Myers of the University of Houston Library. Throughout my fifteen years in ALA, Judy has served as a mentor, a coach, and a source of ideas, as well as a wise and gentle critic. It was through her that I became involved in my first major Web-based database project, well before such things were even talked about.

I also want to thank the staff at ALA Editions for their considerable help and patience in working with me on this project. In particular, I want to thank Laura Pelehach for her kindness and for being able to resolve problems with humor, grace, and incredible understanding. I also want to express my sincere gratitude to Helen Court for her wisdom, experience, patience, and expertise as copy editor of this volume. Her understanding of Web development was incredibly helpful in resolving knotty technical issues. In addition, I would like to thank Russell Harper for helping with the last-minute changes that are inevitable when dealing with open source software. His efforts are greatly appreciated.

I also want to acknowledge several others who have both encouraged and supported my explorations in this technology. They include Sue Tyner (my boss at the University of Texas at San Antonio), under whom I began working in this area and who encouraged my experimenting in it, and Michael Winecoff (my current supervisor), who not only read the book but has supported further work in this area. I also want to thank Ladd Hanson of the University of Texas at Austin, who first introduced me to Web-based database programming and who gave me my first taste of PHP.

I also want to thank those who have read various parts of the book and made good suggestions. Two people were especially helpful in reviewing early drafts of this book and helping me to clarify my ideas. One is my brother, Ronald Westman, from whom I got my first computer and who helped me overcome programming challenges that arose as I wrote this book. Another is Jeffrey Millman of Similarity Systems, who made many wonderful suggestions, pointed out issues with which I would need to deal, and helped me clarify my writing. I also would like to acknowledge Trisha Davis, Allison Pittman, Jonathan Champ, Jo Earle, and Michael Winecoff for reading drafts of the manuscript and making suggestions. Any problems with the contents of this book are due to my not listening.

I also want to express my gratitude to all who have provided ideas, suggestions, and support in the creation of the function file included in this book, especially Seth Hall (who helped to develop the initial code that served as a model for the current library), Jonathan Champ, and Ronald Westman. In particular, I would like to acknowledge the Ohio State University for their permission to use ideas and code that I developed in my work there to serve as the foundation for the creation of this library.

I would like to acknowledge the staff and my supervisors at the Ohio State University (Sally Rogers) and the University of North Carolina at Charlotte (Michael Winecoff) for allowing me to have the time needed to complete this task.

On a more personal level, I want to thank my family for their support and encouragement in a project that was far greater than I initially imagined it would be.

Last, but not least, I want to thank Janis for her wisdom, love, support, patience, and the incredible beauty that she has brought to my life.

# Chapter 1

# INTRODUCTION

Perhaps you've heard of others using databases on their Web sites, but are not sure how they are doing it. You understand that using databases can make site maintenance and data publishing much easier. However, you might be afraid that only extremely technically savvy people, or those able to hire such individuals, can do these things. This book is for you. It is intended for librarians who would like to try their hand at developing database-backed Web pages but are not sure where to start. I deal with a broad range of programming and other technical issues, approaches, and techniques, but I do not assume anything beyond a basic level of familiarity with HTML and the ability to create HTML forms. I explore such concepts as relational databases, Structured Query Language (SQL), data modeling, server-side scripting, "maintaining state," and user authentication. I explain each of these concepts in straightforward English within the framework of creating useful Web pages. Where more detail is needed, appropriate readings, Web sites, and other information sources are provided.[1]

The other part of this title—"Using Open Source Tools"—defines the second goal of the book: to introduce a very exciting and powerful way of developing and distributing software. In these times of expanding budget needs and shrinking revenues, the last thing we as librarians need to do is to spend large amounts of money on hardware and software to enhance our Web presence. The good news is that you can use open source tools to build a complete—and very powerful and dynamic—database-Web presence for the cost of a basic PC (say $1,000). In fact, using the information in this book along with the companion

1

materials available at http://www.ala.org/editions/extras/Westman09108, you too can become your own Webmaster using your own PC. In the process, you can strike a blow for truth, justice, and the library way!

I show you how you can take data from legacy systems and create searchable Web-based resources. I also step you through a complete database-backed Web project from initial concept through data modeling and database creation to programming and actual implementation. The code for creating the project is provided and explained. The idea is that, by using the information in this book, you will be able to start exploring this very useful and exciting world. Along the way, I examine possible pitfalls and problems you may encounter and provide alternative approaches to solving those problems.

Although I focus on open source tools, I concentrate as much on what is being done and why as on the specific details of how it is being done. The goal is to help you understand the process, and thus be able to apply it to whatever programming syntax and platform you choose.

Information for developers and library administrators overseeing this type of project is also provided. This includes the following:

- comparisons of various open source tools currently available
- programming and documentation procedures for the development process
- list of development standards
- forms and templates to define and implement a project of your own

Wherever administrative issues need to be addressed, I present information and recommendations that will enable you to deal with those issues.

The goal of this book is to acquaint you with all of the basic processes involved in creating database-backed Web applications, not to go into any great depth in any particular area. We will look at rather simple applications without a lot of advanced programming or design techniques. The thought is that, by learning the basics, you will be able to investigate any particular area of interest further. To that end, I include a bibliography of Web sites and books for further research in the online companion materials.

## ANOTHER BOOK ON DATABASES AND THE WEB?

Some of you may be asking, "With all of the books currently available that deal with database-backed Web pages, why another one?" This is a fair question. The quick answer is that this book is designed to be different in a number of ways:

I focus on the entire process rather than on individual aspects (such as coding, database design, and the like). Doing so will illuminate all aspects of this type of project.

I explain concepts using familiar, real-world terms and metaphors rather than technical language.

I write as a librarian and for librarians, using library terminology and explaining things with library-based examples and concepts.

I emphasize searching techniques and investigate ways to implement the types of searches that librarians have come to expect from their systems.

I provide information on good programming practices, documentation techniques, and process planning that can be useful to developers and library administrators.

I provide sample forms to help you get started, fully annotated source code for all sample applications, and a PHP programming library that gives you access to some rather advanced techniques and information on how you can use these resources to set up your own database/Web server on your PC.

After working through the examples in this book, you will have the tools with which to begin working in this most exciting area of Web publishing.

## WHAT ARE DATABASE-BACKED WEB PAGES?

The first thing to explain about database-backed Web pages is what they are. Right now you're possibly asking yourself: "Don't you write HTML pages using Web editors, such as Dreamweaver or FrontPage, and then transfer them to a Web server? What do databases have to do with publishing Web pages?"

The answer is that, although they differ in details, all database-backed Web pages are essentially Web-based reports. Many of you are already familiar with the reports (such as overdue notices) that your local online library system produces. You (or those who create your reports) write the programs that tell the system what pieces of information you want. The programs then respond to user input and

• search the database using the query designed into the report

• compile a list of information that matches the designated criteria

- take the data and format them using rules built into the program
- print the report

Web pages are no different in their basics in that they also search a database, embed the results within HTML tags, and output the results to a Web server.

## Approaches

### The Old-Fashioned Way

To begin understanding how database-backed Web pages work, let's look at how a typical Web page is retrieved. As shown in figure 1-1, the publisher (Web page creator), usually using Web-editing software of some kind, creates a file containing the data the user is intended to see, formats it using HTML (1) and places it on the Web server (2). A user who wants to view the information then clicks on a link to request the page (3), which sends a request (via a URL) for that particular page to the Web server (4), and the Web server retrieves that file (5, 6) and sends it to the browser (7) for viewing (8). Note that creating and retrieving are separate processes: the only time the information that the user sees changes is when the publisher edits the page and uploads it to the server.

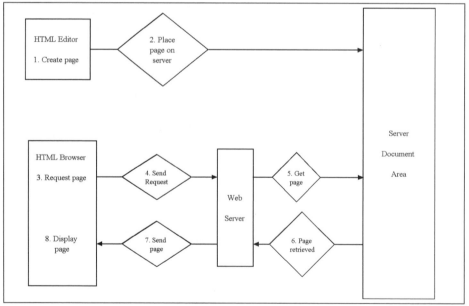

Figure 1-1

### Creating Static Web Page Reports

Database-driven information can be created two ways. In the first, as illustrated in figure 1-2, the publisher enters a query using Web report writing software (1) and the query is then sent to the database (2). The database is searched (3), the results are returned to the report writer (4), which then formats the results as a Web page (5). The publisher then transfers the file to the Web server (6), where the user retrieves it in the same manner as the Web page demonstrated in figure 1-1.

Here again, the process of Web page creation and page retrieval are discrete acts; once the HTML report has been written out and placed on the server, any changes to the database will not be reflected on the Web page until someone executes another report and places the new page on the Web server.

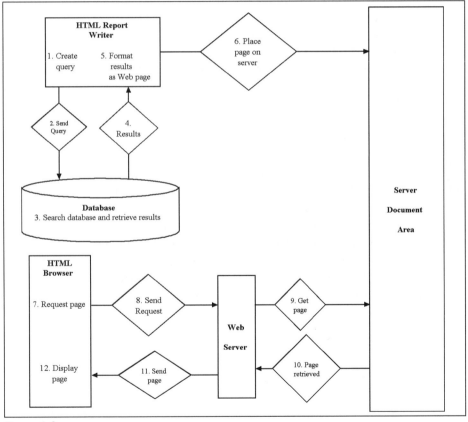

Figure 1-2

This approach can be appropriate with data that doesn't change very often and when only a few pages need to be maintained. If you need several database reports using the same data (such as new book lists organized by subject, author, publication dates, and holding library), you must create each one individually and republish each of them should the data in the database change. This is of course possible, but can be horribly inefficient in terms of time and energy.

### Creating Dynamic Web Page Reports

The alternative is to output the information "in real time" ("just in time" publishing, if you will). Rather than creating a static page that contains the information from the database the way it was when the publisher created it, the user receives a page that contains the contents of the database as it is at the time of the user request, thereby allowing the library to provide the most accurate and up-to-date information possible.

The process of creating a dynamic database-backed Web page is illustrated in figure 1-3. It is similar to that shown in figure 1-2, with one important difference. Once the programmer has written the program to search the database and to output the data as an HTML report, the only person involved in the Web page creation is the user, who initiates the process either by clicking on a link or by filling in a search form and clicking the **Submit** button (1). When this happens, the browser sends two types of information to the server: the name and location of the program that will create the report; and the parameters for that report (2).[2] The server then notes that the requested resource is a program (3) and it then calls the requested program and passes the appropriate parameters to it (4). The program takes the parameters and constructs one or more queries, opens a connection to the database (5), and passes the query or queries to it (6). The database then executes the requested search or searches and creates a retrieval set (7), which it then passes back to the program (8), where the results are formatted as an HTML document (9). The resulting Web page is then returned to the Web server (10), which treats it as a Web page (11) and passes it back to the browser (12), where it is displayed (13).

For this process, you need three things:

1. A database—some way to store the data in a structured manner that will allow for retrieval and output. We will deal with databases in chapters 2, 3, and 6.
2. A program or application—the means to create and pass the user's request to the database and format its output to HTML. We will take a look at these in chapters 4, 5, and 7–10.

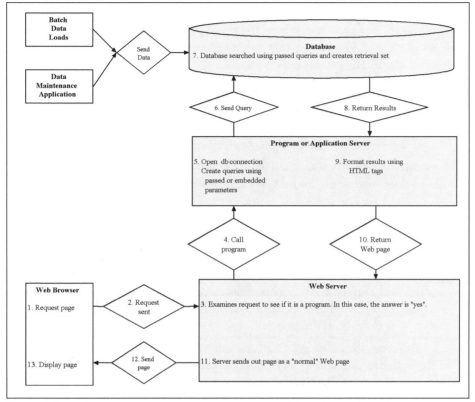

Figure 1-3

3. A Web server—to mediate between the user (Web browser) and the application server or program. In the bibliography, I provide links to a number of sites that provide information on how to set up your Web server. Also, I show you how to configure your Apache/MySQL/PHP installation to use the examples provided in the book in Setup.pdf.

## WHAT CAN DATABASE-BACKED PAGES BE USED FOR?

One of the first things we need to look at is when the use of a database is appropriate. Although it certainly is the latest news in Web publishing, a database is neither a silver bullet nor a tool that can be used in all contexts. There are times when a plain HTML page is a more appropriate approach. We therefore need to ask, "When should I use a database for my Web publishing?" Although it is difficult to provide hard and fast rules, there are certain guidelines that may help. In general, databases can be useful where

*Data are made up of discrete pieces of information about persons or things.* That is, items are described with individual metadata elements. One example is a page with Web sites containing at least three such elements: name, URL, and description.

*Data are highly and regularly structured.* That is, the information has a defined structure that repeats throughout the data. Examples include address and new book lists.

*Information changes often or reuse of the same data in a variety of contexts is desirable.* Using a database permits input/edit screens that make keeping information up-to-date much easier. They also allow you to enter once and use many times. For example, a list of personnel could be used to populate a telephone list, departmental contacts, and the basis for a password file to protect sensitive or otherwise restricted resources.

*You wish to search on discrete elements within the data.* By structuring data, databases make it possible to search and display data as requested by a user. One such example is being able to search a new book list based on subject, author, or date of publication.

On the other hand, databases—particularly the type with which we will be dealing—are not well suited for pages that

*Are very complex and have significant amounts of textual data.* Being highly structured critters, databases don't handle certain types of complexity well. Pages that include many different types of data from a variety of sources and formats may not fit well into a database structure.

*Contain hierarchically organized data.* XML documents, such as TEI documents and EAD finding aids, are not necessarily good candidates for a database (at least for public searching/outputting).[3]

*Are more document-like and require specialized layout.* To take one example, due to their prose-like nature and often specialized layouts, departmental information pages would require significant programming to meet the needs of users.

Time does not permit an exhaustive look at projects that libraries have undertaken. However, I provide a list of sites and articles in the bibliography that contain articles and pointers to various types of sites currently using databases to produce Web pages.

## OPEN SOURCE SOFTWARE

As noted, one of the major goals of this book is to provide an introduction to open source tools. The open source movement is one of the most exciting developments in software in years. Using a model of cooperation and sharing, rather than competition and profit, open source licensing allows users to freely (most of the time) download and to modify and redistribute software without incurring licensing costs.[4] The advantages of such an approach are many and powerful:

Open source provides an extremely low-cost alternative to commercial systems. Using the software tools provided here—along with an open source operating system such as Linux, FreeBSD, or OpenBSD—one can set up a fully functioning Web infrastructure essentially for the cost of an average computer workstation or personal computer.[5]

Open source tools are usually cross-platform and can run on all forms of Unix (including Linux), various flavors of Windows, and increasingly on Macintosh OS X. Thus, any application you develop can be moved to other platforms, should your computing infrastructure change down the road.

Open source products are extremely powerful and provide most—if not all (and in some cases more)—functionality that one can find in commercial products.

Product development is undertaken by individual developers rather than a central commercial entity. Because source code is freely available and modifiable, anyone with the interest and skills is free to do so. This means that, particularly on more popular products such as those detailed here, new features and bug fixes can be added very quickly. In addition, because the source code is available, the user can modify it to do whatever is needed, rather than submit enhancement requests that may or may not be honored.

Open source programs are extremely popular. In fact, the tools used in this book are among the most popular applications—commercial or open source—on the Internet. For example, Apache is running on almost fifty-two million sites (71 percent of all Web servers—more than three times as many sites as Microsoft's Internet Information Server); MySQL is active on more than five million sites with thirty-five thousand downloads daily; and PHP is running on just over twenty-two million domains.[6] This popularity translates into (1) a robust aftermarket of books on these tools, (2) a large number of users with whom you can network to obtain support, (3) a large support base to fix problems and bugs as they arise, and (4) a large number of applications and code libraries available for use in your projects.

Another reason the open source movement is valuable to librarians is the number of similarities between it and librarianship:

Both seek to make their product, be it programs or information, as freely available as possible.

Both are based on a collaborative philosophy, not dissimilar to peer review, in which cooperation rather than profit-seeking and a group approach to developing the product and solving problems are fundamental tenets.

Both seek to disseminate information in such a way that it furthers the quality and diversity of the products and services they provide.

Both seek to empower the user rather than maintain centralized control of development and distribution.

## STRUCTURE OF THIS BOOK

This book is divided into three sections. We first focus on data management tools and techniques. Chapter 2 explores the data storage options, focusing on relational database management system (RDBMS) technologies. We will explore how an RDBMS works and the features it provides; briefly examine Structured Query Language (SQL), the standard language used to interact with RDBMSs; look at features provided by RDBMS products; and briefly look at the various open source alternatives for relational database systems. In chapter 3, we look at what is involved in setting up a database within an RDBMS, using MySQL as our product. In undertaking this task, we will be using another open source product—phpMyAdmin—as our graphical MySQL management tool. I will show you how to create and define a database and its constituent tables; load data into the database; enable database security by creating user accounts; and discuss some of the issues you will encounter in database management.

In the second section, we look at the process of creating programs to search and output data from the database. In chapter 4, I introduce programming (I hope painlessly). My approach is to use a cooking metaphor to introduce the concepts you need to know. In using the familiar to explain the unfamiliar, it is my hope that some of the angst normally associated with programming might be avoided. I conclude by showing you how to "program" the cooking of one of my favorite dishes: *Shrimp Étouffée*. Once we have these basics down, we proceed to chapter 5, where I walk through the creation of a variety of reports you can use to output data from your database. Because searching is an intrinsic part of the process, I also introduce you to basic searching applications.

The third section covers the creation of a complete database-backed Web application. In chapter 6, I address planning issues, data modeling, and database design. This includes forms and grids you can use to gather the information needed to create robust applications. Chapter 7 takes the gathered information and shows how it can be used to create an application. This application will include pages to add, edit, and delete records as well as how to create a front-end to enable end-user searching. which I cover in chapter 9. I also discuss user authentication and security in chapter 8, searching techniques in chapter 9, application development issues in chapter 10, and a number of other topics throughout.

I also provide two forms of supplementary information. First are three appendices:

> a recipe for shrimp étouffée in both traditional and programmed format
>
> programming standards used to create the examples in this book
>
> a glossary of terms

Second are the companion files and resources available online at http://www .ala.org/editions/extras/Westman09108. These include a bibliography of useful resources and updates for this book.

A download file containing numerous types of documents and resources is also available. These include

> *Setup.pdf*—various aspects of setting up the environment used in this book
>
> *Fully annotated source code*—for all example apps and scripts, in ASCII and PDF format

*ala_functions*—a library of programming code (functions) used in this book, in ASCII and PDF format

*Functions_Guide.pdf*—an introduction to these functions

*Data and configuration files*—to set up your own database/Web server applications

*Project planning forms and grids*—used in chapter 6, in Word and Excel format

Throughout this book, I will refer to a variety of PDF files that contain information, examples, and other types of resources. Copies are included in the download file.

## DEVELOPMENT ENVIRONMENT AND TOOLS IN THIS BOOK

All the tools used in this guide are open source. Among their advantages are that they are nicely priced (free for noncommercial use), cross-platform (they run on Windows, Linux, Unix, and Mac OS X), and extremely feature-filled and powerful.

Apache is the world's most popular and widely used Web server. In addition, Apache also incorporates a highly modular design that makes it very easy to integrate other modules and capabilities as needed, something that is very important with the other tools we will be using here.

MySQL is a relational database system (RDBMS) originally created in Sweden that moved to open source licensing in 2000. Both extremely fast (matched only by Oracle) and easy to use, it is the most popular open source database server for Web-based applications.

PHP is a scripting language that integrates with Apache to allow you to embed short bits of programming code directly into HTML-like files. It also has a number of products, libraries, and third-party written applications that can make development easier (or be scavenged for code).

PhpMyAdmin is a PHP-based GUI (graphical user interface) tool that greatly facilitates the administration of MySQL databases. This product will be discussed in more detail in chapter 3.

I also provide programming code created especially for this book to facilitate Web application development. This code, named ala_functions.php, is in fact a collection and is available for download as part of the online companion materials. The file includes instructions on how to set this environment up for yourself on your own computer so that you can work through the exercises in this book.

## TYPOGRAPHICAL CONVENTIONS USED IN THIS BOOK

`This font` is used for code, including field, record, and table names as well as arrays, commands, functions, and variables.

**This font** is used for grid, interface, and menu elements and names.

### Notes

1. The focus of this book is not on providing a complete compendium of every technique and task you might want to undertake. However, I try to provide you with a solid conceptual understanding of database-backed Web pages—an understanding that will allow you to approach other books—such as those in the bibliography available as part of this book's online companion materials—and have an understanding of how to include them in your project.
2. In the form, program name is included as the `action` attribute of the `<form>` tag and the parameters are the names of the various inputting boxes, lists, and checkboxes. In the link, the URL consists of the program name and the parameters are listed at the end as a list of name and value pairs, such as search.cgi?Author=Faulkner&Title=Sanctuary. We go into greater detail on this in chapter 5.
3. Ronald Bourret's *XML and Databases*, cited in the bibliography, provides an interesting and useful distinction between data-centric and document-centric information, the former being much more amenable to relational database technology.
4. There are some copyright and licensing restrictions on certain open source tools, usually restricting the types of copyright restrictions that can be placed on modified code or limiting free use of the package to noncommercial applications. If you want to redistribute the application or use it in work for hire, consult the licensing agreement that comes with the open source tool or tools you are using.
5. If this is to be used in a production environment, you will also need to provide backup and other systems support services.
6. "Webserver Survey," Netcraft, http://news.netcraft.com/archives/2005/12/02/december_2005_web_server_survey.html. Company Fact Sheet, *MySQL*, http://www.mysql.com/company/factsheet.html; Usage stats, *PHP*, http://www.php.net/usage.php.

# 2 DATABASE BASICS

Now that we have an idea of how database-backed Web pages and applications work, let's look under the hood. We begin by examining how we can use databases to store and retrieve data. Although I will be throwing about a lot of technical terms such as Structured Query Language, setting relations, and normalization, my goal is to take some of the mystery out of such words and phrases (see glossary). The concepts they describe are not that complicated and many are quite familiar to librarians (albeit under different names). Understanding them will not only make the rest of this book easier to follow, but also allow you to impress your friends and confound your critics as you talk about "normalizing your data model to ensure its referential integrity."

Here we will look at some essentials of database management systems. We begin by exploring various approaches to storing and retrieving data, focusing in particular on relational database management systems (RDBMS). We then examine elements of database structures and modeling and see how we can use them to design solid databases for use in our Web applications. After that, I introduce you to Structured Query Language (SQL) and show how we can use it to interact with databases. I then present some of the techniques RDBMSs provide for ensuring data integrity and security. We finish up by discussing various open source database implementations currently available.

## DATA MANAGEMENT APPROACHES

Although data management techniques may come in many shapes, sizes, and colors, they all have one basic characteristic in common: they structure the information that they store.[1] To paraphrase a maxim: "a place for every datum and every datum in its place." Putting each piece of data in its own unique and identifiable cubbyhole allows programs to find and display it when requested. You can take two approaches to structuring data: structured text files and database management software. We look at both approaches.

### Structured Text Files

A delimited text file is an ASCII file in which we store data, placing a delimiter (specific character) between each piece of information (field) that we want to store. This effectively tells a program where one field ends and the next one begins. A delimited text file is similar to a spreadsheet, in which each row (or record) represents a single thing (book, or person, for example) and each row has a number of fields (title, author, and the like) separated from each other by the delimiter. You then write programs in languages such as Perl that will parse the data (break them down into their constituent components) and look through those components to find and output the information contained in these files.[2]

In creating delimited text files, you need to observe three rules:

1. The character used for the delimiter must appear only as a delimiter and must not be one used within the data. Otherwise the program, when encountering that character within a field, will assume that the text after the character is a new field—clearly not what you intend.
2. Each line (record) within the file must have the same number of fields. Because computers need to find information in predictable places, if a certain piece of information is not available, you must still add a delimiter to create an empty field to hold that piece of data's place, just as you would do with a spreadsheet.
3. Each line (record) must have its pieces of information in the exact order as every other record within the text file.

In this example, we are creating a text file phone directory comprising three fields (elements of information): `name`, `email address`, and `phone number`. Into this file, we place the name, e-mail address, and telephone number of three people. In building the file, we decide that the first field will always be the name, the second field will always be the e-mail address, and the third will always be the phone number. If we use the pipe (vertical bar) character as our delimeter, our resulting file would look like this:

```
Smith, John|jsmith@mylib.net|555-1212

Doe, July|jdoe@mylib.net|555-2121

Jones, Fred||555-3123
```

Note that Fred does not have an e-mail address. Rather than ignoring that field altogether, we hold its place with a delimiter character in the appropriate spot. If we follow the rules we established in the previous paragraph, programs using this data will assume that the second field is the e-mail address. If we don't add the placeholder, the phone number (555-3123) would be in the e-mail record's position and there would then be no field to represent the phone number.

### Comma-Separated Values

Probably the most commonly used delimited text file format is comma-separated values (CSV). It is used by programs such as Microsoft Access and Excel as one way of exporting and importing data. CSV files have quotation marks around each field and a comma separating the fields. A CSV version of our example above would look like this:

```
"Smith, John","jsmith@mylib.net","555-1212"

"Doe, July","jdoe@mylib.net","555-2121"

"Jones, Fred","","555-3123"
```

Although CSV files are very popular, they do have one drawback: they are built more for traditional database data—such as personnel and payroll systems—than for the more textual type of information librarians deal with. In particular, the use of quotation marks as an end-of-field indicator raises a question. "What if the data has a quote within it?" Remember that the delimiting character or characters should not appear in the data being represented in the file. Placing data with quotation marks within the data in a CSV file can create serious problems during processing. Although there are ways to get around this difficulty, the limitation essentially means that, if you have data you want to transmit from one system to another that contains quotation marks, you will probably need to find another technique for transferring it.

## Database Structure

On the one hand, using text files requires low overhead in terms of their creation and storage. On the other, it demands that the developer write a search engine to extract information. This approach may work well for simple applications, but it quickly breaks down as information becomes more complex or searching requirements become more sophisticated. The alternative is to use database management software. Such systems not only provide structure to the data, making it easier to search and retrieve data, but they also provide tools to facilitate searching, data maintenance, and system security.

Systems vary wildly in capabilities, size, and characteristics, but most database programs have certain structures in common. These include

*Database.* The basic container in a database management system, a database contains the table or tables in which we place our data.

*Table.* Similar to the delimited file, a table is the base unit within a database that contains the actual data. Tables generally store information on a specific and (if the database is well structured) unique[3] entity (concept), such as books, authors, orders, and such.

*Record.* The structure within tables that contains descriptions of individual instances of the entity that the table in question represents, records are the database equivalent of the rows in the delimited file.

*Field.* Database fields are the individual parts of the record that describe specific aspects of the entity being represented in an individual record (such as the individual elements contained between the vertical bars above).

*Index.* Just as books contain indexes to help you find information quickly, database systems create similar indexes that facilitate quick and easy retrieval of information from the database. Some types, such as UNIQUE indexes, can enforce certain rules about data entry. We will look at different types of indexes later in this chapter.

Database products come in many shapes and sizes. Let's now take a look at some of the more popular types and see how they relate to Web publishing.

### Single-Table, Fixed-Field

Database programs that store all information in a single table were very popular in early PC database and information managers. Packages such as PC-File and VP-Info provided a quick and inexpensive way of maintaining simple information collections, such as address lists and phone numbers. Unfortunately, a number of problems limited their usefulness:

> Data in one database created using these packages were inaccessible to any other database.

> Each record was required to contain all possible fields. In most cases, these were fixed length, which meant that it took up the same amount of space on the disk whether the field contained any data or not. Both features meant an often inordinate amount of duplicated information, wasted space, and unused space.

> Customized data entry screens were generally not an option.

> Few if any of these programs are Web aware. To use the data in such systems, you need to extract their information and load it into a Web-aware database.[4]

## Personal Bibliography

Similar to single-table databases, what is known as personal bibliography software has been extremely popular in the library community for a number of years. These packages use variable length fields, which take only as much space as is necessary to store the data. They still have the drawback of using only a single table, but have been invaluable in helping users create bibliographies, pathfinders, and a world of information support tools. Examples include Notebook II, ProCite, EndNote, and LibraryMaster. Such products are beyond the scope of this book, but several tools mentioned in the bibliography can assist you in publishing data from these programs on the Web.

## Personal Information Managers

A type of application very popular in the 1990s, PIMs (as they were called) allowed you to place all sorts of different kinds of unstructured data into the application, including numeric, date, and textual materials. They would then allow you to do a free text search through the database to find the information you needed. Again, as with personal bibliography software, we do not deal with these applications here but tools to help you place such information on the Web are included in the bibliography.

## Relational Databases

Based on the research of E. J. Codd and others, relational database management systems (RDBMS) were first developed in the 1970s. In its simplest form, this approach focuses on efficient storing, searching, and retrieving. Data are broken into separate concepts or components (tables) associated by a series of relationships. RDBMS applications are extremely powerful and flexible. Because of this, they are used throughout the Web, from simple applications to integrated library systems and massive online financial systems.

### Object-Oriented Databases

At the cutting edge of database technology, object-oriented database management systems (OODBMS) have made quite a splash in some quarters. The idea is that data, rather than being stored in records, are stored as objects (individual data elements) that can be brought together on the fly by the calling program. Early OODBMS were difficult to program for and to use. They are becoming more readily usable, but are really designed for large-scale applications, involve complex programming techniques and languages, and provide much more power and complexity than is required by the average library-created application.[5]

### XML Databases

Another new type of database product is the XML database. Designed to store and to search/output XML documents using XPath or XQuery statements (or both), these programs are able to maintain the internal structure of XML documents and serve them up as needed. Their capacity to store and search hierarchically structured data make them well adapted to dealing with such library-based resources as EAD finding aids and TEI-encoded documents. Although there are a number of open source tools—such as eXist and Xindice—available, they address a different set of problems from those we deal with here and we will therefore not cover them.

### MARC Systems

Before proceeding, I would like to briefly discuss the MARC record format and the possible confusion it may create in our later discussions. Some earlier library systems did store their records in something approaching MARC format, but later systems usually do not. Although MARC is used to transfer records into and out of these systems, the way that the data are stored internally is quite different from the single-record MARC screen we have come to know and love. In fact, a growing number of systems are actually using relational database management systems—usually Oracle or Sybase—as their underlying database technology to store the data. Then, when a particular record is requested, these systems use programs to retrieve the data elements from wherever they reside and reconstruct a single MARC record on the fly for display to the user.

It is important to keep this distinction in mind as we proceed through this book. There may be times when the metaphor of the MARC record—which on the surface runs counter to many of the foundation principles of relational database design—may cause some confusion. Examples include the concepts of repeatable fields and subfields, and the idea of storing all data in a single record. In such cases, it may be helpful to remember the distinction between how the information is presented (as a MARC record) on the screen and how it is actually stored in the system.

## RELATIONAL DATABASE MANAGEMENT SYSTEMS

To show how RDBMSs structure data, let's take a look at the differences between an RDBMS product (which is relational) and a single-table database (which is not). We begin by examining how we might use a single-table database to create a checkout system for books. Such a table might look like figure 2-1. As you can see, if a person were to want to check out five books, the system would need to update five records (one for each book), putting the same `patron name`, `patron address`, `patron city`, `patron state`, `patron zip code`, `patron phone number`, and `patron email address` into each record. Talk about wasted time, effort, and disk space (to say nothing of possibility for errors)! Wouldn't it be a lot easier to put the patron information into one place and then point to it when needed?

This is exactly what relational databases permit you to do. Rather than entering that information over and over again, you merely create a second table—a `patrons` table—where information on the patron is kept. When a patron checks out a book, you place a pointer to the `patron` record inside the `books` table. Then, by looking at the book record, you can follow the link back to the `patrons` table to see who has it checked out (see figure 2-2). This is known as linking or setting a relation—a concept we will explore later in this chapter.[6]

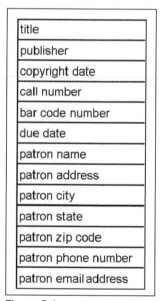

| title |
| publisher |
| copyright date |
| call number |
| bar code number |
| due date |
| patron name |
| patron address |
| patron city |
| patron state |
| patron zip code |
| patron phone number |
| patron email address |

Figure 2-1

| patrons | | | |
|---|---|---|---|
| Field | Data Type | Size | Key |
| patron_id | Character | 40 | P |
| first_name | Character | 40 | |
| last_name | Character | 40 | |
| address | Character | 50 | |
| city | Character | 50 | |
| state | Character | 50 | |
| zip | Character | 10 | |
| email | Character | 50 | |

| books | | | |
|---|---|---|---|
| Field | Data Type | Size | Key |
| title | Character | 100 | |
| publisher | Character | 100 | |
| patron_id | Character | 12 | F |
| due_date | Date | | |
| call_number | Character | 12 | |
| copyright_date | Date | | |

Figure 2-2

Let's now take a look in some more detail at how relational database systems are put together.

## Tables and Records and Links, Oh MY!

Relational database management systems store information in multiple tables with each table representing a separate logical entity (concept) within the database. For example, in a library system, you can have a books table, a publishers table, a subjects table, and so on. For each individual entity within the database, a separate table will be created. There are two reasons why this is good. First is that information on a given entity is stored in only one place. Second is that, by keeping entities separate from each other, it allows the same information to be used in multiple ways. For example, a patron's list could be used to check out books, create a searchable phone directory, build a mailing list, or authenticate users for a library proxy server. Placing this information inside a books record would make this reuse virtually impossible.

Having broken down our information into separate tables, we need to find a way to bring them together as needed. We do this by creating links (relations) between the records that in turn link the various tables. Tables are linked through what are called primary/foreign key pairs—a pair of fields, one in each table, that share a common value. We set relations—as in the example above—by taking a unique value (primary key) from a field in one entity and placing it in a corresponding field in another record in another table (foreign key) so that a link is established between the two records.

For example, in figure 2-2 we place the `patron_id` (primary key) from the `patrons` table into the `patron_id` (foreign key) field in the `books` table for the records that the user wishes to charge out. Then, when we later want to know what books a person has checked out, we look up the name, find out the person's `patron_id`, and then search for all of the `books` records that have that value in the `patron_id` field in the `books` table.

As noted, a primary key is a unique value in a record (the value doesn't appear in that primary key field in any other record in that table) that is used to identify that—and only that—record.[7] In our figure 2-2 example, the `patron_id` in the `patrons` table is the primary key for that table (hence, the P in the **key** column). Just as all U.S. citizens need a social security number to identify them, so tables need primary keys to identify an individual record in the database.

Foreign keys, on the other hand, are fields in one table into which the primary key of another table has been placed, thereby linking records in the two tables with this common piece of information. Because you may have multiple records in one table that point to a single primary key record in another table (patrons may have more than one book checked out, for example), foreign keys are not required to be unique. Thus, in our example, the `patron_id` in the `patrons` table (or `patrons.patron_id`) is the primary key and the `patron_id` field in the `books` table (or `books.patron_id`) contains the foreign key.[8]

One way to look at this is to think of the primary key as a surrogate (or, if you will, a database telephone number) for the record that contains it. As new linked records are added to the system, the database gives this phone number to the new record (placing it in the foreign key field) saying, "If you need this information, call this number."

In looking at figure 2-2, note that the arrow points from the `books` table to the `patrons` table, even though we spoke about taking the `patron_id` from the latter and placing it in the former. This is because the function of the arrow is not to indicate the direction of movement of the linking information, but to show where a field containing such information is pointing.

In the next pages, we will be talking about some of the essentials of data modeling—the process of taking the pieces of information that you want to include in your system and structuring them in a way that will make storage and retrieval of that data more efficient. Although this is a rather cursory treatment of the subject, we will be going into greater depth in chapter 6.

## Tables and Fields

In general, we will be using three types of tables in our applications in this book. Please note that these distinctions may sometimes blur in that a table may serve multiple purposes in a complex application:

*Data tables* are the primary bearers of information within a database. They contain the information content that your application wishes to store and make available.

*Linking tables* define many-to-many relationships, that is, when we have multiple records in one table that are to be related to multiple records in another. We will discuss these in more detail.

*Lookup (or authority) tables* restrict the set of values for a field to a predefined list stored in the table, such as the state abbreviations allowed by the U.S. postal service.[9] We will use these extensively in our programs in later chapters.

## Setting Relations

In establishing links between them, there are generally three types of relationships that can exist between tables:

*One-to-one.* A record in one table is related to only one record in another table. This usually is done where information in the second table amplifies information contained in the first table or where, for security purposes, certain fields have been placed in a table with more restrictions on access. For example, in a personnel system, you may wish to keep public information on an employee (name, phone number, office number) separate from more sensitive information (SSN, salary, job performance rating, and the like). One-to-one tables allow that.

*One-to-many.* A record in one table may be related to multiple records in a second table. In our example above, one book may be checked out by only one person, but one person may have many books checked out.

*Many-to-many.* Multiple records in one table are related to multiple records in another table. Again using our online library system example, a single `book` table record may be linked to multiple `subject` table records and a single `subject` table record may be linked to multiple `book` table records.

Let's take a look at each of these types in some more detail.

ONE-TO-ONE   In general, one-to-one relationships are used with subset tables—tables that contain information that provide additional information on the subject in the primary data table. Figure 2-3 shows how this can be done using a one-to-one relationship.

We create a separate `patron_private_information` table and define additional fields to hold that information. Included in those fields is a `patron_id` field that will be linked to the `patron_id` field in the `patrons` record by having the `patrons.patron_id` primary key placed in it. In figure 2-4, we can see what this would look like with filled-in fields.

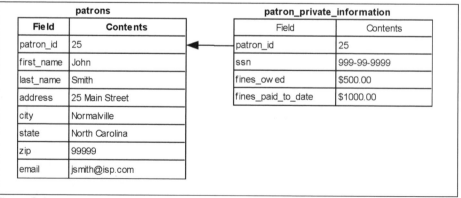

**patrons**

| Field | Type | Size | Key |
|---|---|---|---|
| patron_id | Character | 40 | P |
| first_name | Character | 40 | |
| last_name | Character | 40 | |
| address | Character | 50 | |
| city | Character | 50 | |
| state | Character | 50 | |
| zip | Character | 10 | |
| email | Character | 50 | |

**patron_private_information**

| Field | Type | Size | Key |
|---|---|---|---|
| patron_id | Character | 12 | F |
| ssn | Character | 11 | |
| fines_owed | Number | 8 | |
| fines_paid_to_date | Number | 8 | |

Figure 2-3

**patrons**

| Field | Contents |
|---|---|
| patron_id | 25 |
| first_name | John |
| last_name | Smith |
| address | 25 Main Street |
| city | Normalville |
| state | North Carolina |
| zip | 99999 |
| email | jsmith@isp.com |

**patron_private_information**

| Field | Contents |
|---|---|
| patron_id | 25 |
| ssn | 999-99-9999 |
| fines_ow ed | $500.00 |
| fines_paid_to_date | $1000.00 |

Figure 2-4

ONE-TO-MANY   One-to-many relationships are essentially the same as one-to-one relationships except that a record in one data table may be linked to multiple records in the other table or tables. It involves placing the primary key of your main record into the foreign key field of multiple foreign records.

In figure 2-5, we see an example of this type of relationship. Here we have a **books** table where we store information about printed materials in our collection. Assuming for the moment that a book can have only one publisher, we create a separate table for publisher information. We can use this table to store information about the publisher, such as address, phone number, and the like. Then, when we enter a book into the system, we select the correct publisher from that list and store its primary key as a foreign key in the **books** table.

This type of relationship can be very useful in creating database applications. As we will see later, it allows us to create authority tables, which enforce uniform entry of information and which end users can use to select from when searching a database.

MANY-TO-MANY   As noted, one side of a relationship must always be unique, identifying one and only one record. However, data do not always work that way. Many times a single record in table A may point to multiple records in table B and vice versa. The question then becomes how you can create this type of relationship.

The answer is by creating a third (or linking) table that takes the primary keys from the **books** and **subjects** tables and stores them in foreign key fields in the third table. Then when we need to find associated information, we follow

publishers

| Field | Type | Size | Key | Value |
|---|---|---|---|---|
| publisherno | Integer | 1 | P | 10 |
| publisher | Character | 100 | | Bill's Publishing House |
| address | Character | 100 | | 25 Main Street |
| city | Character | 100 | | Hometownville |
| state | Character | 2 | | Utah |
| zip_code | Character | 10 | | 98789 |
| phone | Character | 12 | | 555-555-5555 |

books

| Field | Type | Size | Key | Value |
|---|---|---|---|---|
| author | Character | 100 | | Doe, John A |
| title | Character | 100 | | Php for Fun & Profit |
| publisher_no | Character | 100 | F | 10 |
| copyright | Character | 4 | | 2005 |
| pages | Integer | | | 1050 |

Figure 2-5

the primary_key -> secondary_key/secondary_key -> primary_key chain to find that information.

Let's see how this works. Using figure 2-6 as an example, let's say the person has chosen to search for a particular Library of Congress Subject Heading (LCSH). The system needs to

1. Find the primary key (`subject`) for the desired LCSH entry in the `lcsh` field.
2. Collect all records in the linking table that have that value as the linked foreign key (`books_subjects_links.subject`).
3. Find out what the `books_subjects_links.bib_no` is for each `books_subjects_links` record retrieved.
4. Use the information it has gathered to retrieve the record for each number it finds where that value can be found in `books.bib_no`.

For each subject that is assigned to a book, a new `books_subjects_links` record is created, placing the value from `bib_no` field in the linking table's `bib_no` field and placing the subject into the linking table's `subject` field. A program can then follow these links from `books` -> `books_subjects_links` -> `subjects` to see what subjects have been assigned to the book as well as going the other direction to see which books have used a given subject heading.

Figure 2-7 shows a variation on this theme—one that provides a more correct way of handling the basic book checkout system presented in figure 2-2. Note several things about the graphic. First, the list has been divided into three separate entities, each of which has its own table: `books`, `checkouts`, and `patrons`. Second, there are three types of tables: data (`books`), authority (`patrons`), and linking (`checkouts`), the linking table—checkouts—defining an intersection (relation) between `books` and `patrons`. Third, `checkouts` is a good example of a table that serves two purposes simultaneously. In addition to

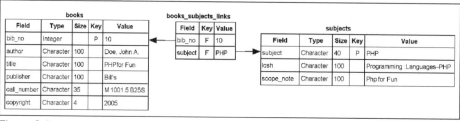

Figure 2-6

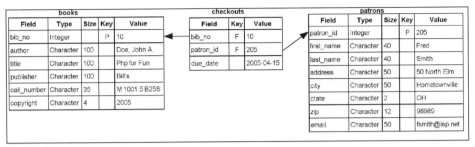

Figure 2-7

being a linking table between `books` and `patrons`, we have also placed the `due_date` field in the same table, thereby having it participate as a data table as well.

### Arbitrary vs. Descriptive Keys

Two types of values can be used in creating primary keys: arbitrary and descriptive. The first can be seen in the `books` table in figure 2.6, where a numeric value (automatically generated by the system) is used for the primary key field (`bib_no`) value. The second can be seen in the `subjects` table, where a meaningful word (`subject`), whose value is guaranteed to be unique, is used as the primary key. Each of these approaches has its pros and cons.

Descriptive keys are useful because they are easier for people to understand and they allow users to more easily see links and debug data problems. However, arbitrary keys can be (are usually) auto-generated by the system, saving you the effort of ensuring that the keys are unique. In addition, because arbitrary keys are not descriptive, they are unlikely to change should the content of the record change. Remember that when a primary key changes, all linked foreign keys must also change. By using an unchanging value for the key, many data integrity issues can be avoided.

### Designing Good Databases

In setting up databases, it is important to follow certain rules to ensure that finding information is both easy and predictable. This process—known as normalization—involves following standard procedures in designing and implementing the database. The following basic rules are recommended:[10]

Do not place more than one piece of information in a single field. Otherwise, it can be more difficult to maintain and retrieve data. Multiple values of the same type for a field should be placed in a separate table and linked to the main table. If you find that you need subfields, you may be better advised to break out the information into separate fields, perhaps into a separate table (in a one-to-many relationship) if you need them to be treated as a unit.[11]

Do not enter the same type of information (user's name, subject heading, for example) into a given record more than once (for example, `subject1`, `subject2`, and so on). Doing so is inefficient and makes searching awkward. If you need to have repeatable fields, you should create a separate table for them and link it to the primary table.

Do not enter the same information in more than one place. If you do, you will need to make changes in more than one table should the data change.

Each table should be "about" only one thing. For example, don't mix books and patron information in the same table.

If information could be used in more than one context, consider moving it to a separate table.

Note that I said that these are guidelines and not laws—the reason being that there may be times that you will choose to not follow one or more of them. The thing is that this should be done only after careful thinking through of the ramifications of doing so and for very good reasons.

## Structured Query Language (SQL)

Now that we have briefly looked at how a relational database structures data, let's look at how we can interact with those structures. To support such interactions, a special language was developed concurrently with the relational database theory.[12] Called Structured Query Language (or SQL), it is used to create queries (requests to the database to do something) that are used in all interactions with the system, and partakes of many of the qualities of a language. SQL was intentionally designed to be understandable and constitutes a database lingua franca that is used in virtually all RDBMSs. There may be individual differences in how each product implements its particular dialect of SQL, but the essentials of the language are the same.

The structure portion of the acronym certainly lives up to its name. In their most basic form, SQL statements are built up from the following structured templates:

- searching

```
SELECT <field names> FROM <table(s)> {WHERE
    <conditions>} {ORDER BY <field(s)>}
```

- adding

```
INSERT INTO <table> (<field names>) VALUES
    (<corresponding field values>)
```

- editing

```
UPDATE <table> SET <field name> = '<corresponding field
    value>', <field name> = '<field corresponding value>'
    ... WHERE <condition>
```

- deleting

```
DELETE FROM <table> WHERE <condition>
```

In the rest of this section, we take a very brief look at basic SQL queries and explain how they work. This is not intended to be a tutorial but instead an introduction that will allow you to understand the examples in this book. For example, in the first bullet above—searching—the last two phrases are enclosed within curly braces, which indicates that the values are optional. This practice will be used throughout the book. To delve into the complexities and richness of SQL, you should consult one of the books or Web sites listed in the bibliography.[13]

## SELECT

The keyword (command) that we use to retrieve records from the database is **SELECT**. The use of the **SELECT** statement is one of the most complex of the SQL queries we will see.[14] This is understandable because it is used to search the database, and searching itself can be quite complex. In the following sections, I illustrate how some very basic SQL searching statements are constructed. Then, in later chapters, I expand on these techniques to show how they can be used in real life.

SINGLE TABLE    The simplest search is to find all records in a table. For example, were we to want to know the names, stored in the **patron_name** field, of all of the patrons in the **patrons** table above, we could use the following query:

```
SELECT patron_name FROM patrons
```

If we wanted to have their address information as well (say for a mass mailing), we would enter the name of each field, separated by commas:

```
SELECT patron_name, address, city, state, zip_code FROM
    patrons
```

If you don't want to type out every field name, you can use an asterisk to retrieve all fields in a table. For example, `SELECT * FROM patrons` would bring back all fields from all records in the `patrons` table.

Usually you want to be more selective, and retrieve information that matches certain criteria. In such cases, you would use the `WHERE` statement. For example, say you want to know all of the books in the `books` table (shown in figure 2-6) published by ALA, but not by anybody else. Using the structure shown in figure 2-7, you would then specify the search:

```
SELECT title FROM books WHERE publisher='American Library
    Association'
```

In this example, the database has been asked to go into the `books` table and select all records in which the `publisher` field is equal to American Library Association. That means that the entire contents of the field must be `'American Library Association'`. Note in the example that we are enclosing search values in single quotes. This is required by the SQL standard.

As librarians know all too well, users either do not always know the entire contents of a given field or would like to do keyword or phrase searches within fields. It was to be able to search parts of individual fields that the `LIKE` statement was created. When searching a table, you may specify a substring by using the word `LIKE` instead of = and then use % as a truncation symbol, before and/or after the string for which you wish to search.

For example, were we to search for all titles that began with the words "Introduction to" we could use the following SQL statement to find all such books:

```
SELECT * FROM books WHERE title LIKE 'Introduction to%'
```

On the other hand, if we were looking for books with the word France anywhere in the title, we might use:

```
SELECT * FROM books WHERE title LIKE '%France%'
```
[15]

One thing I need to mention is that, unlike other database servers (including PostgreSQL), MySQL searches are by default not case sensitive. That is, a search for France will retrieve records containing France, france, and even fRAncE.[16]

However, it is possible to force case sensitivity by using the BINARY operator on one of the elements in the search. For example, the following two (equivalent) searches will retrieve records where France (but not france) is in the title field:

```
SELECT * FROM books WHERE BINARY title LIKE '%France%'

SELECT * FROM books WHERE title LIKE BINARY '%France%'
```

Just as command line searching in OPACs, SQL does enable you to provide multiple conditions with its Boolean operators AND and OR. For example,

```
SELECT * FROM books WHERE title LIKE '%Perl%' AND
    publisher = 'SAMS'
```

would bring up all records from the books table that had Perl in the title field and that were published by SAMS. On the other hand,

```
SELECT * FROM books WHERE title LIKE '%Paris%' OR title
    LIKE '%London%'
```

would retrieve a result that contained all books that had Paris, London, or both in their titles.

Although the use of LIKE does provide a kind of poor person's keyword searching capability, it suffers from one fatal weakness: it is utterly unaware of what constitutes a word or phrase. For example, if you were to use LIKE '%ton%' in the title field, it would retrieve records containing polytonality, atonement, stone, tonnage, Washington, and the like. This obviously is a rather inexact—and not terribly satisfactory—way to implement keyword searching. We will explore some alternatives in subsequent chapters.

Searching for records that do not contain certain values can also be useful. To do this, you can use either of two operators to signify does not equal: != or <>. For example, you can use either of the following queries to find all records in which the e-mail field is not blank (that is, where it contains an e-mail address):

```
SELECT * FROM patrons WHERE email != ''
```

or

```
SELECT * FROM patrons WHERE email <> ''
```

All the above searches bring back records in an unspecified order. However, this may not always be the most useful way in which to view or process records. You can therefore specify the ordering of the records via the use of the ORDER

BY keyword. For example, if you wanted to see all subjects in alphabetical order, you would use the following query:

```
SELECT subject FROM subjects ORDER BY subject
```

You can also order by multiple fields. For example, to print out an alphabetical list of `patrons`, you could use this one:

```
SELECT * FROM patrons ORDER BY last_name, first_name
```

The result of this search would be the entire contents of the `patrons` table, ordered by `last_name` and, within `last_name`, by `first_name`.

MULTIPLE TABLES  Although the previous queries are useful in querying single tables, the full power of relational databases comes in the user's being able to retrieve information from anywhere in the system. Doing this involves being able to search multiple tables at the same time. Note that it is here that we begin to use the primary and foreign keys to which we have been referring so often in this chapter.

To search multiple tables, you need to create your SQL queries to follow the relations to join the tables into a single entity. This allows you to access all other information from the joined tables. It is important to note the differences between these queries and those we have encountered:

> If there are two or more fields in any part of your query with exactly the same name, you need to qualify them by appending the table name in front of them (for example, `patrons.patron_name`). Otherwise, the system will get confused. It is for this reason that I have adopted a standard in this book where each field within a database is uniquely named, thereby eliminating such problems before they begin.[17]

> All tables involved in the join must be included in the tables list coming after the `FROM` keyword.

> All linking information must be contained in the <condition> section of the query after the `WHERE` keyword and each condition must be separated by `AND`.

The condition used to select the records should be the last condition.

TWO-TABLE JOINS  In the following examples, we will use the tables in figure 2-8 to demonstrate how to search using a two-table join. Note that the two fields are the same type (character) and size (ten characters). This is an important practice to follow in that it helps ensure that the same value is placed in each.

| books | | | | | publishers | | | |
| --- | --- | --- | --- | --- | --- | --- | --- | --- |
| **Field** | **Type** | **Size** | **Key** | | **Field** | **Type** | **Size** | **Key** |
| bib_id | Number | 11 | P | | publisher_code | Character | 10 | P |
| title | Character | 100 | | | publisher_mame | Character | 50 | |
| pub_code | Character | 10 | F | | publisher_address1 | Character | 75 | |
| copyright_date | Date | | | | publisher_address2 | Character | 75 | |
| call_number | Character | 12 | | | publisher_city | Character | 50 | |
| | | | | | publisher_state | Character | 50 | |
| | | | | | publisher_zip | Character | 10 | |
| | | | | | publisher_phone | Character | 15 | |
| | | | | | publisher_email | Character | 100 | |

Figure 2-8

The basic syntax for a multiple-table search is

```
SELECT <fields> FROM <all_tables_involved> WHERE <linking
    path(s)> AND <conditions>
```

Let us suppose that we were to want to find all books published in New York. The linking path provides the primary/foreign key path from the main data table being searched (**books**) to the table with the field you are searching on (**publishers**). In this case, the syntax would be

```
books.pub_code=publishers.publisher_code
```

Note that we have qualified each of the fields (**pub_code** and **publisher_code**) with the table where the field is found. Given that the names are different, we could also have made it

```
pub_code=publisher_code
```

However, including the names of the tables where the fields are found helps to make the path clearer. Using this construct, the query to do the multiple-table search would be

```
SELECT books.title FROM books,publishers WHERE
    books.pub_code=publishers.publisher_code AND
    publishers.publisher_city='New York'
```

THREE-TABLE JOINS    The above syntax will work where only two tables are involved in one-to-one or one-to-many relationships. However, there will inevitably be times when you will have many-to-many relationships from which you will want to retrieve records. For example, say you wanted to find all the books that use Anthropology as a Library of Congress Subject Heading in a database structured like that in figure 2-6.

To create a query to search these tables, you would first replace <all_tables_involved> with the names of the three tables. In this case, these are `books`, `books_subjects_links`, and `subjects`. You would next replace <linking_path(s)> with the path the database needs to take to follow the relations. Here, the path would be `books.bib_no=books_subjects_links`  `.bib_no AND books_subjects_links.subject=subjects.subject`. Last, you would replace <conditions> with what you want to look for in the database, in this case, `lcsh='Anthropology'`. The resulting query would be

```
SELECT      Title

FROM        books, books_subjects_links, subjects
WHERE       books.bib_no=books_subjects_links.bib_no
AND         books_subjects_links.subject=subjects.subject
AND         lcsh='Anthropology'
```

We will look at more detailed examples in chapters 7 and 9.

### Database Maintenance

As we discussed, the three main SQL commands for updating the database include `INSERT` (for adding records), `UPDATE` (for updating records in the database), and `DELETE` (for deleting records). Let's take a brief look at each of these in turn.

INSERT   The basic syntax for an insertion query is `INSERT INTO <table>` `(<field names>) VALUES (<corresponding field values>)`.

In this case, `<field names>` is a comma-parsed list of field names for which you wish to add values. Note that using this list is not required. It is, however, needed if you don't want to add values for every field in the table or if for some reason you want to add values in an order other than the order of the fields inside the table.

In the same way, `<corresponding field values>` contains the values you wish to add. If you have defined `<field names>`, you must place the values in the same order as they appear in the field name list. On the other hand, if you don't have a field name list, you must place the value of each non–auto_increment field in the same order as they appear in the table definition. Note that, in entering the values, you must enclose each of them in single quote marks (`'John','Doe','125 Main Street'`).

UPDATE   The command to update the database is similar to `INSERT` except that, rather than having a list of fields followed by a list of values, it uses `SET`

`<field1>='<value1>',<field2>='<value2>'` to define the field/value pairs. In the case of updating a particular record, we use the syntax `UPDATE <table> SET <field name>='<corresponding field value>',<field name>='<corresponding field value>' . . . WHERE <primary key field>='<primary key value>'`. Note we have indicated that the database should update the record where the primary key field has the value of the record that we have edited (otherwise, every record in the table would be updated with the same information).

DELETE   As with updating, the `DELETE` command needs to have a condition telling it which record to delete (otherwise, all records in the table will be deleted!). Again, we use the `WHERE <primary key field>='<primary key value>'` condition to delete only that record we wish to delete.

## Data Security

One of the most important tasks any system has—particularly a Web-based system—is to protect the data from unauthorized access and manipulation. We need to make sure that only those people we want to have access have access to the data. To address this, all RDBMSs support some kind of user security. We will see how MySQL does so in the next chapter.

### Database Integrity

Beyond user security, we need to make sure that the integrity of the data is maintained. It is important not only that the information is inserted into the database correctly, but also that complete and proper relations are set and maintained. If these are not handled properly, severe problems can develop and make a system unusable.

Referring to the checkout system just mentioned, think what would happen if the integrity of the link between the checkout and patron record were to be lost. Not only would you not know who had the book checked out, but you might also not even know that it was ever gone. You certainly want to have the system make sure that that would never happen.

Many RDBMSs have a number of built-in mechanisms designed to maintain data integrity that you can use in addition to those you might program in yourself. The advantages of letting the RDBMS do the work are that it saves development time and avoids problems due to bugs in the coding. In this section, we look at some of those techniques.

TABLE/ROW LOCKING   When working in a multiuser environment, one challenge is to ensure that two people do not try to try to save their edits on the same record at the same time. If that is permitted, the record can be corrupted and the database compromised.

To keep this from happening, database systems permit you to lock the resource you are editing, either at the table or at the row level. Two kinds of locks can be used. What is called a WRITE lock allows you to read/write data to the table/row and prevents everyone else from reading or writing until you finish your work and release the lock. What is known as a READ lock allows you and all others to read the table/row, but prevents everyone (including you) from writing to the table or row.

Locking can be at the table level or the individual record level. Table-level locking is adequate for small-scale applications, but does not work in larger applications in which many users access the database. The good news is that MySQL supports both types of locking.[18]

TRANSACTIONS   When changing data in a database, you want to make sure either that all actions are completed or that none of them are. Incomplete interactions are a major cause of data integrity problems. One useful technique when there are multiple interactions with the database is transactions. Transactions allow all interactions that would modify the database to be performed, but not actually saved to the database until all interactions are successfully completed. The data can then be committed (stored) to the database. If there is a problem with any of the interactions, the system can do a rollback, placing the system in the state that it was before the transaction was attempted. Transactions are particularly useful in systems with large numbers of users or in those that deal with information where retracing steps could be difficult—or even impossible.

For example, perhaps you had a system that tracked the number of vacation days each employee had. Word then came down that everyone was to be given an extra five days of vacation. You therefore go into the database to update it to give everyone those extra five days. However, midway through the process, something happens and the processing stops. At this point, you probably have no easy way of knowing who has been given the extra five days and who has not. In a system that supported transactions, there would be no cause for concern.

FOREIGN KEY CONSTRAINTS   Given that the keys are the mechanism that permits the bringing together of information from multiple tables, it is crucial that those links are carefully and properly maintained. If the value of the primary key is changed without changing the values in all related foreign keys, the relationship is lost and the ability to retrieve that related information is gone.[19]

This integrity support can be done manually with programming. Every time a primary key is changed, a corollary SQL updating query must be run to make the same change for each associated foreign key field, in whatever table it may reside. You can do this, but all such queries must be run successfully and all foreign key fields must be included. If there is any problem (such as neglecting to include all required queries), relational links are broken.

RDBMS products with foreign key constraints, on the other hand, allow foreign keys to be updated automatically. In such systems, tables are defined in such a way that primary key/foreign key relationships are directly established in the table definitions. Whenever a change is made in a primary key, the RDBMS can then automatically make the appropriate changes in the foreign keys.

## Other Features

### Indexes

As with books, journal articles, and the Web, finding information in a database is a lot easier if an index is available. In creating a standard index, the database software creates a list of all of the values contained in a field or fields and collects pointers to the records containing those values. Searching this index instead of the tables can dramatically increase the speed with which records are retrieved. RDBMS products can create other types of indexes as well. In the case of MySQL, there are three others, `PRIMARY`, `UNIQUE`, and `FULLTEXT`.

The `PRIMARY` index is the one that is used for the primary key for a field. It ensures uniqueness and that `NULL` values are not stored there. It is also used in creating foreign key constraints (see below). A `UNIQUE` index keeps track of values that have been placed into a field and does not allow more than one record's field to contain that value. A `FULLTEXT` index is a proprietary type that MySQL provides to support `keyword` indexing. As we will see, this type does have some limitations.

In general, it is a good idea to take a balanced approach to indexing. On the one hand, indexing can make retrieval quicker when searching often-searched fields—particularly in large databases. On the other hand, overuse can slow down record inserts/updates and takes up additional disk space.

### Views

Views (sometimes called virtual tables) are a way of creating structures within the database across table lines. Such structuring involves taking fields from various tables and bringing them together and forming a logical construct (a sort of single virtual table) with which the programmer can interact. Although this is not needed when working with a single table, once you begin working with multiple tables, it can be time-consuming to bring these fields together by hand using joins or other techniques. Views can make this process much easier in that the system does the multitable joins for you to create a virtual table (allowing you to query that virtual table), rather than forcing you to write the SQL join statements by hand. MySQL 5.0 implements views.

### Stored Procedures and Triggers

Stored procedures are pieces (modules) of programming code or SQL queries (or both) stored in the database for use by the database or applications. These modules have a number of advantages:

> They are precompiled and optimized so that they can run faster than ordinary routines.

> They are stored in the database and are available throughout the system.

> They reduce network traffic by allowing the module to be run within the server, rather than requiring that it be called from a network-based application.

> They are reusable and thus can reduce maintenance and recoding.

> They are inside the database and thus can execute code and access tables to which the user may not otherwise have access. This can be extremely valuable in that it can dramatically increase application security.

Triggers are essentially stored procedures that are automatically performed when changes are made to the table to which the trigger is attached. They can be extremely useful in maintaining data integrity and enforcing business rules. Support for both stored procedures and triggers is included in MySQL 5.0.

## Choosing an RDBMS

In selecting an open source relational database management system, you have several choices, each with a varying degree of open source–ness and each with its own pros and cons. The main candidates are

> *MySQL.* Originally an internal database developed at TcX in Sweden, this RDBMS was initially made available on the Internet in the form of Linux and Solaris binaries and later released under the GNU Public License (GPL) in June 2000. It has become the leading open source database management system on the Web. Sites that use MySQL include Yahoo, NASA, the U.S. Census Bureau, and Amazon.com.

*PostgreSQL*. Essentially a third-generation Berkeley database management system (ancestors include Ingres and Illustra, the second was merged into Informix), PostgreSQL is the most feature-filled open source RDBMS system currently available (although MySQL is quickly catching up). Users include Reuters, MIT's DSpace project, Utah State University, and the Biblioteca Civica Pablo Neruda di Grugliasco online library system.

*Firebird*. Released initially as an open source version of Borland's Interbase 6.0 product, this system is now being managed by a separate group. The developers intend to maintain interoperability with Borland's product (which is no longer open source) in any new code that they write. Although a very robust and capable system, it is having a hard time making inroads into the open source arena.

*mSQL (or miniSQL)*. One of the early pioneer free database servers on the scene, mSQL's lack of features makes it mainly a niche market player.

*Ingres*. Older brother of PostgreSQL, Ingres was initially developed at UC Berkeley and later commercialized, eventually being purchased by Computer Associates in 1994. Then, in 2004, CA released a version under an open source license. In November 2005, the software was purchased by Garnett & Helfrich Capital, who then set up Ingres Corp to provide support.[20] Ingres is a highly sophisticated database engine that offers a number of very good features. However, news of its availability came too late to include a review in this book. Links to information on Ingres can be found in the bibliography.

*Genezzo*. A new relational database—written entirely in Perl—that is currently under development and whose goal is both to provide a small footprint and to be able to support shared data clusters.

## MySQL vs. PostgreSQL

The only two serious contenders among open source relational databases at the time of writing are MySQL and PostgreSQL. Both are excellent systems (which I use) and each has valuable characteristics. First, they are easily installed. Although PostgreSQL initially required special libraries to run on the Windows platform, version 8.0 saw the creation of a native version for the platform (see bibliography). Second, both have a number of useful internal features, including functions that can make database development and data processing much easier, and powerful regular expression engines that can allow for sophisticated searching and data processing (as we will see later).[21] Last, they are both truly cross-platform and run on all varieties of Unix/Linux as well as on Win32 and Mac OS X machines. However, several factors led me to choose MySQL:

*It is fast.* Benchmark tests have shown that MySQL is virtually tied with Oracle as the fastest database product available on the market.

*It is more forgiving.* MySQL is somewhat more forgiving of nonstandard or incorrect SQL statements. It is important to bear in mind, however, that this permissiveness can create problems elsewhere.

*It is widely supported.* As noted earlier, MySQL has a significant following, which means that a large (and growing) number of books, Web sites, and other resources are available to help you get started using it.

*It is easy to use.* It has implemented extensions to the SQL command set that, rather than requiring knowledge of complex SQL command syntax, allows the administrator to use such straightforward commands as **SHOW FIELDS IN <table>** to list the characteristics of a particular table.

PostgreSQL has traditionally led MySQL in two areas: stability under heavy workloads and advanced features, such as stored procedures and triggers, transactions, and views. In terms of stability, MySQL has made great strides in its performance and is currently being used for a number of high-volume, large-scale systems. As to features, though PostgreSQL still does have an advantage in some of these areas, it is slowly diminishing with MySQL's inclusion of InnoDB tables (supporting foreign key constraints, field-level locking, and transactions) and the recent release of MySQL 5.[22]

The bottom line is that MySQL is the easier to learn and to begin using. Also, given its popularity, it is much easier to find support for it. The downsides to using it primarily have to do with the features it does not yet support—features that most basic Web applications typically would not use. Besides, given the MySQL rate of growth, it is quite likely that by the time this book is published, many of the remaining features will have been included.

## Notes

1. Although you can put information in an unstructured file and use free-text searching on it, this is inefficient and you lose a great deal of precision in searching.
2. For information on and examples of how to process text files, see Andrea Peterson, *Simplify Web Site Management with Server-Side Includes, Cascading Style Sheets, and Perl* (Chicago: LITA, 2002).
3. The uniqueness is an important concept in maintaining data integrity (something that we will explain). Just as a bibliographic record in an online system represents a single unique entity, so it must in other databases.

4. A Web-aware database is one that allows you to publish information contained in it directly to the Web.
5. Although PostgreSQL, Oracle, and others bill themselves as object-oriented relational database systems, that merely means that some object-oriented elements have been added to a relational database management system—a much different proposition than a pure OODBMS system.
6. This example is not ideal, in that it keeps the `due_date` field in the `books` table. I will illustrate a better way of handling this later.
7. A good example of a primary key is the Bibliographic Record (BR) number in the MARC record. Each BR number refers to a specific record in the bibliographic database. This record, in turn, provides information about the item to which the BR number has been assigned.
8. This formulation—<tablename>.<fieldname>—is a standard way to identify fields in SQL.
9. See http://www.usps.com/ncsc/lookups/usps_abbreviations.html.
10. A set of formalized rules govern normalization. I have included some resources in the bibliography on data modeling. Note, in particular, Michael J. Hernandez, *Database Design for Mere Mortals* (Reading, MA: Addison-Wesley, 1997).
11. There may be times when this approach may seem like using a thermonuclear device to kill a mosquito—as we will see in our discussion on rights in the user authorization application in chapter 8. However, if you want values to be under authority control, you will need to create the second table.
12. For more background on the history of relational database theory and SQL, consult the bibliography.
13. The examples I provide here are rudimentary and only scratch the surface of what SQL can do. For more information, consult the bibliography in the online companion materials.
14. Note that though the SQL standard doesn't require it, for ease of reading, I have put all SQL operators into all uppercase to help distinguish them from other parts of the query.
15. Note the space on either side of the word France. This technique can be used to implement a simple—if not very accurate—kind of keyword searching. The problem is that this search would not pick up a record that began with "France, at the beginning of the 17th century." In any case, there are better ways of doing this (as we shall see later).
16. As of MySQL 4.1, this can be modified by changing the collation (sorting order) when creating the database. See chapter 3.
17. Although such an approach is not mandatory, doing so makes creating the functions used in the library presented in chapters 7 through 9 much easier to program.
18. To use record-level locking, you must use MySQL's InnoDB file type.
19. Note that this is a good reason why one should use arbitrary—and therefore unchanging—primary keys.
20. Information from http://en.wikipedia.org/wiki/Ingres.
21. Regular expressions are a set of advanced pattern-matching techniques that permit sophisticated searching and string manipulation functions. How they work is beyond our scope here, but a number of the functions included in the ala_functions.php file use them.
22. While the main focus of this book is on MySQL, I have also included support for PostgreSQL. This support can be found in (a) the ala_functions.php library, written to use either RDBMS, (b) copies of the examples and data files for use with Postgre SQL, and (c) Setup.pdf and Functions_Guide.pdf in the download materials file, which contain information on the setup and use of PostgreSQL.

# 3 SETUP AND ADMINISTRATION

Now that we have explored the basics of relational database technology, it is time to put that information to use. In this chapter, we take data already stored in another system and move it into MySQL. We will work through selecting appropriate fields, creating data structures to hold that data, taking downloaded data from the legacy system and importing it into newly created MySQL tables, and then establishing user accounts that can access that data via a Web-based output page. In the process, we will be building a database that we can use in chapter 5 to create reports and search pages. We conclude by exploring some of the tasks involved in administering the database, database backup strategies, and setting up user security and access controls.

## PLANNING

Before you create a database—to say nothing of the Web pages that the database will generate—you need to figure how you want to use those pages, what data must populate the database for it to fulfill that purpose, and where to find that data. Say, for example, you want to create an online staff directory for your library. What information would you want included? Certainly you would include the person's name, office address, and telephone number. You might also want to include the e-mail address, job title, type of position (civil service, faculty, administrative, and so forth), or areas of expertise.

In making this decision, it is helpful to define the purpose of your page: a directory, a contact list for departmental home pages, or a resource page to direct users to staff who can assist them. You might also consider how the database might be used in the future, such as an authentication mechanism for interactive Web applications. As you can see, a page's purpose strongly influences what data you need—and thus the database used to create the page.

Once you have what you think is a complete list, sit down, have a latte, and look at what you have written. Is there any information that you might want that isn't there? How many lists do you want? How do you want the list or lists to display and in what order? How do you want to group the items in the list? Do you want to output subgroups that constitute only part of the full list? If so, what piece of information (subject, location, department, or what have you) do you want to use to separate the wheat from the chaff?[1] All these questions have an impact on what data you include in your database.

## SETTING UP THE DATABASE

Once you have decided what to include, you need to determine where to get the data. Additionally, you need to decide how you are going to get the data into your new system. You can take a number of different paths, but they boil down to two basic techniques. You can create the database in MySQL manually, obtain the data from the other system, and then load the data into the database you've just created. Alternatively, you can take the automated route, using products to connect to your current database and then loading the data directly into MySQL, creating your tables and loading the data in a single step.

Although the second option is considerably easier and more efficient for the user, only a few systems can be connected this way. We will therefore focus on the manual option. A list of products that support the second option, however, is included in the bibliography.

### Manual Conversion

A manual data load involves four steps: defining which data elements you wish to include; developing a way to download data from the existing system; setting up your MySQL database, defining the tables and fields to be included; and loading the data. We will take each of these steps in order.

## Defining the Data

In our present staff directory example, we have decided what we want (personnel information with phone numbers) and where to get it (our library's HR system). Next we sit down and identify the fields with the data we want. Having decided that we want to create a simple address list, we look through the available pieces of information. We choose the following fields: `last_name`, `first_name`, `phone`, `email`, `department`, `location`.

In preparing the list of data elements, you will need to know some things about each piece of data to be included in the database:[2]

> *Name.* We all have to have a name and fields are no exception. Otherwise, how will the database know what to look for?
>
> *Type.* What type of datum is it? Is it a word or phrase? a number? a date? Data types most often encountered in relational databases include
>
> - *char*—character data of a fixed length, causes every record in the table to occupy that length, whether it contains data or not, normally limited to 256 characters
> - *varchar*—character data in which there is likely to be wide variation in the length of the data going into that field, particularly useful in saving space, limited to 256 characters in MySQL
> - *text*—can store more than 256 characters of textual data
> - *integer*—numeric whole numbers
> - *float*—numbers with decimals
> - *date*—numeric, calendar dates that allow for doing calculations based on date; normal format in MySQL is YYYY-MM-DD
> - *Y/N or Boolean*—one of two values—on and off—used to indicate whether something is or is not the case; when not available, as in MySQL, can be mimicked by one-character `Y`/`N` field
>
> *Size.* How large is the data segment likely to be? Plan on the largest possible value to avoid data loss. MySQL will not warn you if you try to input more data to a field than it can hold.
>
> *Search.* Do you want to be able to search (or limit output) by this datum? If so, what type of searching? keyword? phrase? comparative (earlier than, less than, and so on)?
>
> *Description.* What is the usefulness of this field within the output? Why is it here? Where will the value for this field come from?

Figure 3-1 provides an example of how we might fill in these values. It has seven data elements (six plus the primary key `phoneno`—a necessary addition for a number of reasons). You also may note that we have put all of the field names in lowercase. The reason for this is that MySQL, even on the Windows platform, does have times when it is case sensitive. Therefore, rather than spending time on dealing with these vagaries, I have standardized on lowercase for all database, table, and field names, something that is fairly normal in relational databases.

| | Name | Type | Size | Search | Description |
|---|---|---|---|---|---|
| 1 | phoneno | Auto | 11 | N | Primary key - system generated |
| 2 | last_name | VC | 50 | Y | Person's last name - from *lname* field |
| 3 | first_name | VC | 50 | Y | Person's first name - from *fname* field |
| 4 | phone | VC | 15 | N | Phone number - from *phone* field |
| 5 | email | VC | 25 | N | On-campus email address - from *loc_email* field |
| 6 | department | VC | 50 | Y | Primary department - from *dept1* field |
| 7 | location | VC | 60 | Y | Office address - from *address1* field |

Figure 3-1

NULL vs. NOT NULL    Before going on, let me take a minute and explain the potentially very confusing concept of NULL versus NOT NULL. Essentially, NULL means undefined—in essence that the individual record being defined "ain't got one of those." Although it is perfectly possible—and for the most part legal in MySQL—to define a field as NOT NULL and then define the default as an empty string, the two are not the same and can cause you problems in the most unexpected ways.

The root of the problem comes in that the difference between a blank string and a NULL value is that a blank string has a value—of a 0-length string—whereas a NULL value has none for that field. It becomes clearer if we look at numbers. The equivalent value of " " in an integer field is 0 (an integer), not " " (a string). If you want to have a lack of value in an integer field—as opposed to a value of 0—you should allow it to be NULL and then indicate that state by setting the value to NULL. The same should hold for all fields. As we go through the book, we will be setting most of the fields we create to NULL (read "NULL entries are allowed").

One aspect of MySQL that makes understanding this more difficult is that MySQL blurs the distinctions between an empty string and a NULL value in ways that can mess you up. For example, in dealing with date type fields, saving an empty string to a MySQL date field causes 0000-00-00 to be stored there. Then, when you retrieve that record and display the date, it will output 0000-00-00, unless you do some filtering before displaying. This behavior is definitely non-standard and can create problems when working with other database systems. While it is nice that it can be so forgiving, it is best to get into good programming habits from the beginning.

In some cases, MySQL will object if you use an empty string instead of a NULL value. For example, when using values as primary/foreign key pairs in setting foreign key constraints, unless you have a record in the authority table with a primary key of " " (something that doesn't make much sense), MySQL will not allow you to set the value of an associated foreign key field to " ". In such cases, you must set the field to allow NULL entries. Therefore, you should only use NOT NULL if the field is to have a default value.

To make matters easier—and to allow things to work properly with the functions library and elsewhere—I strongly suggest that you follow these guidelines in defining your fields to NULL and NOT NULL in MySQL:

> If a field is to have a default value, then set that field to NOT NULL and put the appropriate value in as the default value.
>
> If a field is defined as an auto_increment primary key field, it should be set to NOT NULL.
>
> If a field does not have a default value, then make it NULL (the corollary of this is that if a field is set to NULL, then it should not have a default value). Note that phpMyAdmin will not make this easy in that the drop-down box for setting the value for NULL in the page where you create a table defaults to NOT NULL. This means you have to make a change for every field for which you do not have a default value.
>
> If a field is a date type, never set it to NOT NULL. If you want a default date, have that date sent to the database as part of your programming.

One final point to make about NULL fields: you need to handle searching for records where fields have been set to NULL somewhat differently from the ways we discussed in the last chapter. Specifically, because NULL is the absence of any value, it is somewhat illogical to say "give me records where the value is no value." Rather than doing so, in creating the appropriate SQL statement, you use WHERE <field> IS NULL, not WHERE <field>=NULL.

### Offloading the Data—Text Files

Once you have found the data, you will need to get the information out of that system so you can load it into MySQL. For example, you might use the library's online system to create a new books list. On the other hand, you may have a bibliography residing in a PC-based database or word processing document. In the case of the former, the database software may have a way you can export it to a structured file for loading. In the latter case, you might write macros (miniprograms within your word processor) to go through and put the information into one of the manual load formats described below. The basic idea is that it doesn't matter where the data reside, as long as you can get them out of the system and into the proper format for loading.

There are a number of file formats you can use to transfer data between systems. These include

> *delimited text files*—discussed in chapter 2
>
> *CSV or comma-separated values*—a special type of delimited text file also discussed in chapter 2
>
> *SQL files*—a series of SQL statements—in the form of `INSERT` statements—that can load the data into the database (see examples in the companion materials download file)
>
> *XML files*—a markup language that can be used to encode data for transfer between systems

Data can be output in other formats as well. For example, you might output in MARC or other formats and then run conversion utilities to get the data into the proper shape for importing into the database.[3]

INTERMEDIARY APPLICATIONS    In many cases, tools will create the upload files for you. For example, many integrated library systems (ILS) can save data into intermediary software packages from which a data file can be created in a format appropriate for loading the data into MySQL. Users of RDBM-based systems such as Voyager and ExLibris can use ODBC connections between those systems and MS Access or Excel to obtain data.[4] Other systems, such as those using Innovative Interface's proprietary database backend, enable saving search results to a CSV file to load the data into MySQL.

### Creating the Database (Implementing the Data Model)

We begin by creating the data structures into which the data will be imported. This can be done in one of two ways. If you're adventurous, you can learn all of the appropriate SQL queries for creating databases, log into your database server, and then type in and run each query to create your structures. Although it is good to be able to do this, the process can be very tedious and, unless you are a very good typist, take a long time to get everything right.

DATABASE ADMINISTRATION TOOLS—phpMyAdmin    The alternative is to use a graphical interface—one that allows you to point-and-click and fill-in-the-blanks as much as possible. A number of such tools—often called GUI (graphical user interface) tools—are available for MySQL databases.[5] The one I use—and present in this book—is phpMyAdmin. It provides good features and allows you to accomplish virtually all common (and many uncommon) tasks very easily. Where it doesn't, it provides you with its own version of the SQL character command line, where you can enter commands manually to do something the GUI doesn't currently support.

Figure 3-2 shows the login screen for phpMyAdmin. There are three ways in which you can set up user authentication for phpMyAdmin, but its built-in authentication mechanism is the most flexible and, if you use SSL, the most

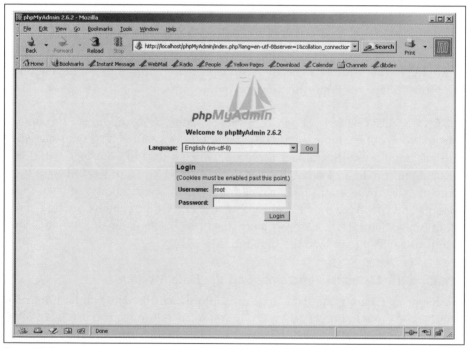

Figure 3-2

secure (see chapter 8 and Setup.pdf in the companion materials download file for more information). This screen uses username and password combinations, defined in the MySQL authentication tables, to provide you access to those databases and fields for which your account specifies permissions.

In this case, because we have already set up a root user, we will use that account and the password you have provided for root. Note that if you have not already done so, you must before going any further (consult your MySQL user documentation on how to do this). Otherwise, anyone on the Internet will have full access to all of your databases and possibly create untold mayhem.

Once you have successfully logged in, you will be presented with the screen shown in figure 3-3. There are several useful points to be aware of about this screen:

> Multiple languages for the interface screens are supported (fifty as of version 2.6.2, which was released as this book went to press). To change the language, click on the drop-down list next to Language(*) to select the language you prefer.

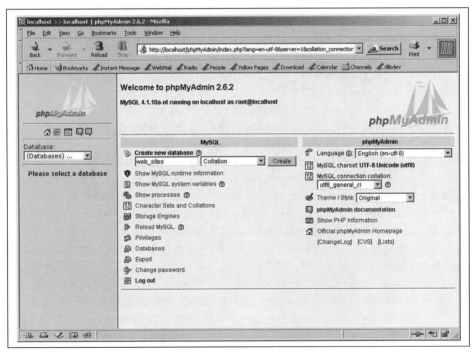

Figure 3-3

Both the MySQL version and the server on which it is running are indicated.[6] Several clickable links enable you to check system status, access documentation on the application, and load the phpMy-Admin homepage.

You can, if you are logged in as root, set up and change users, assign privileges on databases, and examine system diagnostic information.

A drop-down list with a complete listing of all databases on the administered server for which the logged-in user has rights is accessible in the left-hand frame. To work with any of them, simply click on the down arrow to select the database. You are then presented with that database and a complete list of all tables within it.

You have the option of choosing among a potentially bewildering array of possible character sets and collations (sorting rules), all of which were new as of version 4.1. We discuss these options below.

ADDING A DATABASE    You create a new database from this opening phpMy-Admin page by typing in the name of the database—in this case, `web_info`—into the **Create new database** text entry field. When adding the database, we decide what collation we would like to use.

The basis for this question is that different languages often use different diacritics with the same letter. For example, what is a in English can be a, á, à, or â in French. Similarly, o in English might be o, ö, or ø in Norwegian. Once you introduce non–Western European languages, things get even more complicated. Because each of these characters is represented by a different numeric code—none of which are in any particular numeric order—the database must be told what rules to use to sort its output correctly. However strange it might initially seem to U.S. users, the general rule is to either use **latin1_swedish_ci** (ci standing for case insensitive) if you are using **latin1** as the default character set for the database (the most likely alternative), or **utf8_swedish_ci** if you are using **utf8**. In this case, we will just accept the default value, that is, not select anything in the **Collation** drop-down list.

Clicking on the **Create** button to its right takes you to a screen where you can begin adding tables to the newly created database (figure 3-4).

To add our new table, we take our list and use the categories we defined there to create the new database. We begin by entering the name of the table that will contain the data in the **Name** input box. Because the table is to be used

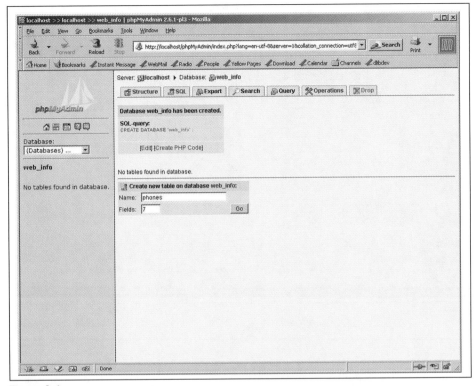

Figure 3-4

for a phone list, we call it `phones`. We then type in the number of fields (7) to be included in the box after **Fields** and click the **Go** button.[7]

Next, we define the seven fields we asked for in the previous step. Figure 3-5 shows this screen. In it we see the values for three columns from our form entered into the field definition form—datum, type, and size—being entered into the **Field**, **Type**, and **Length/Values** columns in the screen. As noted, because we wish to have a default value—the library's main telephone number—defined as the phone number to enter into the record, we define `phone` as `NOT NULL`, giving it the default value. In addition, because it is to be both `auto_increment` and the primary key field, we define `phoneno` as `NOT NULL`. We define the five remaining fields as `NULL`—meaning that they are allowed to have `NULL` values in them.

We finish by defining which fields get which type of indexing: `phoneno` will have the primary key index and set to `auto_increment` and the regular indexes

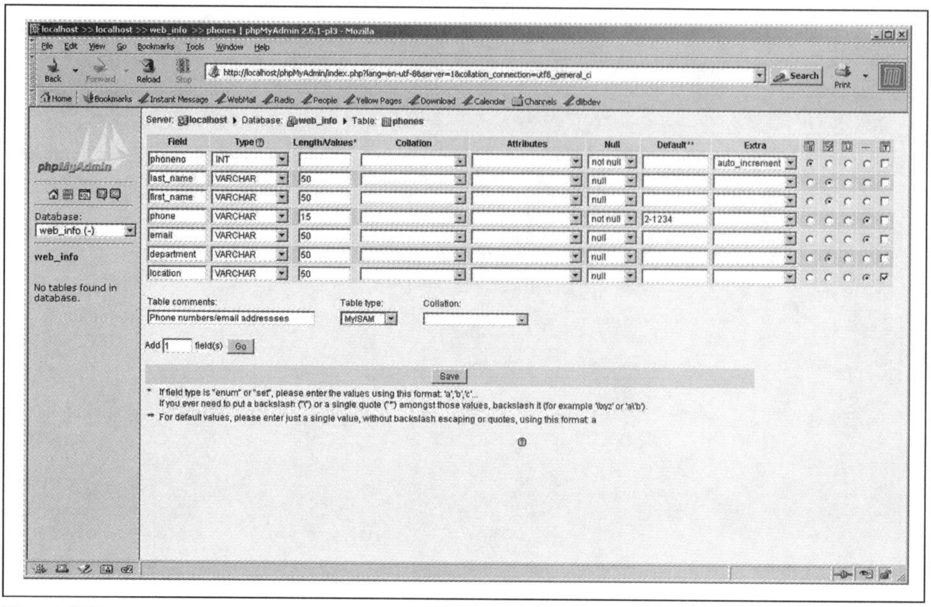

Figure 3-5

in the fields on which we will want to search—`last_name`, `first_name`, and `department`. In addition, we create a `FULLTEXT` index for the `location` field, so that we can keyword search it. Finally, to make sure that our `FULLTEXT` indexing will work properly, we make sure that the `table` type is set to MyISAM (other types do not support `FULLTEXT` searching; see chapter 7 for more information).

Once the user clicks **Save**, the table definition is used to create the table in the database and the user is taken to a page showing the structure of the successfully created table (shown in figure 3-6). Note that phpMyAdmin has printed out the SQL query used to create the table—something that can be useful both for learning SQL and for making sure that the system did what you wanted. You can even cut and paste it into a file for later use.

### Loading the Data

The next step is to take our data and load it into the newly created database. As noted in chapter 2, CSV files are a commonly used format in transferring data between applications. In this case, we have obtained such a file from our personnel database for this project. Figure 3-7 shows the sample CSV file we have

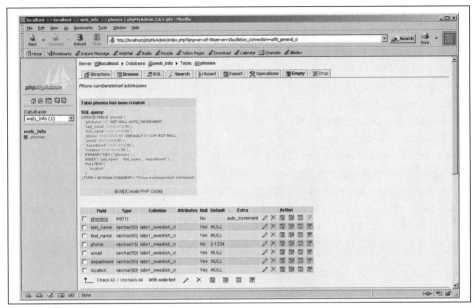

Figure 3-6

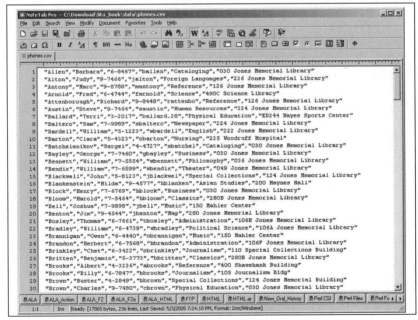

Figure 3-7

obtained.[8] In the first line, we have six entities, each in quotation marks and separated by commas. These correspond to the six fields we created above. (The seventh, `phoneno`, as you may recall, was defined as `auto_increment`. This definition instructs MySQL to automatically create an incremented value for each record it creates to hold the data coming from the CSV file. We therefore don't include it here.)

To get this data into the database, we select the `phones` table, and click on the SQL tab. This brings up the screen shown in figure 3-8. We click on the **Insert data from a textfile into table** link at the bottom of the right-hand frame.

This brings up the screen in figure 3-9, where we tell phpMyAdmin certain things about the file we are importing and how it is to be handled. The first is the file to be loaded and its location. If we do not know the exact path and file name, we can click on **Browse** and look through our local and network drives for the file. Ultimately, we need to navigate to where we unzipped the download file,

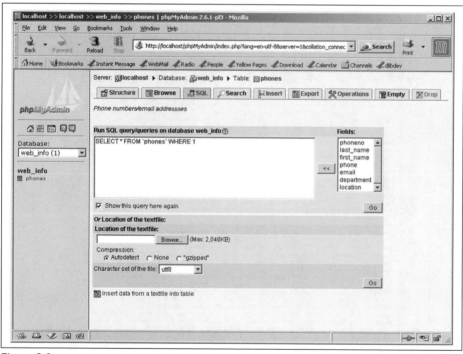

Figure 3-8

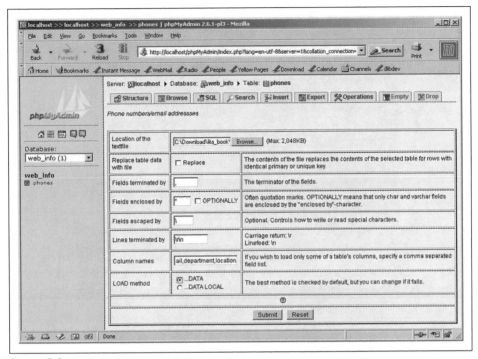

Figure 3-9

selecting the phones.csv file from within that path's data directory (see Setup.pdf for more info). After that, we skip the **Replace** option, and fill in the **Fields terminated by** with a comma, the **Fields enclosed by** with a double-quote, and the **Column names**, with the field names for each of the fields represented in the CSV file, separated by commas, in the same order as they appear in the CSV file (`last_name`, `first_name`, `phone`, `email`, `department`, `location`). Finally, we select `DATA` as the **LOAD** method.

Clicking on **Submit** causes phpMyAdmin to load the contents of the selected file into the `phones` table. To verify, click on **Browse**, and you should see the loaded data (figure 3-10).

## Conversion Programs

Another approach to acquiring data is to use conversion programs to move the data directly into MySQL. This allows you to connect directly to the MySQL

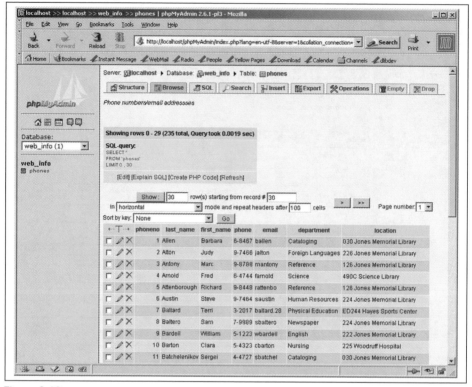

Figure 3-10

server (usually using an ODBC connection); automatically create databases, tables, and indexes; and then load the data into the resulting database. The advantage of this approach is that much of the work described is handled automatically (assuming that the structure and data of the existing database will provide the output you desire). If you have a system that is supported by one of these programs and you merely want to make the database available more or less as is on the Web, this is clearly an attractive alternative.

Several such programs are available (see the bibliography for a list). One I have found very useful is DBManager from DBTools Software.[9] The program is currently available in both freeware and commercial versions, both of which can be used for data migration from a wide variety of database formats (including various versions of MS Access and Excel, dBase, FoxPro, Paradox, and any database that supports ODBC) into either MySQL or PostgreSQL.

## CREATING THE USER ACCOUNT

One final thing needs to be done in MySQL to enable publishing data to the Web. To run a report, you will need to create an account in the RDBMS that has permission to log into the database and execute the desired query. Although you can use any account that has access to the database in question, it is a good idea to create unique user accounts for each application and to provide those accounts only those permissions that are necessary for the application to do its job. Especially if you are working in a multidatabase environment, you don't want people to be able to access—let alone change—other users' data.

To set the user permissions for this database click on **Home** inside phpMyAdmin and then click on the **Privileges** link in the right-hand frame. Doing so brings up the screen shown in figure 3-11.

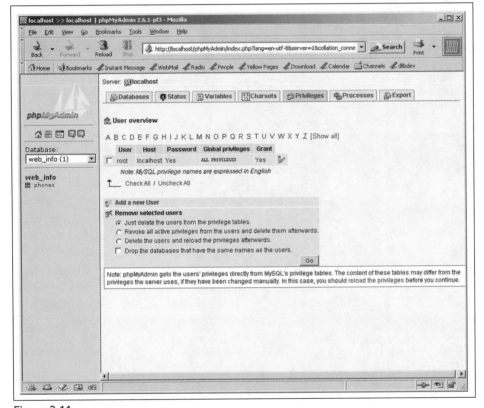

Figure 3-11

This screen allows you to view and edit all of the permissions for all registered user accounts residing in the MySQL database.[10] In addition to being able to edit (add and revoke permissions) and delete existing accounts, you may also click on **Add a new User** link to add an account. Doing so brings up the screen shown in figure 3-12.

There are two parts to this screen. In the first, you can set the **User name** (account name), the host from which they will be allowed to connect, and their password. When creating user names, it is generally a good idea to have the name be based on the name of the application for which you are providing access. This makes it much easier to track and maintain accounts as the number of databases and applications grows. Each field in the form has drop-down option lists in the left column that you can use when creating the accounts.

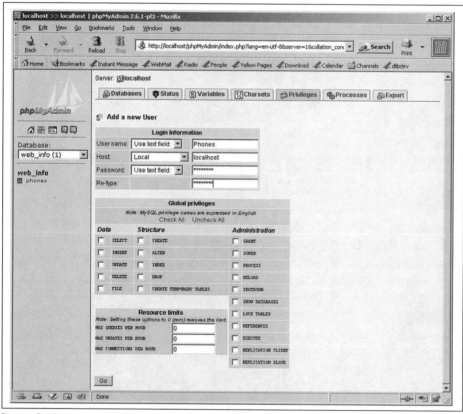

Figure 3-12

*User Name.* We select **Use text field** and give the account the name `Phones`.

*Host.* Because the application that will be running reports will be on the same server as MySQL, we select `localhost` from the drop-down for the host.

*Password.* Again, we use **Use text field** to enter a password, where we type in `Fone_Usr`. If you are placing this on an Internet-available server, you should change the user name and password to something else. Otherwise, anyone reading this book will have access to your database. Note that, if you do make a change, you need to be sure that you place the same information in any scripts that access this database.

*Re-type.* Requires the administrator to verify the password by typing it in again. If it does not match, a Javascript box appears notifying him or her of the fact. He or she is then unable to proceed until the two passwords do match.

The second section asks which GLOBAL privileges (in any and every database that is now or ever will be entered into this system) you wish to assign to the user. These list the SQL commands the user is authorized to run in the system. Because it is best not to grant any global permissions to any users other than database administrators, we do not check any of the GLOBAL privileges.

Once you have clicked on **Go**, the account will be created and the screen shown in figure 3-13 will be displayed.

Because our new Phones@localhost account currently has no privileges to any database, we need to add such permissions here. We do so by first clicking on the **Add privileges on the following database** drop-down list toward the bottom of the page. We then select **web_info**, which causes the database to load in the right frame. If it does not, you probably have Javascript turned off. Just click on the **Go** button. This brings up the screen shown in figure 3-14.

Here we can specify which SQL commands this user will be able to run on this database. As you can see, they are a subset of those commands given above. Because we are setting this account up to only read from the database and then output the results, we click only the **SELECT** box in the left-most column. Once we click on **Go** just below that grid, the new user rights will be added to the database.

Because the privilege tables are normally read only when MySQL starts up, we need to get the database to reread them so that our new user account has access. To do that, we click on **Privileges** at the top of the screen, which brings us

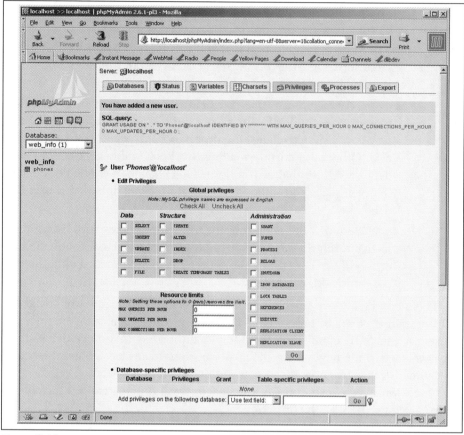

Figure 3-13

the pages we see in figure 3-15. We then click on the **reload the privileges** link (in the note paragraph at the bottom of the right-hand frame). This causes the permission tables to be reread. Our `Phones` user is now ready to go.

## ADMINISTRATION TASKS

For relational database systems to work, they need to be installed and set up; databases, tables, and indexes need to be created and maintained; security access

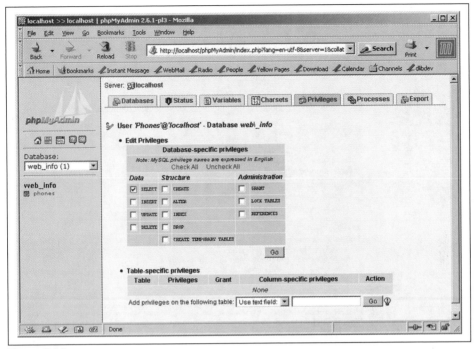

Figure 3-14

needs to be established with user names and passwords created; and other systems support tasks need to be completed. In the following section, we will take a look at some of the database administration tasks you will need to take care of and show you how to do so.

## Creating Indexes

Getting the data into the database is just the first step in making it available to users. Although the data is searchable once it is inside the database, such searching can be terribly inefficient. Left to its own devices, an RDBMS will go through your tables record by record, matching the query terms against the contents in each of those records. Thus the more records you have, the more time it will take to look through all of them.[11]

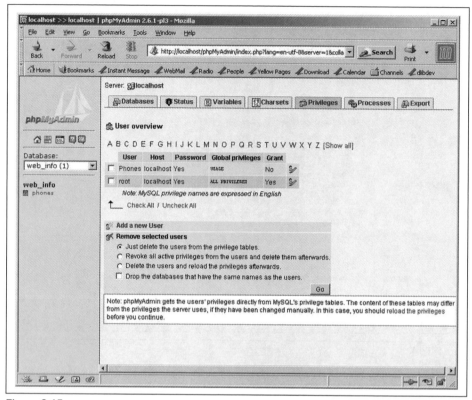

Figure 3-15

The answer to this problem is to use indexes. Just as books have indexes that help you find individual topics within the book and library catalogs provide an index to a library's collection, a database uses its index to match the query parameters and go directly to the appropriate record or records.

As noted earlier, in chapter 2, MySQL supports four types of indexes:

> *Basic.* The basic index covers the entire field, is used to allow ordering by fields, and makes searching those fields faster and more efficient.

> *Unique.* The UNIQUE index adds server enforcement of not allowing more than one record to have the same value in that field.

> *Primary.* The PRIMARY index is similar to the UNIQUE, but indexes the field as the primary key, thus disallowing NULL and duplicate values; note that a table can have only one primary key.

*Fulltext*. The FULLTEXT index capability was added as of version 4 and allows for the indexing of individual words within fields (we will explore it in chapter 5).

You can create indexes when you create the table by clicking the appropriate icon in figure 3.6. You can also use the SQL box and enter the appropriate command there. For example, to add a UNIQUE index on the email field, you would enter one of the two following commands:

```
CREATE UNIQUE INDEX email ON phones(email);

ALTER TABLE phones ADD UNIQUE (email);
```

## Backups

One of the most critical tasks in any computer-based system is to back up the data. Given that computers often get cranky and do things we don't want (or expect) them to do, we need to be able to recover from glitches that occur. To make sure you can do this, you need to have a good backup strategy in place before you begin working with a database management system. When constructing such a plan, you need to keep two types of backups in mind: server and transaction.

### Server Backups

The first of these is the server backups. Although most of you are probably familiar with backing up computers and servers, the situation is slightly different with databases. The problem is that, unlike the average computer application in which, when a file gets backed up, it remains internally consistent with itself, the same thing is not necessarily true of databases. If a database is backed up in the middle of a multitable transaction, the backup may get pretransaction data in some tables and posttransaction data in others. The result can be a data integrity nightmare.

Fortunately, there are ways that this problem can be avoided. The easiest for our purposes is to take the database system offline (or at least locking all tables to prevent them from being updated) and then doing a complete backup. Although the major backup system vendors—such as Veritas—do include the capability of doing what are called hot backups, such programs tend to be written for major players such as Oracle, not open source databases. In addition, given that there are probably long periods when librarians—even techie librarians—are likely to be asleep and not updating the database, you can probably without too much difficulty find a convenient time in which to schedule a job to run automatically to do this task.

In the case of MySQL, its command line client—mysqldump—comes with a multitude of switches (command line parameters) that can be entered in a shell script or batch file to do the trick. For example, the following works quite well:

```
mysqldump --quick --add-drop-table --lock-tables >dump.sql¹²
```

Entering this command into a batch file or shell script, and then running it on a regular basis, will cause all database structures and data to be backed up and ready for easy restoration. The command runs the mysqldump program, telling it to write directly to the disk (making it faster); include **DROP TABLE/ADD TABLE** for each table backed up, making it easier to use in case of having to do a restore; or lock all tables in a database before doing the dump; and write to a file named dump.sql.¹³

### Interaction Logging

Server backups are a good beginning for a backup strategy. You need, however, to do more. For example, say you do your backups on a nightly basis and the server crashes at 4:30 in the afternoon after a busy day of data entry by forty different librarians. Unless you want to keep a one-way ticket to the Bahamas and a numbered Swiss bank account on hand so you can go into hiding from irate colleagues, you will need a second level of backups.

One easy way to do this is to include interaction logging in your applications (something I will show you in chapters 7 and 9). The basic idea is that as each data maintenance interaction (adding, editing, deleting) is entered into the database, each component SQL query involved in that interaction is written to a log file. Then, if disaster strikes, all you need to do is to restore from the nightly backup and then enter the interactions from the log file and you will be up and running again.¹⁴

## Security

The first thing we need to do is to make sure access to phpMyAdmin is limited to only those persons designated as database administrators. Because phpMyAdmin essentially gives you the "keys to the kingdom," anyone who can access it can do anything they wish to any database in the system (including deleting a database!). Mechanisms within phpMyAdmin do allow you to provide different persons administrative access to different databases, but you need to set up some type of access-control mechanism to make sure that unwanted users don't get in. Setup.pdf, part of the companion materials download file, lists the alternative approaches you can take, with some pros and cons on each.

Next, we encounter a topic we covered above: creating secure and limited-access application accounts. It cannot be overemphasized that this should be handled on a need-to-access basis and that you must be as careful as possible in granting permissions to users. For example, if you place a dynamic page that only searches and outputs data, you don't want the account under which that action is taken to have the permission to add, change, or delete data. Remember that PHP requires that the password be written into any script that accesses the database. That is, anyone with access to the directory in which such a script resides can read the script and see the password. We discuss ways to keep these scripts secure in chapter 8.

Finally, you will need to control which Web users have access to the data maintenance applications you write. This involves user authentication (making sure the person is who he or she claims to be) and authorization (seeing if that individual is allowed to undertake the requested action). We discuss these concepts—and show you how you can implement them in your application—in chapter 8.

Now let us examine how we can go about getting the data back out in the form of Web pages.

## Notes

1. The list of fields we are going to include here is very small. I strongly recommend that you read chapter 6 on data modeling before proceeding with a real project, especially one presenting any possibility of added features, data elements, or interaction with other applications.
2. In many cases, the system in which the data currently reside may already have some of these—especially type and size—already defined.
3. There are a number of tools out there, particularly in the Perl world, that can help you do this. It is not a trivial task, however, and we do not pursue the approach here.
4. Open DataBase Connectivity—a protocol, developed by Microsoft, to permit real time communication between different types of databases running on different operating systems and platforms. Widely used in the field, particularly in some of the conversion applications listed in the bibliography.
5. See the online bibliography for a listing, including phpMyAdmin.
6. In this case, localhost is another name for the computer on which phpMyAdmin is running—any other host being given an IP address or DNS name. In other words, MySQL and phpMyAdmin are running on the same server.
7. Although it is good to know what fields you want when you first create the database, don't worry if you might want to change things down the road, because phpMyAdmin makes it very easy to modify table structures after the fact.
8. This is available in the data directory in the companion materials download file.
9. DBTools Software, http://www.dbtools.com.br/EN/dbmanager.php.
10. You may see more users on your screen than appear here. The reason is that MySQL ships with permissions that constitute a possible security risk. I suggest removing all but

root@localhost as we have done here and adding new users only as needed with minimal permissions.

11. This of course is not necessarily a problem with the phone list example here, but thinking through such things is a good habit.

12. In real life, you will need to add two parameters: one for the user account and one for the password. Rather than using the root account, you should create a separate backup account that has GLOBAL SELECT and LOCK TABLES privileges. See Setup.pdf for more information.

13. This locks tables only within a single database. If you have applications that update tables in multiple databases, you will need to use another approach, such as shutting down access to all databases while doing the backups.

14. Such logs are also extremely useful in tracking down and correcting system and data entry problems.

# 4 INTRODUCTORY PROGRAMMING

Now that we have looked at how we can set up a database and populate it with data, it is time to do something with the data.

Report writing is central to any database-backed Web page, whether it's a stand-alone page or a complex search screen within a large application. Any time you create a query, send it to the database, and then format the returned results, you are creating a report. There are three basic methods you can employ to create a report.

First, you can use proprietary tools. A number of database applications, such as FilemakerPro and ProCite (as well as third-party tools such as Crystal Reports) provide built-in tools to query a database and output the results without any need for programming on the user's part. These tend to be commercial, and while a few are open source, I will not deal with them in this book. However, the bibliography offers a listing of some of the major tools and sites where you can obtain more information.

A second approach is CGI programming. Here, stand-alone programs written in a traditional programming language are used to create the entire report. This program can be invoked either as an `action` parameter in a form or by calling the program directly. The Web server, which has been configured to do so, passes control off to this program. The program then creates and executes the search, retrieves the data and creates the page, and then sends the page back to the server, which then sends it to the user. Given that every step must be implemented using the language's particular syntax, this is a programming-intensive approach.

In the Web server–based scripting approach, the Web server has been outfitted with special modules to handle database requests and other types of programming tasks. Programming instructions are embedded directly into an HTML-like page that is given a special extension (such as search.php rather than search.html). When the user requests this special page, the Web server notes the special extension and then sends the request to the appropriate module. The module then processes the page, running the code inside the code areas as needed and returning the results to the server where they are in turn passed on to the user. The beauty of this approach is that the languages involved are easier to use and (because you don't have to program the HTML sections) easier to develop, and that the module (being part of the Web server) performs its task quickly. This is the technique I will be showing you.

As you can tell from these descriptions, the approach we will be using involves programming. Therefore, it is a good idea to begin exploring how you (yes, YOU) can become a programmer.

## PROGRAMMING?! *YIKES!!*

I can see it happening as I write this. The mere mention of the P word brings on the same physical symptoms as the phrase math test or hearing a police siren coming up behind you while you are driving: your breathing gets shallow, your eyes glaze over, and your fight-or-flight response is engaged as your brain goes numb. This is one area where we feel that the term Idiot's Guide is all too appropriate.

The truth is, programming is not a big deal. Anyone who has ever cooked a dinner, given driving directions, or done training has programmed. Programming is simply writing out step-by-step instructions to tell the dumbest entity on the planet (a computer) how to do something. If you start out with the assumption that you are smarter than a computer (which, if you're reading this book— or any book—or if you're breathing for that matter, you are), you have already won half the battle!

Once you realize who the boss is, you just need to figure out how to let IT in on the secret. This will involve deciding what you need the computer to do, learning the language (words and grammar) that the computer can understand (because it certainly can't understand English, at least not yet), and patiently (and *that* is the key concept) writing out a step-by-step recipe telling it what to do at each step of the way.

We will now look at some of the techniques and concepts we use when telling computers what to do. (That is why programmers do what they do: they get to tell them what to do. Talk about a feeling of power!) To show that it is the syntax, rather than the activity, of programming that is unfamiliar, I will demonstrate each programming technique and concept below using a cooking analogy. Appendix A pulls all of these together and shows how a recipe, written in programming style, looks and compares it to a more traditionally formatted recipe. My hope is that, by seeing the two juxtaposed, you will have a better feel for (and less fear of) what programming actually is.

## BASIC CONCEPTS

### Values

We first need to define several basic concepts we will be using from here forward. Knowing these terms will go a long way toward understanding how programming actually works (and can be useful at cocktail parties as you wow your colleagues with your computational savvy). We will begin by looking at the ways that values are stored and transmitted within a program, focusing primarily on variables and arrays.

### *Variables*

Variables are the building blocks that contain the individual values the program will use to do its job. They are, if you will, the containers into which you put your raw ingredients with the expectation that they will be transformed into something edible. For example, when creating certain types of sauces, there are three categories of things (variables) you need to have to make the sauce: a fat, a thickening agent, and a liquid. Another way of looking at variables is to think of them as containers into which you place a value: a fat container, a thickening agent container, and a liquid container. Note that different kinds of sauces might start with different values for each of these containers (hence the term variable). What a cook (programmer) does is to take those variables and assign values to them, depending on what the desired end result is. Thus, for a white sauce, the three variables might be given the following values:

```
$fat = "4T butter";[1]
$thickener = "4T flour";
$liquid = "8C milk";
```

On the other hand, if a brown sauce were needed, the variables might be these:

```
$fat = "2T oil";
$thickener = "2T flour";
$liquid = "3C beef broth";
```

Note that I have created the variables ($fat, $thickener, $liquid) by placing a dollar sign in front of the variable name. This illustrates two principles. The first is the use of the $ in front. This tells the computer (and the programmer too, for that matter) that the thing $fat is a variable, not the word fat. Although not all programming languages use a dollar sign to denote a variable, PHP does (as does Perl). I have therefore used that formulation here so that it may become more familiar to you.

The second principle is that the word I used for a variable actually describes that which the variable is to represent. Although you could call it $x, $big_foot, or even $mother_of_all_variables, such a name won't help you as you use the variable in writing the program. Nor are you likely to remember what it represents when you return to the program down the road. By using a variable name that clearly describes the information that it contains (such as $fat), you are writing what is known as self-documenting code. This is a concept we use throughout this book.

You may have noticed that, in assigning values to a variable, I place the variable on the left side of the = and the value that will be assigned to that variable (poured into that container, if you will) on the right. This is about the closest you will ever come to a universal truth about all programming languages: content to the right of the = is assigned to the variable to the left of it.

## Arrays

An array is a set of variables that contain related items of information. Arrays differ from variables in that, though variables track individual entities, arrays organize sets of values that go together in some way and that need to be handled together. When we program database searches, we will use arrays to store the individual records before processing them.

To return to our cooking metaphor, when creating a dish, you might keep all of the spices together in small bowls on your counter, using them as needed. For example, an Italian dish might have oregano, basil, thyme, marjoram, and garlic. If you were to create an array to keep the names of all of the spices needed for a dish, you could assign each element individually:

```
$spices[0] = "2T oregano";
$spices[1] = "4T basil";
$spices[2] = "4T thyme";
$spices[3] = "1T marjoram";
$spices[4] = "3 cloves garlic";
```

Another option is to assign the elements in a single statement:

```
$spices = array("2T oregano","4T basil","4T thyme","1T
    marjoram","3 cloves garlic");
```

Either way, in using an array, when you need to add the spices, you can refer to them as `$spices[0]`, `$spices[1]`, `$spices[2]`, and so forth instead of using 2T oregano, 4T basil, 4T thyme, and so on. Note that we are using a number as the index (array address, if you will) of the individual elements (or values) of the array. This technique is useful if you will be stepping through the array one at a time and don't need to look for any particular value.

An alternate approach to indexing arrays—associative arrays—is supported by a number of languages, including PHP. An associative array is one in which we associate a name with the value being stored in the individual element, rather than a number. For example, if we were creating an array of the values needed to make a sauce, we could create it like this:

```
$sauce["fat"] = "4T butter";
$sauce["thickener"] = "4T flour";
$sauce["liquid"] = "8C milk";
```

Thus, referring to `$sauce["fat"]` would get us the value 4T butter, `$sauce["thickener"]` would be 4T flour, and `$sauce["liquid"]` would be 8C milk. This technique makes it much easier to access and output items in an array—such as the results of a database search—by using a name that we know (the field name) rather than having to know where in the array a particular value is to be found. The formulation `$result_array[<field_name>]` gives us access to each field of the results. Thus, in handling output from a database search, we can use `$record["title"]` to obtain the title field, `$record["author"]` to get the author, and so on. In this case, by referencing `$sauce["fat"]`, we would obtain the value 4T butter. This is a remarkably powerful and useful technique and one that I use throughout the book. You will have many opportunities to see it in action.[2]

## Coding

Let me now demonstrate how to do something with variables and arrays. Building on our sauce example above, let's "program" a white sauce we can use to make macaroni and cheese. As noted, creating the program involves writing out each action that needs to be performed to get the desired results. To start, I will use pseudo-code to demonstrate the concept. Pseudo-code is a technique in which you describe what needs to be done in a programming-like way without getting into the intricacies of a particular programming language. I will show you a more programming-like way of doing this later in the chapter.

```
1.  $pan = "4 quart sauce pan";
2.  $how_hot = "medium high";
3.  $heat_source = "stove";
4.  $sauce["fat"] = "4T butter";
5.  $sauce["thickener"] = "4T flour";
6.  $sauce["liquid"] = "8C milk";
7.
8.  Place $pan on $heat_source;
9.  Turn on $heat_source under $pan to $how_hot;
10. $roux = $sauce["thickener"] + $sauce["fat"];
11. Place $roux into $pan;
12. Heat the $roux;
13. Heat $sauce["liquid"];
14. $white_sauce = $roux + $sauce["liquid"];
```

Lines 1–6 set the variables for the program. These include the type of pan ($pan), the temperature at which to make the sauce ($how_hot), what you're cooking on ($heat_source), and the array of items with which to start the sauce ($sauce). Lines 8–14 then describe the steps to be taken with the variables. When this "program" is run, the program substitutes the contents of each variable for the variable name. Thus, line 8 becomes "Place 4-quart sauce pan on stove" and line 9 becomes "Turn on stove under 4-quart sauce pan to medium high."

### Decision Blocks

Anyone familiar with cooking is aware that the previous recipe does not provide enough information as written. You could perform each step in succession, but the results would be far from satisfactory. For this recipe to work, we need to tell the cook (the computer) certain things, including

How long should the heating in line 12 continue?

Does one add $sauce["liquid"] all at once?

How does one know if the process is working correctly?

For each of these questions, instructions need to be included in the program so that the cook (being a computer, not a very bright cook) can proceed properly. The following code shows how we might flesh out the needed information:

```
 1.  $pan = "4 quart sauce pan";
 2.  $how_hot = "medium high";
 3.  $heat_source = "stove";
 4.  $sauce["fat"] = "4T butter";
 5.  $sauce["thickener"] = "4T flour";
 6.  $sauce["liquid"] = "8C milk";
 7.  $half_cups = 16;
 8.
 9.  Place $pan on $heat_source;
10.  Turn on $heat_source under $pan to $how_hot;
11.  $roux = $sauce["thickener"] + $sauce["fat"];
12.  Place $roux into $pan;
13.  $roux_status = "raw";
14.  while ( $roux_status == "raw" ) {
15.      stir $roux;
16.      $temp = temp( $roux );
17.      if ( $temp < 350 ) {
18.          print "Not Yet";
19.      } elseif ( $temp >= 350 && $temp < 400 ) {
20.          $roux_status == "cooked";
21.      } else {
22.          $roux_status = "burned";
23.          throw_away( $roux );
24.          exit;
25.      }
26.  }
27.  Heat $sauce["liquid"];
28.  $bechamel = $roux;
```

```
29. for ( $x=0; $x < $half_cups; $x++ ) {3
30.     $bechamel = $bechamel + 1/2 cup ( $sauce["liquid"] );
31.         stir $bechamel for 30 seconds;
32.         print "You have added $x cups";
33. }
```

In this example, lines 1–7 set the values for each of the variables and lines 9–33 contain the expanded steps. These steps are implemented as decision blocks. Note that this example has three decision blocks—places where the computer decides what to do, whether to continue what it has been doing, or to do something new. These three types of blocks (`while`, `if`, and `for`) are those we will use most often in this book. Before examining them more closely, let us take a look at how a block is structured.

All decision blocks have the same structure:

```
1. conditional ( condition ) {
2.     "Do something!";
3. }
```

There are four things to note here:

> *conditional*—`while`, `if`, or `for`
>
> *condition*—the condition the computer should check to see if it should execute this block
>
> The entire block of code is contained in a block—between the { and } characters—that is executed if the condition is met. If the condition is `for` or `while`, then it continues to be executed for as long as the condition in line #1 is true (if the condition is `if`, then the block is run only once). This means that the block starts at the first line and continues executing until the last line before the } character and, if appropriate, checks the condition again at the top of the block to see if it is still true. If so, it goes through the block again. If not, it goes to the first command after the block closes.4
>
> Here the { and } characters are used to denote the beginning and end of the block, the way it is done in C, C++, Java, PHP, Python, and other C-like languages. Note that Pascal uses `begin/end`.

Before continuing, I would like to point out a formatting convention that, though not required, does make programming code a lot easier to read: within the first decision block (lines 15–26), the lines are indented three spaces and, within the blocks within that block (lines 18, 20, and 22–24), the lines are indented again. Although the programming language does not require this, indenting makes it easier to see where decisions are being made, what is being done at each possible point, and where blocks begin and end. I strongly suggest that you follow this practice.

Now let us take a closer look at the conditional statements:

while  (lines 14–26). This block says, "As long as the $roux_status is raw, keep on cooking." Because we initialized—gave an initial value of—raw to $roux_status at line 13, the first time we get to line 14, it enters the loop. If you don't do this—or you gave it any other value—it would never enter the while loop at line 14. It then proceeds through to the end of the block (line 26). When it goes there, it goes back to 14 and checks to see if the $roux_status is still raw. If it is, the program goes through the block again and continues to do so until the condition is no longer true. For this status to change, a test needs to be run each time through the block to see if the status should be changed. This is done in line 16, where the temperature of the mixture is taken. If you do not do this, the status will never change and so the program will never end (you will have entered what is called an infinite loop).

if  (lines 17–25). An if block says "if a condition is true, then, do something once" (where there are multiple possibilities, you can use one or more elseif statements to do subsequent checks of the value). In line 16, you get the temperature of the roux and then proceed to your if statements. In this case, the condition is checking the value by taking the temperature of the roux. If the temperature is less than 350, then the first condition if block is entered and the cook is told "Not yet"[5] and the program skips the other two conditions (lines 19 and 21), jumping down to line 25 (the closing of the if/then/else block at which point it returns to line 14, where the status is checked. Because it has not changed, it enters that block again. Also note that this block actually has two more tests. If the temperature is not less than 350, then check to see if the temperature is between 350 and 400. If so, it enters the second block, where the $roux_status value is set to cooked (at which point, it goes to line 26 and then back up to 14 to check the status again. Because the status is now cooked, the program skips down to line 27 (the first line after the while loop) and proceeds to the next task. However, if it finds that $temp is more than 400, that means that the process has somehow gotten away from you and has burned. You then change the $roux_status to burned, throw the $roux away, and exit the program (presumably to start over).

for (lines 29–33). In a for block, you know the number of times you need to go through the block (in this case, the number assigned to a sentinel variable $half_cups). In the opening statement, you initialize a counter variable, ($x=0); you tell it to run as long as the counter variable is less than the sentinel variable ($x<$half_cups). You then tell it to increment the counter variable by one each time the block is run ($x++). Then, each time you go through the block, you add 1/2 cup of liquid and stir for 30 seconds, at which point you start the block over and see if your counter variable is now equal to (not less than) your sentinel value, $half_cups. Once it is equal, that means that all of the liquid has been added and the sauce is made.

When going through a for block, it was noted that a counter variable is used to keep track of how many times the block had been executed. This makes the counter variable a valuable resource when used within the block with a numerically indexed array. This is because, as you go through the block, $x is increasing in value by 1 each time through the block. You could then use $x to go through an array one at a time, using the variable as the index to the array to access the array values. For example, if you were making an Italian dish, you could access the array as follows:

```
1. $num = count( $spices );
2. for ( $x=0; $x<$num; $x++ ) {
3.    add $spices[$x];
4. }
```

The first time through the loop (when the value of $x was 0), line 3 would read $spices[0] (whose value is 2T oregano) and it would be executed as:

```
add 2T oregano
```

The second time, the value of $x would be 1 and, because the value of $spices[1] is 4T basil, it would be executed as:

```
add 4T basil
```

and so on. This is a technique we will be using often.

## Operators

Because a computer is, by nature, a glorified calculator, one would expect that any decisions it would need to make would look suspiciously like a math formula. Sure enough, they do. Although the differences between languages can be quite significant, the concepts remain the same. In the case of words, when you want to see if the words or phrases match, you need to check and see if they are equal; if they are different, they are unequal. With numbers and dates, you need to know whether a number is equal to, greater than, or less than (or a date later or earlier than) another. Different programming languages use different operators to denote equal to, greater than, less than, and so on. For example, in PHP, checking to see if `$x` and `1` are equal, you would use `if( $x == 1 )`, whereas, in Visual Basic, you would use `if( x = 1 )`. It is important that you learn how the language you are using does comparisons.

You can also use PHP functions inside `if` statements. For example, one function we use quite a bit is `isset()` to check to see whether a certain variable has been defined: `if( isset( $username ) )`. What this means is if the variable `$username` has been set, then do something. Alternately, if `$username` does not have a value associated with it (or if the value is 0), the code within the block will not be executed.

## Functions

The previous example required quite a few lines of code. If one were using them in many different programs, it would take significant time, energy, patience, and fortitude—to say nothing of serious carpal tunnel insurance to protect one's wrists—to do so much typing. Besides, each time you make a new copy, you take the chance that something will not copy correctly, creating a potentially unpalatable bug in the resulting concoction. Furthermore, even if everything does copy correctly, what happens when you want to make changes? You will have to find and correct each copy manually, one at a time.

Luckily, there is an easy way around this that allows you to reuse that code without having to key it in multiple times. The technique involves taking often-used code and placing it in a separately named block, called a function. Once the code is in a function, it can be called by invoking the function each time it is needed. Breaking larger tasks into smaller tasks and then writing a function for each smaller task is what is known as structured programming. Structured programming makes writing and debugging a program much easier, increases the flexibility and reuse of code, and reduces the number of times the same routine code appears within a set of programs.

If you think about it, this is not all that different from the way we human beings go about things. We don't think through each step it takes to complete a task. For example, if we need to go to the store, we could create a mental list of every step it takes to get there:

```
Get up out of your chair
Walk into front hall
Stop in front of dresser
Put hand out into bowl
Put hand on keys
Take keys into hand
Pull arm back to body
and so forth.
```

You get the picture. If we had to go through that type of mental list for every task we undertook, we would never get anything done. Instead, we take all of the steps needed to accomplish something, put them together as a single entity, and define them as a task (the human equivalent of function) and even give it a name: go to the store. Then, when we need something, we just (at the risk of sounding like Commander Data) run the `go_to_store()` function in our mental sub-processor unit and it gets done.

Note that we usually have a purpose in undertaking an action. For example, `go_to_store()` is a rather generic function and doesn't really get us very far (so to speak) with so little knowledge of what we want to purchase. Therefore, when we run a function, we usually run it with certain ideas in mind—in this case, to go get something we actually want to buy. For this to happen, we need to run `go_to_store()` with that object in mind.

In the programming world, these ideas are known as parameters—things we pass to the function so that it can do what we want it to do. In this example, we might include the parameters grocery store and food for dinner to the `go_to_store()` function. This way, not only do we know the general task to be done, we also have the actual "what to do" included. The way that we would notate this in programming might be:

```
$store = "grocery store";
$to_purchase = "food for dinner, chips for party, birthday
    card for Jim";
go_to_store( $store, $to_purchase );
```

In this function call, two parameters are passed to the `go_to_store()` function. The first, `$store`, tells the function where we want to go and the second, `$to_purchase`, tells us what to buy when we get there. With these two pieces of information, the function can do its job.

When writing a function, parameters are always placed within parentheses as they are here. Even when there are no parameters to be passed—as in the earlier `go_to_store()` example—we must add empty parentheses as a way of indicating to the computer that there are no values to pass. Although these may seem counterintuitive, they are necessary to keep the computer happy.

As you will see, being able to call a function instead of having to write explicit code every time you wanted to go to the store makes life considerably easier. For this reason, a common practice in application development is to put functions you use often in a separate file that can be accessed by any program. This allows the code to be reused by, rather than rewritten for, many different programs. In addition, if a change needs to be made (say you decide that you should actually stir for 20 seconds instead of 30 for all roux in all recipes), only one line needs to be modified for the change to be effective in all programs that call the function.[6]

I have created, for this book, a programming library in the companion materials download file—ala_functions.php—that includes a large number of functions useful in developing database applications. In chapters 7, 8, and 9, I will show you how to use some of them.

## Putting It Together—Making a Sauce

The following code snippet demonstrates this concept by taking the basic sauce-creation logic and placing it into a function called **make_sauce()** that takes the basic steps and abstracts them into a stand-alone entity. You will have different ingredients, depending on the type of sauce you want to make. This is where variables prove so handy. What you do is to create a set of variables that will contain the basic information you want the program to use when making the desired roux. To change the type of sauce you are making, you merely change the values in the variables passed to the function:

```
1. function make_sauce( $sauce ) {
2.     $fat = $sauce["fat"];
3.     $thickener = $sauce["thickener"];
4.     $liquid = $sauce["liquid"];
5.     $pan = $sauce["pan"];
6.     $how_hot = $sauce["how_hot"];
```

```
7.     $done = $sauce["done"];
8.     $half_cups = $sauce["half_cups"];
9.     $heat_sauce = $sauce["heat_source"];
10.    Place $pan on $heat_source;
11.    Turn on $heat_source under $pan to $how_hot;
12.    $roux = $thickener + $fat;
13.    Place $roux into $pan;
14.    $roux_status = "raw";
15.    while ( $roux_status == "raw" ) {
16.        stir $roux;
17.        $temp = temp( $roux );
18.        if ( $temp < $done ) {
19.            print "Not Yet";
20.        } elseif ( $temp >= $done && $temp < $done + 20 ) {
21.            $roux_status == "cooked";
22.        } else {
23.            $roux_status = "burned";
24.            throw_away( $roux );
25.            exit;
26.        }
27.    }
28.    Heat $liquid;
29.    $product = $roux;
30.    for ( $x=0; $x < $half_cups; $x++ ) {
31.        $product = $roux + ( $liquid * 1/2 cup );
32.        stir $product for 30 seconds;
33.        print "You have added $x cups";
34.    }
35.    return( $product );
36. }
```

Note that line 1 of the previous example includes the name of the function
make_sauce( ) and that immediately following the name, it has the word
$sauce inside parentheses. Here, $sauce is the array of values that is passed to
the make_sauce( ) function. In the program that calls make_sauce( ), an array
named $sauce is created and is filled with the various pieces of information that
the make_sauce( ) function will need to do its work. Note that the sauce array
contains eight values. When the calling program is invoked, it in turn sends the
$sauce array to fill the associated parameters:

```
1. $sauce["pan"] = "4 quart sauce pan";
2. $sauce["$how_hot"] = "medium high";
3. $sauce["heat_source"] = "stove";
4. $sauce["fat"] = "4T butter";
5. $sauce["thickener"] = "4T flour";
6. $sauce["liquid"] = "8C milk";
7. $sauce["$half_cups"] = 16;
8. $sauce["done"] = 375;
9. $bechamel = make_sauce( $sauce );
```

You may have noticed that line 35 of the function contains the line return ( $product ). Many functions return a result to the calling program. In the case of making a gravy, it would not make sense to go to the trouble of sending all of these values off to the make_sauce() function if one didn't expect a sauce as the result. This is what the return( value ) does. It takes the results of the function and returns them to the calling program.

On the other end, line 9 of the calling program contains the line bechamel = make_sauce( $sauce ). This essentially says: call the make_sauce() function, pass it to the $sauce array, and place the result in the $bechamel variable.

Note, if we were making a beef gravy, we would just store different values to the various parts of the $sauce array as follows:

```
1. $sauce["pan"] = "iron pot";
2. $sauce["$how_hot"] = "medium high";
3. $sauce["heat_source"] = "stove";
4. $sauce["fat"] = "8T beef fat";
5. $sauce["thickener"] = "8T flour";
6. $sauce["liquid"] = "12C beef broth";
7. $sauce["$half_cups"] = 24;
8. $sauce["done"] = 375;
9. $gravy = make_sauce( $sauce );
```

## Function Libraries and Applications

As noted, you can take individual functions and place them into a separate file, from which they can be included in any application file in which you need to use them. These libraries (and I will not insult your intelligence by explaining why a collection of functions might be called a library) are extremely valuable because you do not have to reinvent the wheel.

Gathering your own functions into library files is only the beginning. A number of other developers have also created their own function libraries and have made them available on the Internet. By finding and using these libraries, modifying them for your needs, you can save even more time and trouble. The bibliography lists just some of the libraries available.

Beyond just libraries, a number of development platforms—particularly Perl, PHP, and Python—are being used in the cooperative development of full-blown applications. These can range from library-specific applications such as MyLibrary to more general programs such as shopping baskets, help desk apps, and the like. The bibliography also lists some of the Web sites where one can find such applications.

## Program Structure

Just as there is a structure to cooking (you can't knead the bread until you have made the dough), so there is a basic procedure for writing a program. When designing any program, you need to take a step-by-step approach to the entire process. Then, within each step will be additional steps that need to be undertaken if the larger step is to be successful. In larger programs, these smaller steps may in turn have steps within them, and so on. This type of structured approach is essential to good program development and one that will be used throughout this book.

We can see this structured approach in action more clearly by examining the process of cooking a dish. In this case, I will show a structured approach to fixing Shrimp Étouffée. Figure 4-1 breaks the process of making this dish into its component parts. Each box, reading from left to right and up to down, represents one of the steps in preparing étouffée and each is keyed to a step in the traditionally laid out recipe in appendix A.[7]

By taking this approach, application development is much less scary. Instead of having a monolithic program that needs to be created, you define each of the smaller—and hence more manageable—steps and knock them out one at a time. Then, before you know it, you have written a program!

## Deciding Which Tool to Use

Before proceeding, we should take a look at the various open source tools available for use in development. All of these tools are also cross-platform—meaning that you can run them on Windows, Unix/Linux, and Mac OS X computers. Although PHP is the tool that I will be spending the most time on,[8] it is by no means the only one you can use. In fact, you can find strong proponents of any

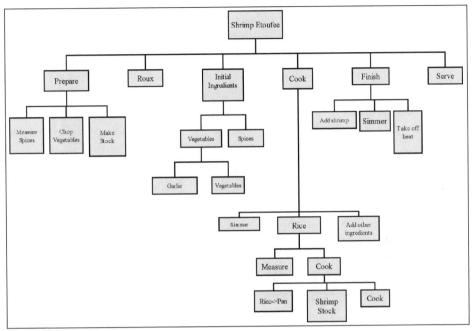

Figure 4-1

of these tools, each person giving strong reasons why their favorite is the "mother of all development tools."9 Although each tool (including PHP) has certain strengths and weaknesses, we won't go into those details here:

Space doesn't permit such comparison.

Such a comparison could easily descend into technical details.

Comparisons made as this book is being written will probably not be valid once it has been published (things happen quickly in the open source world).

There are enough true believers for any particular programming language (including myself) that you are in serious danger of starting a flame war from somebody who doesn't agree with your evaluation of their favorite tool.

I therefore limit myself to providing several points to consider in deciding which tool to use:

*Ease of learning*. How long does it take to get up to speed with a language? Does it require specialized skills?

*Maintainability*. How easily can the applications written in the language be supported and maintained by the developers or by others? How expensive will it be to hire/support somebody to work in the language?

*Readability*. Does the syntax make it easy to understand what is going on in the code? Does the language use idiosyncratic operators that are hard to understand or that are inconsistent in their meaning?

*Rapid development support*. Does it make it easy to develop applications quickly? Do you need to spend a lot of time writing and testing code?

*Error handling*. Does the tool have mechanisms that will allow you to gracefully handle unexpected events and problems, providing useful information to developers and, for public applications, appropriate messages to users?

*Cross-platform*. Does it support more than one type of server? Can it run on multiple operating systems?

*Built-in functions*. Does it have a wide variety of functions built into the system that you can use or is it up to you to write them yourself (or find someone who has already done so)?

*Flexibility and extensibility*. Will it handle all of the things you need to have it do? Does the language allow for the creation of function libraries or modules?

*Performance*. How well does it perform, particularly given multiple users?

*User base*. How popular is it and how many people are using it? In and of itself, this is not important. However, the more users there are, the more likely it is to be developed further; the more people out there who can get you through problems; and the more likely you are to find people who are able to program in it.

*Libraries, modules, and third-party applications*. Are there libraries and other code out there that you can obtain and add to your application (thereby avoiding having to reinvent the wheel)?

There are essentially seven open source language tools you can use to develop your project. The first two—gcc/g++ and Java—are industrial-strength, professional programming languages. The other five—tcl, Perl, PHP, Python, and Ruby—are essentially Web server–based scripting languages that allow Web development without demanding the computational or intellectual overhead of the first two. These can be used via the CGI interface and each—to varying degrees—can be integrated into the Apache server (and some with other Web servers) as an included module. In addition, with the exception of tcl, all five include object-oriented programming (OOP) capabilities, thus making it more likely for you to be able to find OOP libraries that will make your development work easier.

### gcc/g++

These two tools, respectively, are the gnu C and C++ compilers. You can use these languages in developing your project, but I wouldn't suggest it unless you have a lot of money and/or a predictable source of really good C programmers. The reason is straightforward. It is true that C and C++ are widely used in industry and business and produce fast,[10] extremely powerful, and flexible applications, but they require long development time and have the steepest learning curve of any of the tools listed. As a result, they can be a support nightmare if you don't have appropriate expertise available (such expertise being not inexpensive). Additionally, given that they support only the CGI interface, they are not particularly well adapted to Web programming. Essentially, they should be considered only if you have long-term in-house support for C and/or C++ development and will be using them for building in major Web-based applications.[11]

### Java

Created by Sun Microsystems, Java is a cross-platform, object-oriented language that is currently the hottest programming tool for professional (read "expensive to hire") developers.[12] It comes in a wide variety of flavors and can be used as a CGI application, embedded within HTML pages (using Java Server Pages), or can even support complete Web-based applications, forgoing HTML altogether. In addition, it arguably has the best XML support of any language at this point (although Perl and PHP 5.0 are beginning to give it a run for its money). However, as with C/C++, Java is a professional developer's tool and is therefore probably beyond the scope of what you might want to consider for your projects.

### tcl

Long known as a Unix scripting language (often in conjunction with tk, a graphical interface development language), tcl (pronounced tickle) has a small but scrappy following. Also, because it has been around for some time, it has undergone years of development and has built up quite an installed base. It also gathered a number of adherents after the AOLServer added a tcl interpreter within the server (a precursor of the mod_* Apache modules). Tcl allows you to follow different programming models and offers a great deal of flexibility in how you create your applications. It is available both via the CGI interface and as a server module.

## Perl

The most mature of the Web-development languages, Perl has a very wide following and provides the greatest power and flexibility of any of the scripting tools mentioned here. Thanks to the CPAN (Comprehensive Perl Archive Network), a tremendous number of libraries and modules have been created that support virtually anything you might ever want to do, from Unicode to XML. However, this power and flexibility comes at a price. Its syntax, which shows its roots in Unix tools such as sed and awk, can be terse to the point of incomprehensibility. Although it has traditionally been used as a CGI tool, the development of mod_perl, and the subsequent creation of Apache::ASP and Mason, have made Perl-based server modules possible.[13]

## PHP

PHP is another C-like scripting language that has become extremely popular in recent years, as is clear in the steadily increasing number of bookstore and library titles, many in conjunction with MySQL. Because it supports both CGI and server-side approaches, PHP is extremely popular with Web developers.[14] It is also especially easy to learn and use. Another characteristic that has helped in its popularity, especially with database developers, is that its support for database access is integrated into the system, rather than available through installed third-party modules. Although it initially had some problems in being taken seriously, PHP's respectability has been helped considerably by Yahoo and other large organizations, such as Lufthansa and NASA, switching over to it. PHP still has fewer libraries available at this time than Perl, but the launch of the PHP Extension and Application Repository (PEAR), designed to follow the CPAN model, should help close this gap.

## Python

Python is an object-oriented programming language that has generated quite a bit of interest in the Web development community. Third-party modules have been created, including a number for database access, though the number and scope do not currently equal those available for Perl or even PHP. Python is held to be easy to learn. One does, however, need to understand the basics of object-oriented programming. Python also is used by a number of companies, including Google.

## Ruby

Ruby is characterized on its Web site as a "complete, pure, object oriented language—not in the sense of Python or Perl, but in the sense of Smalltalk." As with most of the other tools in this section, support for database access is provided via third-party libraries that you download and include in your Web pages or programming code. Even more so than with Python, you will need to learn how to write object-oriented programs to use Ruby.

Although all of the products listed have significant strengths, I think that PHP provides the best balance of performance, robustness of development efforts, size of user community, ease of use, and reasonable learning curve of the products listed. By embedding programming instructions within HTML pages, PHP makes it much easier for those who are just getting started. Once you have a feeling for how things are done in PHP, you may want to explore some of the information and links in this book and try some of these other tools.

## Notes

1. I am taking extreme poetic license here. In real programming, the number of an item is usually separate from the type of item that it is. For example, the proper way to state 4T butter would probably be `4t * $fat`. I bend the rules a bit here to make things easier to understand.
2. This syntax for accessing array elements is based on PHP. You will need to check appropriate documentation if you are using another language.
3. The way to read this line is "starting with `$x` equal to 0, and as long as the value of `$x` is less than the value of `$half_cups`, and adding 1 to `$x` each time through this loop, do the following." The phrases are not in the usual order, of course, but remember that we are dealing with a glorified calculator.
4. This is not exactly true of the `for` loop. The differences will be explained.
5. I do not know whether 350 is the temperature at which the roux would in fact be done. This, though, is a programming manual, not a cookbook.
6. Start thinking of functions as your friend. As you go through the exercises in this book—or take on new projects of your own—and as you design the flow of the program, be sure to consult the list of functions available in the language you are using to see if there are functions that you can plug into certain steps. The O'Reilly Pocket Reference series is a good place to start. See also the list online at http://us2.php .net/manual/en/funcref.php.

7. My apology to all Louisianans out there if this is not a proper Cajun recipe. It's the best this Yankee can come up with.

8. Thanks to its relatively low learning curve and flexibility, it is in my opinion the tool best suited as an introduction to Web programming for beginning programmers.

9. In fact, one of the characteristics of the open source community is an almost missionary zeal in support of the developer's and user's viewpoint. The development language of choice is no different.

10. These are, though, not that much faster when compared to languages embedded within the server, such as mod_php, mod_perl, and others listed here.

11. One further complication is that to run gcc on a Win32 platform, you need to install the cygwin utilities from RedHat and then download the appropriate files and libraries and install them on your computer. Not a task for the faint of heart.

12. While not currently an open source language, Sun seems to be moving (as of March 2006) toward making Java open source. In addition, Java is used extensively in a large number of open source applications.

13. Both are available for users of the Apache Web server equipped with mod_perl and Apache::ASP libraries.

14. It can be run as a module on Apache, Netscape, and IIS servers.

# 5 CREATING REPORTS

Let's take what we have learned and put it to use. In this chapter, I show you a variety of reports that you can create using PHP. We will begin by creating a simple page to demonstrate the basics of writing a Web-based report. Next, we examine how to create pages using search parameters hard-coded in the page, by passing values to the page via the URL, and then by using input from a form. We will then build on that knowledge to create searching applications. (The annotated source code for all these scripts can be found in Reports_Source.pdf in the companion materials download file.)

## CREATING A BASIC REPORT

### Report Structure

In our first example, we will create a phone list from the database we created in chapter 3. The structure of this program is fairly simple, and is broken down into four parts:

> *Connecting to the database*—establishing a connection by sending the database in question a username and password (required by most RDBMS products)

*Creating and sending a query*—writing a properly formed SQL query and then submitting it to the RDBMS

*Creating the Web page*—taking the results you receive back from the database and using them to create an HTML page

*Outputting the results*—the Web server sends the resulting page back to the user

Figure 5-1 graphically represents this process (moving top to bottom and left to right). I have broken down the sample examples into the three steps—connecting to the database, creating and running the query, and creating the Web page (as noted, the Web server takes care of the fourth step)—to make what we are doing more clear.

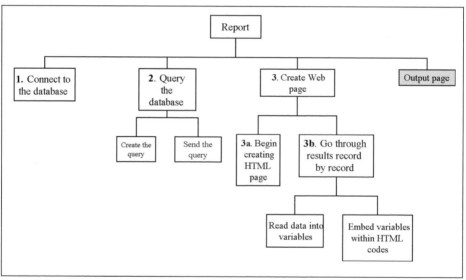

Figure 5-1

## Creating the Report Program

Let's begin by using this structure to create a report to output data from the telephone database we created in chapter 3. If you look at report.php in Reports_Source.pdf, you will see all of the commands used to create the report, broken down into the three steps. These files include annotations ("commenting" the code—always a very good thing to do when writing programs) that describe what each step does.

To place these comments in the file in such a way so as not to confuse the PHP server application, we need to surround them with special characters that tell the module to ignore anything between them. In this book, we use four types:

#    Placing this character on the first position on a line causes the line to be skipped. We use this character, along with full lines of # before and after the comments to help them stand out. For example, the major sections of code we discussed above will have such comments at the beginning of each section.

/* .. */    Placing /* on the line before a comment, */ on the line after, and then placing an asterisk in the first position on each line in between identifies the block to the PHP module as a comment. (The asterisks at the beginning of intermediate lines are not required but do help to distinguish them from lines of code to the reader.) We use this style of comment to explain subunits within the major sections of the pages.

//    Double forward slashes anywhere in a line will cause the PHP module to ignore everything after it on that line. For that reason, we will be using it to explain individual lines of PHP code, also known as inline comments. For example, when the PHP engine comes to

```
$x = $x+1;              // add one to $x
```

it will compute $x = $x+1 and then skip to the next line.

<!-- -->    We use traditional HTML commenting style for comments in HTML areas.

When we run the script, the code creates a page that looks like the one in figure 5-2.

Let's examine this script to see how it works. First we set up a PHP area by placing the opening PHP tag (<?php) on line 1 and the closing tag (?>) on line 21. Anything that we type in between these two tags will be interpreted as PHP code. Within this area, we will undertake the tasks listed in the first two boxes listed in figure 5-1: we make the connection to the database and send the query to the server.

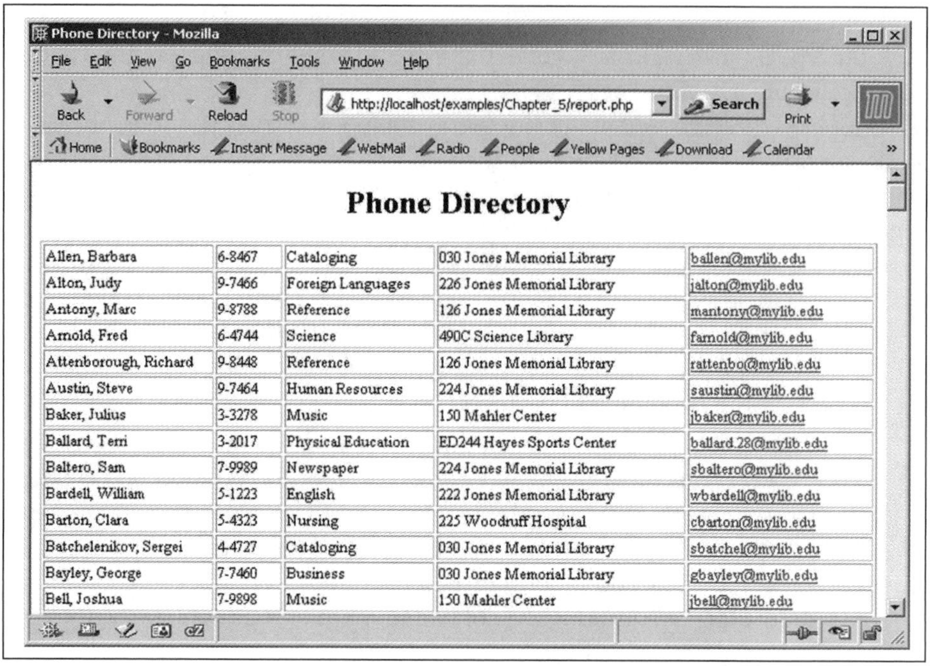


| | | | | |
|---|---|---|---|---|
| Allen, Barbara | 6-8467 | Cataloging | 030 Jones Memorial Library | ballen@mylib.edu |
| Alton, Judy | 9-7466 | Foreign Languages | 226 Jones Memorial Library | jalton@mylib.edu |
| Antony, Marc | 9-8788 | Reference | 126 Jones Memorial Library | mantony@mylib.edu |
| Arnold, Fred | 6-4744 | Science | 490C Science Library | farnold@mylib.edu |
| Attenborough, Richard | 9-8448 | Reference | 126 Jones Memorial Library | rattenbo@mylib.edu |
| Austin, Steve | 9-7464 | Human Resources | 224 Jones Memorial Library | saustin@mylib.edu |
| Baker, Julius | 3-3278 | Music | 150 Mahler Center | jbaker@mylib.edu |
| Ballard, Terri | 3-2017 | Physical Education | ED244 Hayes Sports Center | ballard.28@mylib.edu |
| Baltero, Sam | 7-9989 | Newspaper | 224 Jones Memorial Library | sbaltero@mylib.edu |
| Bardell, William | 5-1223 | English | 222 Jones Memorial Library | wbardell@mylib.edu |
| Barton, Clara | 5-4323 | Nursing | 225 Woodruff Hospital | cbarton@mylib.edu |
| Batchelenikov, Sergei | 4-4727 | Cataloging | 030 Jones Memorial Library | sbatchel@mylib.edu |
| Bayley, George | 7-7460 | Business | 030 Jones Memorial Library | gbayley@mylib.edu |
| Bell, Joshua | 7-9898 | Music | 150 Mahler Center | jbell@mylib.edu |

Figure 5-2

First we make the connection in lines 13–14, using the parameters we set in chapter 3, as shown in example 5-1.

Example 5-1

```
13  $db = mysql_connect( "localhost", "Phones", "Fone_Usr" );
14  mysql_select_db( "web_info", $db );
```

Line 13 uses PHP's `mysql_connect()` function to connect to the database server using three parameters: the host (in this case, `localhost`), the username to connect as (the one we created in chapter 3, `Phones`), and the username's password (`Fone_Usr`, also set up in chapter 3), assigning the resulting connection to `$db` (note that if you changed either the username or password in creating the database, you will need to replace what is here with what you used at that time). Then, in line 14, we use PHP's `mysql_select_db()` function to use that connection to tell the MySQL database server that we want to use the `web_info` database and assign that connection to the `$db` handle (a handle is essentially a variable that you use to communicate with the database).

Next, we create our SQL query and send it to the MySQL database server. This is done in lines 19 and 20 (see example 5-2).

Example 5-2

```
19  $query = "SELECT * FROM phones ORDER BY last_name,first_name";
20  $result = mysql_query( $query, $db ) or die( mysql_error() );
```

Here we create a variable name $query and assign it an SQL query that asks for all fields (SELECT*) from the phones table (FROM phones), sorted by last_name and, within that, the first_name (ORDER BY last_name, first_name). Then in line 20, we use PHP's mysql_query() function to send the $query to the database (via $db), storing the results to $result.

Once we have our data, we proceed to the next step and create the actual report page. First, we define the HTML area into which we will embed our search results in lines 28–34 (see example 5-3).

Example 5-3

```
28  <html>
29  <head>
30  <title>Phone Directory</title>
31  </head>
32  <body>
33  <center><h1>Phone Directory</h1></center>
34  <table border="1" width="100%">
```

Next we read the results into variables and output the values embedded within HTML codes. We do the first in lines 43–47 (see example 5-4).

Example 5-4

```
41  <?php
42  while ( $row = mysql_fetch_array( $result ) ) {
43      $name = $row["last_name"] . ", " . $row["first_name"];
44      $phone = $row["phone"];
45      $department = $row["department"];
46      $location = $row["location"];
47      $email = $row["email"];
48  ?>
49      <tr>
50          <td><?php echo "$name" ?></td>
51          <td><?php echo "$phone" ?></td>
52          <td><?php echo "$department" ?></td>
53          <td><?php echo "$location" ?></td>
54          <td><a href="mailto:<?php echo "$email" ?>@mylib.edu"><?php echo "$email" ?>@mylib.edu</a></td>
55      </tr>
56  <?php
57  }
58  ?>
```

As you may recall from chapter 4, one of the techniques to output arrays is a while block, permitting us to access the contents one item at a time. What this block is saying is this: While there is still a record to process, use PHP's mysql_fetch_array() to extract one record—in the form of an array—and store it to an associative array named $row.[1] Then, just as we did with the $sauce array in chapter 3, we can take each element in the $row array and save it to a variable for outputting.

Using `mysql_fetch_array()` to give us associative arrays (as described in chapter 4) allows us to use the field name to access the field's value. Next, we go through each field we want to output and save its value to a variable with the field's name. In line 43, we actually place two fields into the first variable (`$name`): the `last_name` and `first_name` fields so that we can treat name as a single entity. We do this by joining them (concatenating) by taking the `$name` variable and

- assigning the value of the `last_name` element of `$row` to it
- concatenating (adding) a comma and space at the end of `$name`
- tacking on the `first_name` from `$row` to the end of `$name`[2]

The final task is to output the values in our Web page. Although there are a number of ways to do this, here we temporarily break out of the PHP block (line 48) and output the variables using HTML tags (lines 49–55). Then, so that PHP doesn't become confused as to where things end, we close the `while` block we began in line 41 in lines 56–58 (opening up a PHP block so that the brace will be interpreted as a PHP curly brace).[3]

Note that lines 49–55 are not within a PHP area. We therefore use `echo` with each variable within a PHP block (`<?php echo $variable ?>`) to print out the actual value. While we could have remained in the PHP block, that would have required more typing (using `echo` for the HTML tags). This technique of using `<?php echo $variable ?>` can be very useful and one that we will be using quite a bit in accessing PHP variables inside HTML areas.

One additional thing I have done to make this list more useful is to turn the e-mail address into an actual `mailto` link in line 54 in example 5-4. We do this by simply wrapping the output for the `$email` variable in the appropriate HTML code.

## Obtaining Selective Output

Now that we have a basic report, let's be a bit more selective about what we output. After all, one of the advantages of using a database is that it allows you to retrieve only those records that match what you want to retrieve. As you may recall from chapter 2, we create those subsets by adding a `WHERE` condition to the query in the form `WHERE <fieldname> = '<condition>'`. Then, when the database is searched, the search engine filter retrieves only those records that match that condition.

## Hard Coding

There are three ways you can set the condition. One way is to hard code the query. For example, say you want to create a staff page for the Music Library (as we have done in mus_lib.php). You would simply go into the PHP script above and change lines 20–22 to read as shown in example 5-5.

Example 5-5

```
20  $query = "SELECT * FROM phones
21           WHERE department='Music'
22           ORDER BY last_name,first_name";
23  $result = mysql_query( $query, $db ) or die( mysql_error() );
```

You would then get the screen shown in figure 5-3.

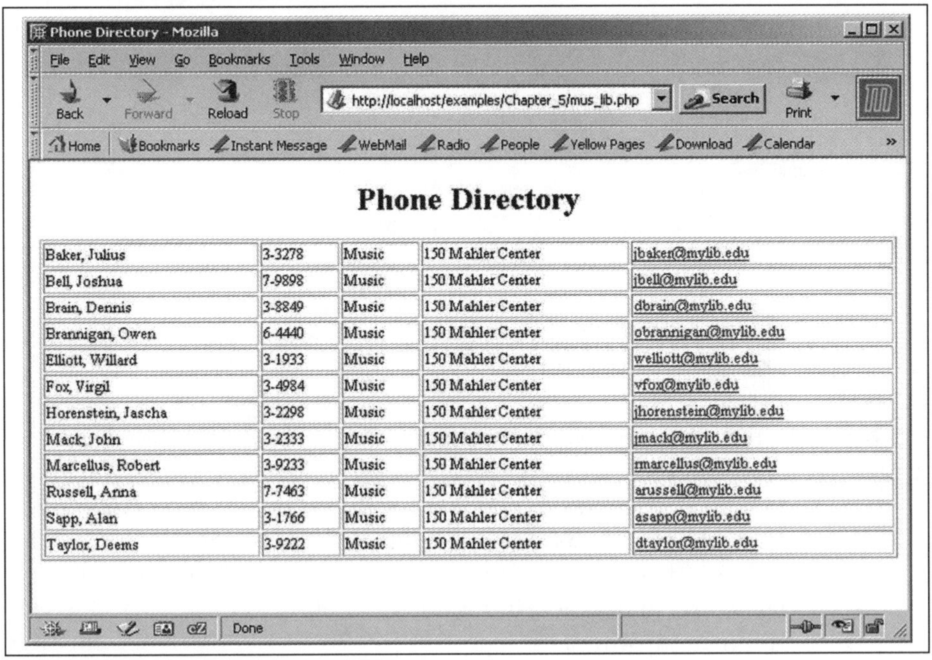

Figure 5-3

## Passing Parameters via URLs

Besides hard coding a condition into a script, we can also pass a parameter to the page via the URL and the page can then use it as the basis for its query. An extremely useful technique, this enables us to automatically generate a page containing a defined subset of a database by simply passing the page a parameter that defines that subset. By allowing us to encode this search into a URL, we have much more flexibility in how we use our database.

For example, say we were responsible for the Music Library's Web pages and wanted to include a link to a Music Library staff directory on our department home page. We could create such a link by embedding the following URL in that page:

```
<A HREF="url_report.php?department=Music">Directory</A>
```

To process this request, we need to copy the report.php to url_report.php and then make appropriate changes to url_report.php:

> Because variables passed via URLs are passed using the GET method, we first make sure that such a value has been passed (see line 20 of example 5-6). If so, we save it to a variable named $department (line 21). If not, we indicate to the user to provide a value and how to do so (lines 24–25) and exit (line 26).

Example 5-6

```
20  if ( isset( $_GET["department"] ) ) {
21      $department = $_GET["department"];
22      $department = urldecode($department);
23  } else {
24      echo "You will need to provide the name of a department in the form ";
25      echo "<b><i>url_report.php?department=&lt;department name&gt;</i></b> as the URL";
26      exit;
27  }
28  $query = "SELECT * FROM phones
29              WHERE department='$department'
30              ORDER BY last_name,first_name";
31  $result = mysql_query( $query, $db ) or die( mysql_error() );
```

> Note that some of the departments in the department list have two words in their name. However, we can't create a URL string containing a space in the middle of it (for example, `<a href="url_report.php?Department=Special Collections">Special Collections</a>`) because the browser won't process anything after the first space it encounters. Therefore, a URL for this resource must replace spaces with %20 (the hexadecimal code for space): `<a href="url_report.php?Department=Special%20 Collections">Special Collections</a>`. However, we need to turn it back into a space before sending it to the database. Therefore, in line 22, we use PHP's `urldecode()` function to do that transformation for us.

> Finally, we need to modify the query so that it uses the parameter that has been passed to it (line 29).

Before proceeding, I would like to briefly explain the concept of superglobals. Superglobals (reserved variables) are global associative arrays built into PHP to make certain types of information available between PHP pages. In the case above, $ GET is an array that contains all of the information being passed to the action page via the GET method. There are a number of these superglobals we will be dealing with throughout this book.[4]

Although we won't spend a lot of time exploring variations of embedding search parameters within a URL, it is an extremely powerful and useful tool in Web database development. It allows you to pass parameters via the URL, permitting you to create canned searches of your database and embedding them as hyperlinks either in Web pages or, if appropriate, in the 856 fields of MARC bibliographic records in your online catalog.

## Search Input Form

Although the previous examples do some valuable things, they are only a beginning. After all, you won't want to (let alone be able to) create a report for every query that a user could possibly want. Better to set up a way by which a user can enter his or her search parameters. After all, isn't that what databases are supposed to do?

To enable end-user searching of a database, we need to have two files: one a form into which users can enter their search terms (input form) and one that will take those search terms, query the database, and output the results (action page). The first thing we do is create the query form (report_query.php). Although it is fairly straightforward, there are a couple of aspects we should take note of. First, in line 7 (example 5-7) we have defined the action (the name of our action page) as report_ search.php. The other is that, in line 23 (example 5-8), we have created a text <input> box with the name of **department**.

Example 5-7
```
 7    <form method="POST" action="report_search.php">
```

Example 5-8
```
23              <input type="text" name="department" size="30" maxlength="80">
```

This name here will be the name of the variable that will be passed to the action page. We use the name of the field (with the same capitalization) that will be searched. As you will see, doing this greatly facilitates your work with databases and makes your code much more supportable.

Although this page has a .php extension, it does not contain any actual PHP code. This is extremely important to note, particularly once we get to chapters 7,

8, and 9. Creating HTML pages with the .php extension opens the door to a number of possibilities, including

- pages with global variables, headers and footers, and other features that PHP can make available to you
- PHP-based authentication and authorization mechanisms to restrict access to the pages (something not possible with .html extension files)[5]

## Action Page

Once we get the user input, we need to do something with it. This is where the action page we have named report_search.php comes in. The following figure demonstrates the basic structure of an action page in a searching application. As you can see in figure 5-4, it is a slight variation on the report structure discussed above, the only difference being getting the user input.

To create our action, we take url_report.php and copy it to report_search.php. Then, because we have defined the **method** in report_ query.php as **POST**, we need to modify line 20 (example 5-9) to use the $_POST array instead of the $_GET array we were required to use when taking values from a URL string.

Example 5-9

```
20   $department = $_POST["department"];
```

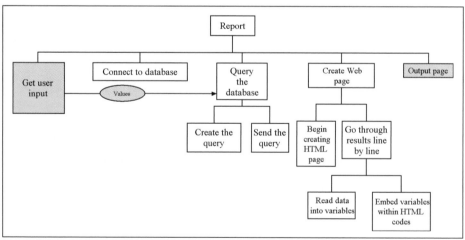

Figure 5-4

Now, if we enter `systems` into the **Department** text box in the `$report_query` search inputting form, we get the result shown in figure 5-5.

Before proceeding, let me point out a naming convention used here that will be used throughout the book. All input forms meant to gather user terms (and then pass them on to a searching action page) will have a base name of query.php with an identifier (in this case, report_) as a prefix to indicate its role in the application. The action pages that do the search and output results will use search.php (with the same identifier prefix) as their base name. This practice allows you, first, to group pages based on what part they play in the greater application and, second, to have a predictable way of naming files so that you will be able to tell by looking at the name what each one of them does.

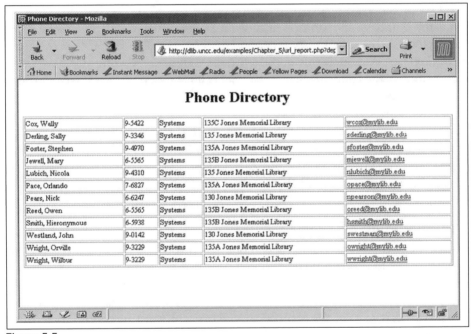

Figure 5-5

## CREATING SEARCHING APPLICATIONS

I have now given you the basic structures you need to create database-searching applications. In the rest of the chapter, I show you some ways you can expand on these ideas to implement more sophisticated searching techniques. We begin by adding more fields to the search form.

In looking at these different approaches, we will limit ourselves to applications that use a single table. Searching multiple tables is more complex because it involves joins to carry out the search. I have found that it is better to start slowly and cover the basic elements of searching applications. We explore searching multiple-table databases in chapters 7 and 9.

Note that the examples that I provide in this book involve using SQL to search relational databases. This approach can be both RDBMS-specific (if one uses proprietary features—as I do—in their programming) and demanding on the programmer, who must be able to write sophisticated queries to retrieve the desired information.

One possible alternative is to write report programs that extract information from the database and store it in individual files. You would then use a Web search tool, such as Swish-e, to index and search those files (rather than the database directly). Although this approach does require recreating the files when information in the database changes, it does offer some advantages. Not only does it give you access to some pretty sophisticated searching techniques (including the ability to index and search HTML, XML, and PDF documents), it relieves the programmer of having to write the search engine. Although describing how this can be done is beyond the scope of this book, I have included more information in the bibliography and some setup and configuration instructions in Setup.pdf, part of the companion materials download file.

## Inputting Multiple Values Using AND

So far, all of the searching we have done has involved a single search term or phrase posed to a single field. Although this can be useful, it is simplistic and doesn't allow for much refinement of the searching process. To search multiple terms, we need to provide a mechanism by which multiple terms can be entered. Then we need to take the search parameters and construct appropriate SQL queries. In this section, I will provide some examples for doing just that.

### Multiple Text Boxes

In the next example, I will construct a search form (multi_query.php) that will allow the user to search four fields: first name, last name, department, and location. Although the form is fairly straightforward, when writing the action page (multi_search.php), we need to take into account that the user may fill in any, all, or even none of the fields on the page. We then need to take appropriate action based on their input. Example 5-10 demonstrates the last of the three cases: the user has input nothing. Because we need to have something to search, at least one of the fields needs to have a value.

Example 5-10

```
19   $first_name = trim( $_POST["first_name"] );
20   $last_name = trim( $_POST["last_name"] );
21   $department = trim( $_POST["department"] );
22   $location = trim( $_POST["location"] );
23
24   /*******************************************************************
25    * Next, we construct the $where string to check each one of the form's
26    * fields.  If it finds a value, it adds an appropriate WHERE condition
27    * to the $where_ary
28    *****************************************************************/
29   if ( $first_name == "" && $last_name == "" && $department == "" && $location == "" ) {
30       echo "Please enter a query";
31       exit;
32   }
```

What the block between lines 29 and 32 is essentially saying is that if `first_name` is blank and `last_name` is blank and `department` is blank and `location` is blank (&& being MySQL's Boolean AND operator), then tell the user "Please enter a query" and exit the program. We can assume that the program will skip this block, if any of the fields is not blank, and go on to line 55 (see example 5-11). To make this work, we need to make sure that there are no extraneous spaces in the queries, such as the user accidentally hitting the space bar at the end of their input. We do this by using PHP's `trim()` function to eliminate any spaces before or after the terms in lines 19–22 when we read in the query parameters.

Example 5-11

```
34   $w = 0;
35   /*******************************************************************
36    * Then, we see if the second search has a field and value.  If so, we attach
37    *      it to the end of the $where string.
38    *****************************************************************/
39   if ( $first_name !="" ) {
40       $where_ary[$w] = "first_name = '$first_name'";
41       $w++;
42   }
43
44   /*******************************************************************
45    * Then, we do the same with the Last_Name
46    *****************************************************************/
47   if ( $last_name !="" ) {
48       $where_ary[$w] = "last_name = '$last_name'";
49       $w++;
50   }
51
52   /*******************************************************************
53    * Then, we do the same with the Department.
54    *****************************************************************/
55   if ( $department !="" ) {
56       $where_ary[$w] = "department = '$department'";
57       $w++;
58   }
59
60   /*******************************************************************
61    * Then, we do the same with the Location.
62    *****************************************************************/
63   if ( $location !="" ) {
64       $where_ary[$w] = "location='$location'";
65       $w++;
66   }
```

The next section of code (lines 34–66), shown in example 5-11, checks each variable coming from the form to see if the user has input something for that field. For each one it finds, it adds a WHERE condition to an array ($where_ary) of WHERE conditions. In the first one, it checks to see if $first_name is blank. If not, it saves first_name = '$first_name' to the $where_ary[$w] element ($w being equal to 0 at that point, having been set to that value in line 34) and then adds 1 to $w (making it equal to 1). The program then goes through the rest of the list of fields, adding an element to the $where_ary array and adding 1 to $w for each field for which a value has been entered by the user.

When we're through, we have an array of WHERE conditions to add to the end of our SQL query. At line 71 (see example 5-12), we begin a for block that will go through the $where_ary array one element at a time and add its content to the $where statement. In line 72, the program checks to see if this is the first element to be processed. The reason for this is that we need to have an AND between all elements (but not before the first one). By processing the first condition or element separately, we can place the condition field = 'value' at the beginning of the WHERE statement. Then, for every statement that comes afterwards, we just tack AND field = 'value' on to the end of the statement (as we do in lines 74–76)—thereby allowing us to not add more ANDs than we need.

Example 5-12

```
68  /************************************************************
69   * Now we go through the $where_ary, constructing our $where statement.
70   ************************************************************/
71  for ($x = 0; $x < $w; $x++) {
72      if ( $x == 0 ) {
73          $where = $where_ary[0];
74      } else {
75          $where .= " AND $where_ary[$x] ";
76      }
77  }
78
79  /************************************************************
80   * Now we put all of these things together, create our query and send it
81   * to the database
82   ************************************************************/
83  $query = "SELECT * FROM phones
84              WHERE $where
85              ORDER BY last_name,first_name";
86  $result = mysql_query( $query, $db ) or die( mysql_error() );
87  $num_rows = mysql_num_rows( $result );
```

Once we have built a $where statement, we use it in constructing our query (lines 83–85) and send it to the database (line 86). Then, in line 87, we use PHP's mysql_num_rows() function to store the number of records retrieved by our query to $num_rows. If the number is 0, we inform the user in lines 109–112 (example 5-13) that their search has been unsuccessful and that they should try again (and exit the program). If it is not, then we proceed to create the screen as in earlier examples.

Example 5-13

```
109   if ( $num_rows == 0 ) {
110       echo "Your search retrieved no results. Please go back and try again";
111       exit;
112   }
```

## Adding Features

The previous examples have given us the basic concept, we now explore more real-world techniques that can help your users find information. In the next example application—multi_keyword—we will explore two such techniques: drop-down lists and keyword searching.

DROP-DOWN LISTS    There may be times when your users don't know the alternatives or the values in the database. In such cases, it can be helpful to give them a list from which they can select, rather than making them guess what may be in there. HTML forms provide a wonderful technique for doing that: the select list. Example 5-14 modifies the previous form to make a list of what is in the database and to create an alphabetized drop-down list from which the user can select.

Example 5-14

```
22   Department: <br>
23   <select name="department">
24       <option></option>
25   <?php
26       $db = mysql_connect( "localhost", "Phones", "Fone_Usr" );
27       mysql_select_db( "web_info", $db );
28       $query = "SELECT DISTINCT department FROM phones ORDER BY department";
29       $result = mysql_query( $query, $db ) or die( mysql_error() );
30       while ( $row = mysql_fetch_array( $result ) ) {
31           $department = $row["department"];
32           echo "<option name=\"$department\">$department</option>\n";
33       }
34   ?>
35   </select>
```

In lines 22–35 of multi_keyword_query.php, we can see how this can be achieved. In this example, we treat the department field in this way by creating a select list, filling it with data from the database. Lines 22–24 and 35 provide the HTML structure for the list. In lines 25–34, we create a PHP block where we do a mini-report containing all three sections of a full report: making a connection to the database (26–27), creating the query (28), running the query (29), and then embedding the results in HTML, this time as a set of <option> tags (30–33).

Although the outer parts of it are like any other select list, there are a few things to note within the PHP block:

We create our query using the DISTINCT SQL operator. This tells the database to give us a list of all unique values within the department field, eliminating all duplicates. In addition, we sort the output by the `department` field.

We go through the results record by record—while ( $row = mysql_ fetch_array( $result ) )— saving the current record as an associative array to $row and then reading the `department` field value into the `$department` variable.

The values for each record are plugged into an <option> line and output to the screen.

The new line parameter \n is added to the end of each <option> line to make debugging easier. Although making no difference to the HTML output, it does make it easier to read the page source from within your browser's **View Source** window by creating a new line after each option. Otherwise, the entire block will be on one long line.

KEYWORD SEARCHING    Another feature we will want in a searching application is to be able to search by keyword rather than requiring the user to search by the entire contents of the field. There are three ways to implement keyword searching in MySQL:

1. Use the LIKE operator. As we saw in chapter 2, this is clearly an unsatisfactory technique to use because it often returns counterintuitive results. It also takes truncation out of the hands of the end-user.
2. Use MySQL's FULLTEXT indexing capabilities. Although a proprietary technique within MySQL, many other products do offer similar capabilities. This is the approach I demonstrate in this chapter. For it to work, you need to go into phpMyAdmin and add a FULLTEXT index to the field you wish to search in this manner (which you should already have done as part of the database creation step in chapter 3).
3. Use regular expressions. Regular expressions are a very powerful—if not easily learned—technique built into many systems, including MySQL. Because of their complexity, we won't be able to deal with them here. I have, however, created several functions for chapters 7 and 9 that use them.

The syntax for FULLTEXT index searching in MySQL on a field where multiple conditions are included is:

```
MATCH (<field_name>) AGAINST ('+<value_from_form>' in BOOLEAN
    MODE)
```

In multi_keyword_search.php, I have modified the multi_search.php file to support a keyword search of the `location` field. Once we have created the `FULLTEXT` index on the `location` field in phpMyAdmin (which we did when we created the database in chapter 3), all we need to do is to modify the step (in lines 65–68) in multi_keyword_search.php where the `WHERE` condition for `location` is created to enable keyword searching (see example 5-15).

Example 5-15

```
65  if ( $location !="" ) {
66      $where_ary[$w] = " MATCH (location) AGAINST ('+$location' in BOOLEAN MODE) ";
67      $w++;
68  }
```

Now, by entering Jones into the **Location** box, we get a listing of all personnel in Jones Memorial Library, no matter their room number. In fact, we could even enter Jone*, using the asterisk as our truncation symbol.

When using `FULLTEXT` indexes, you need to keep several things in mind—things that may have an impact on the desirability and usefulness of the feature (note that none of these apply to the third option that we discussed earlier in this chapter: using regular expressions):

> It will ignore any word of three letters or fewer (unless it has a truncation operator). However, this can be changed by changing ft_min_word_len (the minimum word length parameter) in my.cnf.[6]

> It will fail if your search contains any word that appears in more than 50 percent of the records in the table you are searching.

> It does not permit features such as transactions and foreign key constraints. We will discuss this limitation further in chapter 7.

## Using AND and OR

All the searches we have done until now have placed a Boolean `AND` between the terms we have been searching. Although using `AND` can help refine your search, there may be times you want to expand your results set by `OR`'ing terms together. Before proceeding, you need to go through what is known in programming (and other) circles as operator precedence. Simply put: do you want to group the terms that have been `OR`'ed before or after you group the ones that have been `AND`'ed?

For example, let's say we have a sentence: Sarah and Jim or Bill got married. This could either mean "Sarah and Jim got married OR Bill got married (to somebody else)" or it could mean "Sarah married either Jim or Bill." Because, as we have already noted, computers aren't the brightest bulbs in the shop, we need to be explicit about who goes with what, or the computer will do it its own way (which may not make the three people in question very happy). In the following example, we make the decision that we will OR our terms before we AND them (leading to the second interpretation of our nuptial dilemma).

In terms of what the inputting form looks like, I have made a couple of changes that give the user more control. First, the user may want to look for two different last names and not care about departments. In using this form, the user is allowed to choose the fields to be searched, including being able to select the same field more than once. I do this in two steps. First, rather than hard coding the field names, I create a drop-down `select` list from which the user selects a field, that field name being stored to `Fieldx` (see example 5-16). Then, when the form is processed by the action page, the field name represented by `$Fieldx`— rather than a hard-coded field name—will be entered into the query.[7]

Example 5-16

```
12   <select name="Field1">
13     <option></option>
14     <option value="first_name">First Name</option>
15     <option value="last_name">Last Name</option>
16     <option value="department">Department</option>
17     <option value="location">Location</option>
18   </select>
```

Then, to pass on what the user wants as the operator, we create a drop-down list using the variable names `Operator1`, `Operator2`, and so forth (example 5-17).

Example 5-17

```
24   <select name="Operator1">
25     <option></option>
26     <option value="AND">AND</option>
27     <option value="OR">OR</option>
28   </select>
```

Users also often have different needs for how they want to sort their output. One way to enable this is to provide a drop-down where they select the order they want. Then, when the form is submitted, their information is passed to the action page and the appropriate sort can be undertaken. I have provided an example of this in example 5-18, where a drop-down list for an `order` variable has been created.[8]

Example 5-18

```
90  Order by:
91  <select name="Order">
92    <option value="last_name,first_name">Name</option>
93    <option value="department">Department</option>
94    <option value="location">Location</option>
95  </select>
```

Once we have made these changes and filled in the form with a sample query, we get the screen shown in figure 5-6.

When we get to the action page (and_or_search.php), we encounter another variation on our query construction step. Here, we need to construct an intermediate string that we can then break up into constituent elements to construct our final query. Figure 5-7 provides a basic road map to the process.[9]

Here, we first check for each of the four potential fields coming in for new user input. In the first field, we make sure that the user has both selected a field name and input a value. If not, we ask the user to enter a search, after which we exit the program.

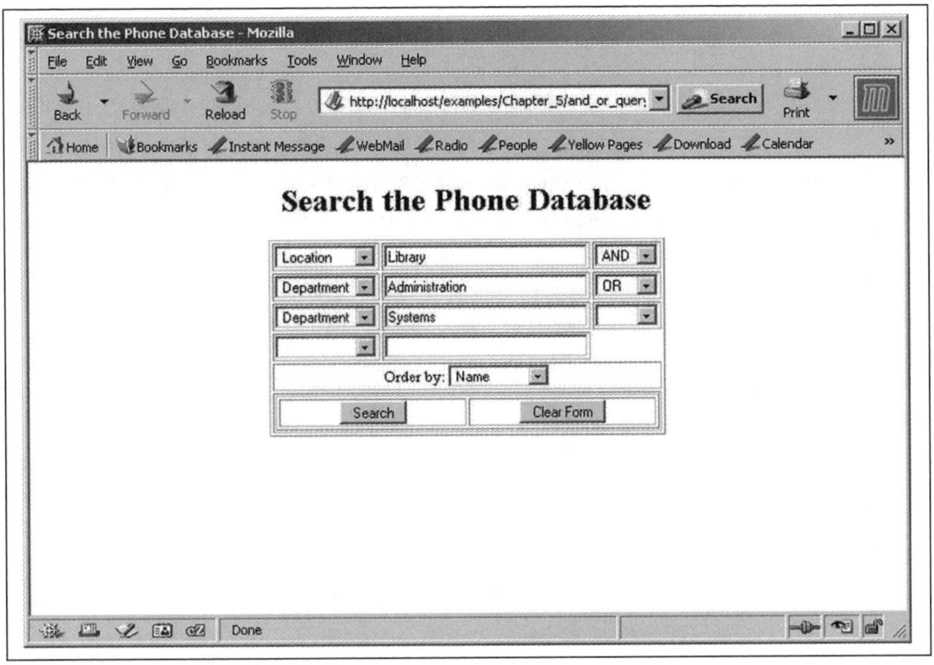

Figure 5-6

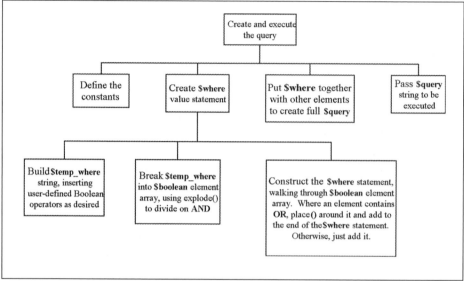

Figure 5-7

If there is a search, we use the value of $Field1 in creating the WHERE condition, rather than defining one beforehand (because we don't know what that's going to be before the user selects it).

Within each of the four if areas, we check to see if the field the user selected was location. If so, we use FULLTEXT syntax for the WHERE condition; if not, then we use the normal field='value' format.

For each parameter, we add its search element (either field='value' or the FULLTEXT-formatted element) to the end of the $temp_where_str variable.

In our search above, once the entire search entered into the above figure has been processed, the $temp_where_str variable has the following contents:

```
MATCH (location) AGAINST ('+library' in BOOLEAN MODE)

AND department = 'Administration' OR department = 'Systems'
```

Next, we need to use the $temp_where_str string to create a where statement implementing our desired operator precedence in lines 95–107 (example 5-19).

Example 5-19

```
95   $boolean = explode( " AND ", $temp_where_str );
96   $num = count( $boolean );
97   for ( $x=0;$x<$num;$x++ ) {
98       $or_pos = strpos( $boolean[$x], " OR " );
99       if ( $or_pos > 0 ) {
100          $boolean[$x] = "(" . $boolean[$x] . ")";
101      }
102      if ( $x == 0 ) {
103          $where = " $boolean[$x] ";
104      } else {
105          $where .= " AND $boolean[$x] ";
106      }
107  }
```

Because we have decided we want values to be OR'ed first, we need to break up the $temp_where_str string on the lower precedence operator—in this case, AND, using PHP's explode() function to split on AND to create an array of elements.

```
$boolean = explode( " AND ", $temp_where_str );
```

This takes the $temp_where_str variable we have created, splits it into separate entities (dividing on AND), and then saves the results to the $boolean array. The contents of that array would look like this:

```
$boolean[0] = MATCH (location) AGAINST ('+library' in
    BOOLEAN MODE)
```

```
$boolean[1] = department = 'Administration' OR department =
    'Systems'
```

Next we find out how many items there are in the $boolean array, using the PHP count() function, and assign the number to $num (line 96). We then use $num in a for loop to go through the array, looking for OR'ed statements. To find them, we use PHP's strpos() function to find the position within the element where OR might be found and store that number to $or_pos. If it is not found, then the value saved to $or_pos will be 0 and control will drop down to the next if statement. If it does find one (that is, when $or_pos is greater than 0), it knows that there is an OR there and puts parentheses around the entire element (so the database will put them together first) and saves the result to $where (putting an AND in front of it if this is not the first time through the loop).

The first time the block executes, it will check for the presence of OR and, not finding it ($or_pos==0), it will skip to the next if statement. Because this is the first time through the block, $x will equal 0, and $where will be set to the value contained in $boolean[0]. Then, the second time through, the script will see that $or_pos is greater than 0 (actually, that OR is in position 30), and will place parentheses around $boolean[1]. Then, because $x is equal to 1 the second time through the loop, it will append AND $boolean[1] to $where in line 105. The contents of $where now read:

```
MATCH (location) AGAINST ('+library' in BOOLEAN MODE) AND
    (Department = 'Administration' OR Department =
    'Information Technology')
```

One further thing needs to be noted. This search page has a large number of values coming in from the input form. Rather than localizing each one separately, we employ a trick that we will be using throughout the rest of the book.[10] We use PHP's list() function to take the superglobal—in this case $_POST— and go through it one element at a time, turning each element in the array into a local variable/value pair (example 5-20).

Example 5-20

```
24    while ( list( $key, $value ) = each( $_POST ) ) {
25        ${$key}=$value;
26    }
```

When it comes in, both elements of the key/value pair are strings. However, we want to turn the key string into a variable with the name of the key string (for example, "key" -> $key). For example, if we have a name/value pair of author/ Dickens, we would like to be able to create an $author variable and give it the value Dickens.

The technique that we use on line 25 to make this happen—and one that is invaluable in writing PHP applications—is the technique of taking a string and turning it into a variable of the same name. By taking the value of $key, wrapping it with curly braces, and prefixing it with a $, this transformation is magically accomplished. For example, see the following code:

```
$title = "The Brothers Karamazov";
$field_name = "title";
echo $field_name;     // would give you "title"
echo ${$field_name}   // would give you "The Brothers Karamazov"
```

This chapter has provided a brief overview of some of the techniques that you can use to search a MySQL database, but we have only scratched the surface of the possibilities. Although useful search interface is one of the more difficult and complicated aspects of database programming, you should be able to get a good start using some of the ideas here.

## Notes

1. You may have noticed a pattern here—three variables named `$query`, `$result`, and `$row`. In fact, using query, result, and row as the base for variable names. Then, when multiple queries are being handled at the same time, we simply add a prefix to describe which query is being referenced—a good example of self-documenting code.
2. This is done using the period, PHP's string concatenation operator. If you want to join things together, you put them in a row and place a " . " between them. For example, if we say `$x="10 million"`, and then `$message="You have won " . $x . " dollars"`, then `$message` would be "You have won 10 million dollars."
3. One of the beauties of PHP is that you can break into and out of PHP blocks any time you need to. All you need to make sure of is that you close off all of your loops. If you do not, the script won't work.
4. Specifically, `$_GET`, `$_POST`, `$_SESSION`, and `$_SERVER`. For more information, see the PHP manual at http://www.php.net/manual/en/reserved.variables.php or http://www.linuxgazette.com/issue86/lechnyr.html.
5. You can configure Apache to send all HTML files to the mod_php processor, but this might have an unexpected and not altogether desirable impact on your Web server's performance.
6. "Fine-Tuning MySQL Full-Text Search," *MySQL Reference Manual*. Available at http://dev.mysql.com/doc/mysql/en/fulltext-fine-tuning.html. See Setup.pdf for more details on my.cnf. In some post-4.1 versions, the configuration file is named my.ini.
7. The x in `$Fieldx` is a variable to indicate a number, such as `$Field1`, `$Field2`, and so on.
8. I did not include a blank <option> line, making the first one the default value. We therefore won't have to check to see if the field is empty in the action page.
9. In the interests of saving space, I detail only the steps involved in creating the WHERE statement.
10. Localizing is a way of saying "taking a superglobal variable and making it local."

# 6

Chapter

## PROJECT
## DESIGN

Now that we have covered the basics of designing and implementing databases and of writing reports and simple search applications, it is time to work through an actual project. Here I introduce you to the development process, discussing each step in planning such a project and pointing out questions you need to ask and tasks you need to undertake. We begin by considering an overview of the development process, its goals and challenges, examining the importance of doing it correctly. We then move through a sample project, looking at typical issues you may encounter.

To help you get started, I have developed several forms to help you in gathering specifications and designing your database. These not only prompt you for the types of information you need to gather, but are also integrated into the application development process described in chapters 7 and 9. As we go through this chapter, I will refer to completed PDF versions of these forms. Blank versions, named Planning_Form.doc and Grids.xls, are available as part of the companion materials download file.

## OVERVIEW

The goal of the design process should be a set of specifications that detail the formal requirements and technical specifications of the proposed application, provide a roadmap that programmers can use to code the application, and serve as the basis for documenting the system once it is in place. These specifications should be the result of discussions with the user or users for whom the proposed application is being built.

It is critical to undertake this planning process before attempting to implement a project. If you don't, you may run into significant problems down the road. A good analogy is building a house. If you were to decide to build a house, it is doubtful that you would simply go to the lumberyard, buy a lot of wood and nails, carry the stuff to your proposed site, and start hammering away. Rather, you would first decide what you want included in the house (bathrooms, dining room, large kitchen, deck), how much space you need, and the types of things you would like to be able to do in the house. Then you would get together with an architect to discuss your ideas. The architect would then take those needs and develop a preliminary set of plans and layouts. You would then go back and forth with the architect until the house fit your needs. Once agreement was reached, a final set of plans and blueprints would be created that you would each sign off on. Those documents would then be given to the contractors to begin building the house.

The same sort of process should be used when building a database application. You, as the architect (developer), need to work with the future homeowners (users) to define what they want in the house (application), usually in stages:

1. Define the goal and purpose of the project—that is, what the users want the application to do, why they want to do it, what will be necessary to create it, and what, if any, systems already exist that could be used or adapted for use in the project.
2. Determine, from users and others, what data to include in the application.
3. Define how the application will work and how the data fit into the application—that is, find out about current workflows and processes and design a system that will either fit or enhance them.
4. Present these to the users for feedback, then incorporate their input with your research to develop a model. At this point, users should be able to provide you not only with possible corrections but also with additional ideas about what they need.
5. Based on this feedback, take what they have given you, further refine your ideas, and make appropriate changes.
6. Repeat steps 4–5 until you reach agreement. Although it can be disheartening (or even threatening) to be told that your ideas don't work,

this iterative process allows both users and developers to come up with the best possible system.

7. Finalize design documents and have all parties sign off on them. Depending on the organization, this agreement can be at any level of formality (and legality). However, having things in writing helps to avoid a number of problems, including differences in understanding as to what was requested and mission creep (when features keep being added as the project is underway). This agreement should include appropriate time lines with target dates and, in the case of complex or large-scale applications, scheduling for implementation of modules.

It's worthwhile to keep a few fundamentals of this process in mind as you move forward. First, keep the project user driven. Not only do users know their needs better, getting their full input up front minimizes the number of changes that will need to be made once the application is in development. Involving them also helps them feel and take ownership of the application, thereby creating buy-in to its use. Second, make sure that the project you undertake is do-able. You should balance exploration of all the possibilities with not raising unrealistic hopes. Particularly when undertaking your first project, there are learning curves to overcome, infrastructure to develop, and personnel to organize and train. Starting small allows you to get your feet wet without engendering expectations you might not be able to meet (with the resulting loss of interest in this and further projects). Third, break complex projects down into subprojects and prioritize user requirements. Features often can be developed separately and sometimes even postponed to later versions.

Although it is important to design the application as completely as possible before beginning programming, it would be naive for us to assume that there will not be changes to the specifications as development goes forward. As users see the application taking shape, new possibilities that can make a critical difference in how the eventual application will function can occur to them. Although this can create problems, the impact of those problems can be minimized in various ways:

Following the data modeling and design principles described in chapter 2 permits new fields and even tables to be easily added.

Working through the initial application design process using screen mock-ups allows the user to see things in a manner that is more familiar to them.

Letting users know the cost and time requirements for making changes after development is underway helps them determine whether the proposed change is worth it.

Requiring that all proposed changes be written up and signed off on by both parties makes sure that all sides know what changes are to be made, eliminating having to redo poorly understood requests.

Batching changes and new features so that they can be done at the same time permits efficient testing and sign-off, an organized approach that is critical for the users' and the developer's sanity.

Developing a long-term mechanism for dealing with modification requests not only enables you to establish priorities but also reassures users that their needs are being listened to and will eventually be addressed.

One other important point is defining who your users are—particularly when working in a library setting where a substantial percentage of the people using the application will be members of the general public. This is one of the first (and most important) decisions you need to make. If it is a purely internal application for administrative purposes, then the target group is clear. However, if you are building a system with a public access component, then your audience will be larger. Although it is advisable to work with staff members who work with the public at the beginning of a project, you should build in ways in which your patrons will also be able to provide input during both the development and the implementation phases. This can be done either through usability tests and focus groups or by inviting input from them on an informal basis.

Following these guidelines and procedures should greatly facilitate the process, and help avoid unneeded and costly delays due to having to add features after the design phase is finished.

## DEFINING THE PROJECT

When starting out, the first thing to do is to gather information about the proposed project. This involves the developer getting together with the user or users for whom the database application is being developed and asking questions about the current environment, needs, and the types of tasks for which the proposed program will be used. Questions can include: Is there a preexisting database (either paper or computer-based) that could be used as a model? to obtain data? What sorts of outputs are desired? Web pages? reports? EAD documents? Are there administrative functions that it will need to perform? If so, what sorts of safeguards are needed for the data? Is a database even the appropriate tool for the job? It is important to ask such questions at the beginning. Although a project may sound simple when proposed, the devil, as they say, is always in the details. Not only is having this information useful when developing the application, it helps in planning and prioritizing the project.

In carrying out these interviews,[1] it is helpful to write out a list of questions beforehand to guide the session and make sure that all the critical questions are asked. Planning_Form.doc in the companion materials download file contains one possible form. This, if used in the initial discussions on any database project you might undertake, prompts for the types of information needed to begin a project. Not only does the form help focus initial questions, it can also serve as a central point of focus throughout the life of the project.

Not all of the questions need to be asked during the first meeting. In some cases, when one has multiple potential projects, you may wish to fill in only those sections that allow developers and administrators to compare the relative importance, costs, and timeframes of different projects, thereby enabling them to prioritize.

The form has six sections:[2]

1. Basic information. What staff and others are involved in the development process? What is the desired launch date?
2. Rationale. Why is the project being undertaken? Information can range from general observations to full mission statements. The goal is to have enough detail to evaluate the project's importance and to help guide the process.
3. Details. What information should it include? What types of uses and outputs will there be? What are the size and complexity of the database and security needs? Note that you may also want to take the **Initial Fields List** grid from Grids.xls (available in the companion materials download file) with you to jot down the information as your users mention it.
4. Present situation. What is the current situation? Are there systems already in place that relate to this need or that could be adapted to that purpose? that could be a model for a new system?
5. Implementation requirements. What special needs does this application have? Are there systems with which this new one will need to interact?
6. Planning. Who can or should be involved? What timeline is realistic? What resources are needed?

Planning_Filled.pdf in the companion materials download file includes a copy of this form, filled out with information that we will be using in our sample application throughout this and the next chapter. Because I have included a complete description of each element in the file, we won't go through the form here. However, because I will be referring to it throughout the process, you might want to print it (as well as the other forms listed in this chapter) for easy reference.

## Using Graphic Images

In addition to the textual description of the planning process provided in the form, there are two points where it can be useful to create a graphic representation of the information. The first of these has to do with the description of current workflow. The graphic in figure 6-1 represents the way in which new resource links are currently being added to the Web site.

In looking at this diagram, we can see that there are two major areas where the process could be made more efficient. First is that funneling all Web sites through the Webmaster creates a serious bottleneck. It requires at least double data entry: the person doing the suggesting writing out the e-mail and the Webmaster having to type (or at least cut-and-paste) the information into at least one Web page. Second is that having to manually edit HTML pages, though not rocket science, can be tedious, time-consuming, and prone to error.

A second area where a graphic can be useful is in mapping out the project planning timeline. Such a representation allows people to have a clearer picture of how things go together, see who is responsible for what, and understand how each of their tasks fits into the overall plan. Although there are a number of ways we could do this (flowcharts, GANTT diagrams, and so on), I find that the easiest way to create this type of "picture" is to use a PERT chart.[3] For example, tak-

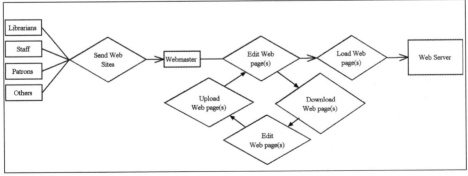

Figure 6-1

ing the information from our sample planning document, we could create the graphic representation of the process shown in figure 6-2.

In this diagram, each step of the process is represented by an oval defining steps in the process with arrows leading from one step to the next. Each oval provides the following information: what the step is; who is involved in undertaking the step; and the target completion date for the step. In several cases, three dates are given: the most optimistic date (BT), worst-case scenario date (WT), and best-guess date (AT). It also represents sub-processes, such as the data modeling that needs to be completed before proceeding to the next step.[4]

Once you have completed the basic information sections of the form, it can be submitted to whatever review process the library has in place. Because this project may potentially require resources allocated from several areas of the library, it is important to gain approval for the project from the administration and affected areas up front. Otherwise, the developers may find that support goes away (or is never there) with the result of much lost time and effort as well as a great deal of frustration.

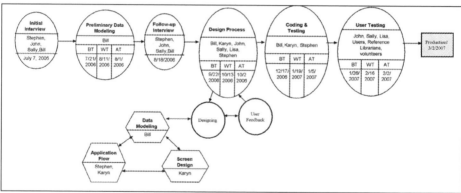

Figure 6-2

## DEFINING THE DATA MODEL

Once you have the go-ahead to start the project, you need to begin designing the application. The first thing that the developer should do is to take the ideas gathered in the initial interviews and to begin building a data model. Although a fancy-sounding concept, a data model is essentially only a list of all pieces of information the user needs to include in the database, organized in ways that will make it easy to store and retrieve that information. The developer creates this model using concepts and techniques we learned about in chapter 2 and applying them to the information gathered from the users.

## Gathering All the Pieces

The first step in building a data model is to create a list of all of the elements to be included in that model. Although the list acquired during the planning discussion is a good start, it is probably not going to be complete. We therefore need to find other ways to gather the information. The elements include

- lists gathered during interviews
- keywords in the mission statement and project objectives sections
- parameters and output defined in existing reports
- types of desired functionalities (multimedia apps will require pointers to digital objects, for example)
- capacity for interoperability with other systems or metadata standards (such as EAD, Dublin Core, OAI, or VRA Core)
- fields implied by certain types of information (such as Web site information, which would logically require a name and a URL)
- developer's intuition and experience from other similar projects

As an example of the second point, looking at the planning document for our Web sites project, we find the following phrases in the Project Objectives statement: "Allow for creation of dynamic Web pages with links to Web sites; Allow me to search for sites based on subject, type of site, or descriptions of the sites." In these statements are several terms that provide an initial list of elements we know will be included in our application: links, Web sites, description, type of site, and subject.

We now take those terms to begin looking for entities or discrete concepts around which we can group our terms. In looking at our list, we see that it contains three possible entities: Web sites, type of content, and subject. The central concept is Web sites. In coming up with concepts, it is important to recall our discussion of entities and foreign keys in chapter 2. Although it is true that type of content and subject can be characteristics of an individual Web site, it is also true that more than one Web site could have the same subject or type of content. We therefore establish them as separate entities.

Note that the same cannot be said of the other two items in the list, links (URLs) and description. These are pieces of information that are essentially characteristic of an individual Web site. We therefore define them as elaborating the Web sites entity. Breaking these into entities and putting these in a graphic form, we see the beginnings of our data model (see figure 6-3).

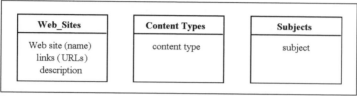

Figure 6-3

With this preliminary list, we return to the users and obtain further information on each of these entities. We ask them to elaborate on the three entities we have extracted, again noting any additional items in our list, asking what other information might be needed. After some discussion, we might come up with a list that would include the following:

> *help page*—to help user utilize the resource
>
> *LCSH* (Library of Congress Subject Heading)—allowing interoperability with the library's online catalog
>
> *subject scope note*—describing particular subject heading
>
> *content type scope note*—describing content type
>
> *requires proxy?*—whether resource requires a proxy server for off-campus access
>
> *restrictions on use*—whether restrictions, other than IP-based limitations, will apply to access
>
> *support name*—name of person who will assist users in using the site
>
> *support e-mail*—that person's e-mail address
>
> *support phone number*—his or her telephone number

In looking at this, we see that the help page, requires proxy, and restrictions all are essential characteristics of a Web site. The LCSH and subject scope note, on the other hand, are characteristics of subjects. Content type scope note is characteristic of types. With support name, e-mail, and phone number, we encounter something that is clearly a separate concept. We therefore create a fourth entity for it. Now our model looks like figure 6-4.

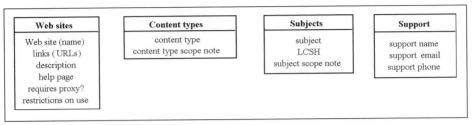

| Web sites | Content types | Subjects | Support |
|---|---|---|---|
| Web site (name)<br>links (URLs)<br>description<br>help page<br>requires proxy?<br>restrictions on use | content type<br>content type scope note | subject<br>LCSH<br>subject scope note | support name<br>support email<br>support phone |

Figure 6-4

There may also be more administrative data that the user will want to include. These can include such things as the date the record was added, which we add to the appropriate group.

Another item to be included is whether a particular piece of information needs to be searchable. Searching can be done in one of two ways: by including a characteristic, such as subject heading, or by excluding based on a missing characteristic, such as not outputting subscription sites to off-campus users where accessing those sites is not allowed. Although the first is useful, it is all too easy to focus only on it and neglect the second.

To find out what types of data might be useful in filtering, it is helpful to determine under which conditions we would not want an item to be displayed. Users might also want to use other characteristics on which to group resources (excluding those not a member of the group). We thus add three more fields to the list:

> *Status* enables assigning various statuses to a site (for example, active for a site that was available, down for a site with a problem, and trial for a resource the library is evaluating).

> *Subscription* enables creating a list of just those resources to which the library subscribes and for which off-campus access is not allowed.

> *Alphabetical_list* enables creating a list of most-used titles in alphabetical order.

It might also be that, as you delve deeper into the possibilities of a project, you need to change the list you have created. For example, in our project, one thing that our users have said to us is that they would like to be able to put other things into the database, such as links to books in the online catalog. Doing this will require two steps:

1. We change the name of the group from **Web Sites** to just plain **Sites** and the name **Web site** within the first group to **name** (to avoid confusion).
2. We add the element **format** to identify type of site (book or Web site) and, because it is a separate concept, put it in a separate concept named **Formats**.

The process of obtaining all data elements continues until both users and developers are satisfied that all useful pieces of data have been included. After adding the information we have gathered so far on this sample project, our preliminary data model looks something like figure 6-5.

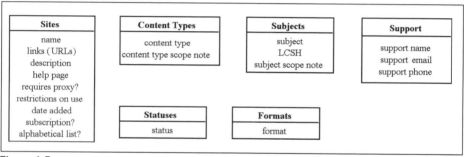

Figure 6-5

In creating these groupings, it can be helpful to use something like a spreadsheet that allows you to enter data, and then sort by individual columns. To help you with this, I have included the **Initial Fields List** grid in Grids.xls in the companion materials download file. This allows you to play around with the **Concept** column, trying out alternative groupings.

First fill in the appropriate columns with the data you collect. You can then assign the concept for each data element in the **Concept** column and then sort to see if things fit correctly. If not, change the grouping and then re-sort until you are satisfied with the groupings.

Once the basic fields have been defined (or even as they are being defined), it is important to define certain characteristics about each data element. We can use the **Initial Fields List** grid to enter this information. In addition, there may be certain constraints (commonly referred to as business rules) to which data should conform:

Is the data element mandatory or optional?

| Table | Type | Field | Length | Type | Uniq | Auth | Search | Req | Null? | Default | Limit | Key | Index | Constraints |
|---|---|---|---|---|---|---|---|---|---|---|---|---|---|---|
| sites | | name | 125 | V | | | Y | | | | | | | |
| | | url | 125 | V | | | | | | | | | | |
| | | description | | T | | | Y | | | | | | | |
| | | help_page | 125 | V | | | | | | | | | | |
| | | requires_proxy | 1 | C | | | | | | | | | | |
| | | restrictions_on_use | | T | | | | | | | | | | |
| | | added_date | | D | | | | | | | | | | |
| | | subscription | 1 | C | | | | | | | | | | |
| | | alphabetcial_list | 1 | C | | | | | | | | | | |
| | | | | | | | | | | | | | | |
| subjects | | subject | 100 | V | Y | Y | Y | | | | | | | |
| | | lcsh | 100 | V | | | Y | | | | | | | |
| | | subject_scope_note | | T | | | Y | | | | | | | |
| | | subject_scope_note | | T | | | Y | | | | | | | |
| | | | | | | | | | | | | | | |
| content_types | | content_type | 100 | V | Y | Y | Y | | | | | | | |
| | | content_type_scope_note | | T | | | | | | | | | | |
| | | | | | | | | | | | | | | |
| supports | | support_name | 100 | V | | Y | Y | | | | | | | |
| | | support_email | 100 | V | | | | | | | | | | |
| | | support_phone | 100 | V | | | | | | | | | | |
| | | | | | | | | | | | | | | |
| statuses | | status | 50 | V | Y | Y | Y | | | | | | | |
| | | | | | | | | | | | | | | |
| formats | | format | 50 | V | Y | Y | Y | | | | | | | |

Figure 6-6

Are there certain types of values to which the data element should conform?

Is input limited to a specific range of values? Does it need to be under authority control? If the answer is yes, it might be desirable to create an authority table and allow users to select only from entries in that list. In our sample application, we will create a separate table for `statuses` and use it to populate the appropriate field in `sites`.

Should access to this data element be restricted? Because this database is going to be on the Web, it is important that any proprietary or confidential information not be included in public data output from the proposed application.

After putting in as much of the information as we can and doing a final grouping, the resulting grid looks like figure 6-6.[5]

## Building the Model

Now that we have our basic data groupings, we need to transform them into a data model, structuring them to build an application—taking these different entities and relating them. Part of this process involves naming our fields and concepts, which we do by taking the terms we have been using and applying the naming conventions listed in our programming standards document (for example, making everything lowercase and replacing all spaces with underscores; see appendix B for more information). We first need to make sure that each entity (table) has a field (or possibly fields) that uniquely identifies it (that is, has a value that no other record in the table would have) to serve as the primary key. If such a field does not exist, we need to create one. If we need to create one, we will use arbitrary numeric keys (as noted in chapter 2). We do so for several reasons:

> They will not need to be changed should content within the record change because they are not based on content.
>
> They can be easily generated by the system.
>
> They are guaranteed to be unique.
>
> Numeric keys are faster to process than nonnumeric keys.

The first point is the most important. It is generally a bad idea to allow users to change the primary key for a table for much the same reason as why one isn't permitted to change their Social Security Number. Doing so can create a multitude of data integrity issues and many developers and many database administrators have hard rules against being able to change a primary key.

However, there are advantages to using meaningful keys, particularly in searching and outputting information from databases. We will therefore take a mixed approach. To show how one can use arbitrary keys in one-to-many relationships, I have set up the `formats` and `statuses` tables to use nonarbitrary keys. Then, in chapter 7, I will show you two ways that demonstrate how, if you do decide to use meaningful keys, you can maintain data integrity.

In the other tables, we create an arbitrary key field for each of the tables by adding an integer field, provide each field with significant names made up of the singular form of the table name (`support`, `subject`, and so on) with `no` (to designate number) as a suffix (for example, `supportno`, `subjectno`, and `content_typeno`), define each as its table's primary key, and choose auto_increment under the **Constraints** column in the field generation form.

In the case of `subjects` and `content_types`, we have decided to support items having more than one of any of these values assigned to it. Conversely, those values will usually be assigned to more than one item. As we saw in chapter 2, this many-to-many relationship dictates that we create a linking table into which we can place a foreign key field for each data table's primary key. Laying this out so that the links between the various primary and foreign keys are shown, we come up with the representation shown in figure 6-7.

In creating linking tables, I find it useful to create table names that contain the names of the tables it links with the authority table's name second (for

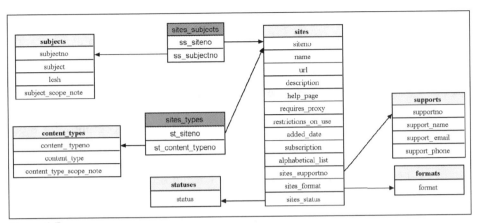

Figure 6-7

example, `sites_subjects`). Not only does this let the viewer know that it is a linking table, it also specifies which tables it links. This can be very valuable in the programming and debugging process.

Next we make places for the foreign keys. We do so by determining what the nature of the relationship between the two tables is going to be (that is, where the foreign key will be placed) and creating the foreign key field accordingly. If it is part of a one-to-one or a one-to-many relationship, then we add an appropriate foreign key field in the foreign key table, making it the same type and size as the primary key value that will be placed there; otherwise we create a linking table, also with fields of the same type and size as the primary key fields.

When creating the foreign key field names, I take the name of the primary key field and prepend the foreign table's name along with an underscore (for example, `sites_supportno`) to ensure that each field in the database has a unique name. When this would result in a field name that is too long, I use the initials of the table followed by an underscore (for example, `st_content_typeno` instead of `sites_types_content_typeno`).

In addition to the graphic representation, you need to build a complete table and field list before moving on. As with other steps in the process, I have provided a form in which to enter this information in Grids.xls (see Table_Definitions.pdf in the companion materials download file for a completed example). The following outlines the process by which the **Table Definitions** grid is defined:

1. Sort the **Initial Fields** grid by **Concept**, modifying each **Data Element** name to all lowercase and replacing spaces with underscores.
2. Cut and paste data from the **Initial Fields** grid into the **Table Definitions** grid (in this case, columns B–J in the **Initial Fields** grid are pasted into C–K in the **Table Definitions** grid). This works because the two sets of columns have the same structure.
3. Enter the lowercased name of each field group's concept into the **Table** column in the first row of each group of fields in the **Table Definitions** grid.
4. Add whatever primary or secondary key fields we need to establish relations between the tables, denoting in the **Key** column whether it is a primary or foreign key. If it is a foreign key, place the table and field name of the associated primary key (in `Table.FieldName` format) in the **Constraints** column.
5. Define the type of index (Primary, Unique, Keyword, Standard)—if any—for that field in the **Index** column.[6]
6. List what if any constraints (business rules) there are on that column in the **Constraints** column. For example, if a field is to be either yes or no, we add a constraint `Y/N`.
7. Fill in any other column that has not been updated.
8. Indicate the type of table (Data, Authority, Linking) for each concept group in the second (**Ttype**) column. Note that you may need to place more than one code here if a table has more than one role (e.g., a checkout record).
9. Create entries for the linking tables, making sure that we make the data type in the foreign key field the same type and size as the primary key field with which it will be linked.

Figure 6-8 shows what the **Table Definitions** grid looks like after entering our parameters. We will use this table in defining our database at the beginning of chapter 7.

## DESIGNING THE APPLICATION

Once the initial data model has been agreed upon, the next step is to design the application that will maintain and publish the data. To do this, you need to first

| Table | Type | Field | Length | Type | Uniq | Auth | Search | Req | Null? | Default | Limit | Key | Index | Constraints |
|---|---|---|---|---|---|---|---|---|---|---|---|---|---|---|
| sites | D | siteno | 11 | I | Y | | | Y | N | | | P | P | auto_increment |
| | | name | 125 | V | | Y | | | | | | | K | |
| | | url | 125 | V | | | | | | | | | | |
| | | description | | T | | Y | | | | | | | K | |
| | | help_page | 125 | V | | | | | | | | | | |
| | | requires_proxy | 1 | C | | | | | | | | | | Y/N |
| | | restrictions_on_use | | T | | | | | | | | | | | |
| | | added_date | | D | | | | | | | | | | | |
| | | subscription | 1 | C | | | | | | | | | | Y/N |
| | | alphabetcial_list | 1 | C | | | | | | | | | | Y/N |
| | | sites_supportno | 11 | I | | | | | | | | F | S | supports.supportno |
| | | sites_format | 50 | V | | Y | Y | | | | | F | S | formats.format |
| | | sites_status | 50 | V | | Y | Y | | | | | F | S | statuses.status |
| subjects | A | subjectno | 11 | I | Y | Y | Y | Y | N | | | P | P | auto_increment |
| | | subject | 100 | V | Y | Y | Y | Y | N | | | | | |
| | | lcsh | 100 | V | | | Y | | | | | | S | |
| | | subject_scope_note | | T | | | Y | | | | | | S | |
| content_types | A | content_typeno | 11 | I | Y | Y | Y | Y | N | | | P | P | auto_increment |
| | | content_type | 100 | V | Y | Y | Y | | N | | | P | | |
| | | content_type_scope_note | | T | | | | | | | | | | |
| supports | A | supportno | 11 | I | Y | Y | Y | | N | | | P | P | auto_increment |
| | | support_name | 100 | V | | Y | Y | Y | N | | | | | |
| | | support_email | 100 | V | | | | Y | N | | | | | |
| | | support_phone | 100 | V | | | | | | | | | | |
| statuses | A | status | 50 | V | Y | Y | Y | Y | | | | P | P | |
| formats | A | format | 50 | V | Y | Y | Y | Y | | | | P | P | |
| sites_subjects | L | ss_siteno | 11 | I | | | | | | | | F | S | sites.siteno |
| | | ss_subjectno | 11 | I | | Y | | | | | | F | S | subjects.subjectno |
| sites_types | L | st_siteno | 11 | I | | | | | | | | F | S | sites.siteno |
| | | st_content_typeno | 11 | I | | Y | | | | | | F | S | content_types.content_typeno |

Figure 6-8

determine the application flow. Begin by defining what if any workflow exists. If one does not exist, the developer works with the user to define one. Once you have a workflow, you proceed to map out each process that will be involved in maintaining and using the application, defining each step needed to carry out that process. You then need to define the pieces of data from your data model that need to be included within each step. You then create a user interface using mock-ups or sample screens to implement the forms that will be used to implement the queries involved in each step.

We will now take a look at each of these steps in turn. One thing to remember is that, although a book provides information in a linear way, reality is not always that clear cut. These three steps can be done in any order, or even simultaneously. The important thing is that each one is given its proper weight.

Please note that part of the process of creating the application is defining appropriate navigation elements for your application's pages. This is a topic unto itself and not one we can cover here. Many good Web interface design books are available to help you with this part of the project.

## Application Flow

Defining application flow means defining the processes involved in entering, editing, and outputting data into and from the database and defining the data involved in each step. In creating this representation, each step will use a unique view—or set of fields—in carrying out its "mission."[7] It is not necessary to define what fields will be associated with each view at this point. That will be done in the next step.

One point of clarification: view names have initial capital letters, whereas table names are all lowercase. One reason is that we need to be able to distinguish between the two. The other is that there is not necessarily a one-to-one relationship between views and tables. The **Sites** view, for example, includes data from tables other than the `sites` table.

At the highest level, our application has two main areas: data maintenance and the public interface. Figure 6-9 is a graphic representation of this top level, providing an overview of our application. On the left-hand side, we see the two subgroups of processes needed for creating and maintaining the two main resource groups in the database: the **Authority** views and the **Sites** view. The first group, labeled **Authority Data Maintenance**, is where we maintain the data used in the option lists, checkboxes, and the like in our forms for adding and editing **Sites** records. It provides the names of each of the five views to be used in maintaining these tables. Although the view names in the authority maintenance apps are the same as the table names (and will include only fields from that table), the situation as we shall see is a bit more complex in the second group—**Sites Data Maintenance**—where we will manage the information stored in multiple tables.

On the right side of figure 6-9, we see two outputs identified in the planning document: **Dynamic Pages** (for outputting resources by subject) and **Public Searching** (to create a public search application). In each case, a view name describing the task that view undertakes has been provided. Note that the arrows in the left half point in both directions, indicating that data can flow in both directions (retrieving records from the database and sending records/updates to the database). Those on the right side, however, point away from the database, indicating that we are selecting records to be output with no data going in the other direction.

Figure 6-10 details the form and action page pairs included in a basic database maintenance application: adding (**Add form** and **Insert action page**), searching (**Query form** and **Search action page**), editing (**Editing form** and **Update action page**), and deleting (**Delete form** and **Delete action page**). Let's take a more detailed look.

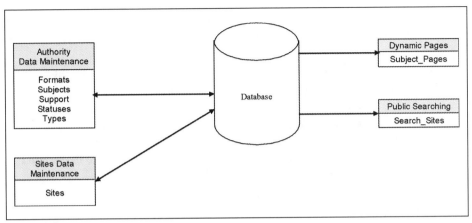

Figure 6-9

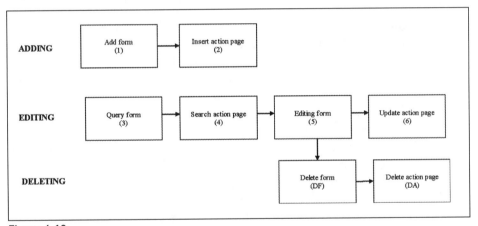

Figure 6-10

## Adding a Record

The first pair, used in adding records to the database, involves the following steps:

1. When an **Add form** page is loaded (1), it sends a set of queries to the database asking for authority lists that it can make into option lists, checkboxes, and so on. The results of these queries are then embedded into the **Add form** page.

2. The server does each of the requested searches and returns the results, which are then used to create authority lists so that the user can use them in inputting data.
3. The user fills out the various fields in the form and clicks on **Submit**, causing the user input to be passed to the **Insert action page** by either GET or POST (2).
4. The **Insert action page** then constructs the appropriate INSERT SQL queries and sends them to the database to add the record.
5. The result of the query is passed back and a response page, based on the success of the queries, is created and sent to the user.

## Editing a Record

Although similar in some ways to adding a record, the process is somewhat more elaborate in that the user needs to be provided with a way of selecting records:

1. A **Query form** is created to allow user input (3), obtaining authority table information for authority lists as needed.
2. The user fills out the page and clicks **Submit**, which sends search parameters to a **Search action page** using either GET or POST (4).
3. The **Search action page** takes the parameters passed to it from the **Query form**, constructs a query (or queries), and sends the query or queries to the database.
4. The database executes the queries and returns the results, which are then formatted. This formatting will include a hyperlink—using each record's primary key—to an **Editing form**, where the user will be able to modify the record's content.
5. The user clicks on this link, which loads the **Editing form** (5).
6. The **Editing form** retrieves the same authority lists as the **Add form**, but also the requested record and associated (linked table) information and displays the current state of the data on the update screen.
7. The user makes the appropriate changes in the record and submits the changes.
8. The changes are passed to an **Update action page** (6) that creates the appropriate queries and sends them to the database.
9. The database executes the queries and returns the result.
10. An output page with the result is presented to the user.

Note that these processes are usually carried out on the same set of data. It therefore makes sense for us to treat them as a unit (view).

*Deleting a Record*

On the other hand, users can also be given a link at the top of the editing page (or on the **Search action page**, for that matter) that allows them to delete the record. If they click on that link, they can be taken to a page where they can verify their decision. Here they are given two alternatives. Those choosing to delete the record are sent to a **Delete form** (DF) to verify that the record should be deleted. If the answer is Yes, the **Delete action page** is run (DA) where the record is deleted and corresponding linked records are appropriately updated or deleted, depending on the type of links involved. If not, a number of options are available, such as returning to the search results or the home page.

## Views—Bringing Data and Application Together

Now that we have decided on the views we want, we need to define the content. This means looking at each view and deciding what fields need to be included in each step of the view and how each field participates in that step. To make this easier, I have included three more forms in Grids.xls that you can use to define your views:

> *Views* defines the fields used in each view and the tables into which the data will go. Their primary use is in creating data entry forms and detailing how the data in those forms are to be handled. They also allow you to specify what fields are used in each task and how those fields participate,

> *Queries* defines the queries to be used in each view, particularly those that create authority record selection lists.

> *Links* defines the names of tables and fields used in implementing many-to-many links within the database, to be used in adding, querying, and updating multitable views.[8]

Copies of these grids, filled out with data for this sample project, are included in the companion materials download file.

*Defining the Views*

The first thing to do is to enter the names of the various views to be included in this application in the leftmost column in the **Views** grid, maintaining a row for each field to be added to the view and a blank row between the views. (If you need to add a row, you just need to right click on a row number on the left edge of the Excel screen and select **Insert**. Another row will be inserted.)

Let's begin with the **Subjects** view—the view that will be used in maintaining the `subjects` authority list.

1. We begin by placing the name of the view—**Subjects**—in the first column, first row of the section. This defines the beginning of the **Subjects** view.

2. Next, we cut and paste the names of the appropriate fields from the **Table Definitions** grid's **Field** column that we wish to include in this view and place them in the **Name** column.

3. We next do the same with contents from the **Table Definition** grid's **Length** column (that defines the number of characters in the field), pasting it into the **Max** column in the **Views** grid. Because the size of the column is the largest input we should allow in the form, this helps ensure that, as we build our form, we won't make any input box bigger than the capacity of the field into which the data will be going.

4. Next, we define the input types for each of the fields, using the codes in Views.pdf in the companion materials download file. Because the first field in the list—`subjectno`—is to be assigned by the system, we

> leave the **IType** (input type) column blank (because we aren't creating an input element for it)
>
> place the field name inside parentheses (to indicate that we are not creating an input box in the form)
>
> give it a variable type (**VType**) of `INT` (for integer)
>
> enter the name of the table into which the value will be placed into the **Table** column
>
> place `(AUTO)` in the **(Value)** column, to indicate the value will be automatically generated
>
> place `auto_increment` in the **Notes** column to indicate how it is being generated

5. Next, we go to the second line and enter the data for the next field (subject), giving it an **IType** of `T` (text), and **VType** of `STR` (string). Because we won't know the value for the **Size** column until we do the screen design, we skip it for now. We finish by placing the name of the table into which it will be inserted in the **Table** column.

We then fill in the rest of the data for this table into the **Views** grid. Because `scope_note` is to be a field with `textarea` type, we use an **IType** of `TA` (for textarea). Again, we skip the **Rows** and **Cols** until we do the interface design. Once we have finished with **Subjects**, we proceed to do the same for the rest of the authority tables. Figure 6-11 shows us what the **Views** grid should look like at this point.[9]

Now we will look at the **Sites** view. This view is a bit more complex for a number of reasons: it uses authority lists from other tables, includes a wider variety of variable and input types, and updates multiple tables.

We begin by entering all of the fields from `sites` that will be used in this view, filling in the appropriate values for **View**, **Name**, **VType**, **Max**, and **Table** columns. In three fields—`requires_proxy`, `subscription`, and `alphabetical_list`—the information we obtained from our initial interviews was that values should either be yes or no. We therefore define them as a `Y/N` **VType** and define **Size** or **Max** values of 1 for them. In creating the `added_date` field, we will be using a different generated value—one using `$today` as a variable inside the application, its value being set (as described in the **Notes** column) with PHP's `date()` function.

Next, we need to deal with those fields that use authority tables for inputting. First, for each field that will use an authority list for inputting, we create a four- to six-letter code and place it in the **Auth** column. This code provides a pointer to the **Queries** grid, where the parameters for the search to create the list will be defined. We begin with **Subject**, assigning it the code of `qsubj`, entering it into the **Auth** column. We then do the same for **Content_Type** (`qctyp`), **Support** (`qsupt`), **Status** (`qstat`), and **Format** (`qfmt`).

We then need to define the type of HTML input tag (**IType**) to be used in our forms in this view. In the case of the three fields where the foreign key is

| View | Action | IType | Auth | Name | VType | Size | Max | Rows | Cols | Add | Query | Display | Edit | Link | Table | (Value) | Notes |
|------|--------|-------|------|------|-------|------|-----|------|------|-----|-------|---------|------|------|-------|---------|-------|
| Subjects | M | | | (subjectno) | INT | | | | | | | | | | subjects | (AUTO) | auto_increment |
| | M | T | | subject | STR | 50 | 100 | | | | | | | | subjects | | |
| | M | T | | lcsh | STR | 50 | 100 | | | | | | | | subjects | | |
| | M | TA | | subject_scope_note | STR | | | | | | | | | | subjects | | |
| Content_Type | M | | | (content_typeno) | INT | | | | | | | | | | content_types | (AUTO) | auto_increment |
| | M | T | | content_type | STR | 50 | 100 | | | | | | | | content_types | | |
| | M | TA | | content_type_scope_note | STR | | | | | | | | | | content_types | | |
| Support | M | | | (supportno) | INT | | | | | | | | | | support | (AUTO) | auto_increment |
| | M | T | | support_name | STR | 50 | 100 | | | | | | | | support | | |
| | M | T | | support_email | STR | 50 | 100 | | | | | | | | support | | |
| | M | T | | support_phone | STR | 12 | 12 | | | | | | | | support | | |
| Statuses | M | T | | status | STR | 50 | 50 | | | | | | | | statuses | | |
| Formats | M | T | | format | STR | 50 | 50 | | | | | | | | formats | | |

Figure 6-11

placed directly into a corresponding field in the `sites` table (`sites_format`, `sites_supportno`, and `sites_status`), we need to choose an input type that allows you to select only one value from the authority list. Because we can choose either select list (`S`) or radio buttons (`R`), we decide to use select list for each.

In the case of `subjects` and `content_types`, we are setting many-to-many relationships. We therefore need to take several steps. First, to allow the user to select multiple values, we need to set **IType** either to `C` (for checkboxes) or `M` (for combo boxes). For our sample application, we will choose `C` for checkboxes. Second, because the input from the form could contain multiple values, we need to make the variable type one that can handle more than one value. Recalling from chapter 4 that we use arrays to handle such data, we make the **VType** `ARY`. Next, so that PHP can handle the values as an array, we need to place square brackets (`[]`) after the field name (for example, `subjects[]`) so that PHP will handle it as an array and not a single-value variable. Finally, because this information is stored in another table, we put the name of that table into the **Table** column. Once we have completed our work, the **Views** grid should look like figure 6-12.

We now need to define the appropriate query parameters in the **Queries** grid for the authority lists for which we created codes in the **Views** grid. For each

| View | Action | IType | Auth. | Name | VType | Size | Max | Row s | Cols | Add | Query | Display | Edit | Link | Table | (Value) | Notes |
|---|---|---|---|---|---|---|---|---|---|---|---|---|---|---|---|---|---|
| Subjects | M | | qsubj | (subjectno) | INT | | | | | | | | | | subjects | (AUTO) | auto_increment |
| | M | T | | subject | STR | 50 | 100 | | | | | | | | subjects | | |
| | M | T | | lcsh | STR | 50 | 100 | | | | | | | | subjects | | |
| | M | TA | | subject_scope_note | STR | | | | | | | | | | subjects | | |
| Content_Type | M | | qctyp | (content_typeno) | INT | | | | | | | | | | content_types | (AUTO) | auto_increment |
| | M | T | | content_type | STR | 50 | 100 | | | | | | | | content_types | | |
| | M | TA | | content_type_scope_note | STR | | | | | | | | | | content_types | | |
| Support | M | | qsupt | (supportno) | INT | | | | | | | | | | support | (AUTO) | auto_increment |
| | M | T | | support_name | STR | 50 | 100 | | | | | | | | support | | |
| | M | T | | support_email | STR | 50 | 100 | | | | | | | | support | | |
| | M | T | | support_phone | STR | 12 | 12 | | | | | | | | support | | |
| Statuses | M | T | qstat | status | STR | 50 | 50 | | | | | | | | statuses | | |
| Formats | M | T | qfmt | format | STR | 50 | 50 | | | | | | | | formats | | |
| Sites | M | | | (siteno) | INT | | | | | | | | | | sites | (AUTO) | auto_increment |
| | M | T | | name | STR | 50 | 125 | | | | | | | | sites | | |
| | M | T | | url | STR | 50 | 125 | | | | | | | | sites | | |
| | M | TA | | description | STR | | | | | | | | | | sites | | |
| | M | T | | help_page | STR | 50 | 125 | | | | | | | | sites | | |
| | M | Y | | requires_proxy | Y/N | 1 | 1 | | | | | | | | sites | | |
| | M | TA | | restrictions_on_use | STR | | | | | | | | | | sites | | |
| | M | | | (added_date) | DATE | | | | | | | | | | sites | $today | date("Y-m-d") |
| | M | Y | | subscription | Y/N | 1 | 1 | | | | | | | | sites | | |
| | M | Y | | alphabetical_list | Y/N | 1 | 1 | | | | | | | | sites | | |
| | M | S | qfmt | sites_format | STR | 50 | 50 | | | | | | | | sites | | |
| | M | S | qstat | sites_status | STR | 50 | 50 | | | | | | | | sites | | |
| | M | S | qsupt | sites_supportno | INT | | | | | | | | | | sites | | |
| | M | C | qsubj | subjectno[] | ARY | | | | | | | | | | sites_subjects | | |
| | M | C | qctyp | content_typeno[] | ARY | | | | | | | | | | sites_types | | |

Figure 6-12

code you entered into the latter, you define a line in the **Queries** grid, filling in the following columns:

*View.* The view in which this query will be used. Because authority query results may be used in multiple views, we place them all in an Authority view.

*Act.* The action for which this query is being used. In this case, we enter Q (for query) for each of the queries.

*Auth.* The four- to six-letter code entered into the **Views** grid. For example, we enter `qsubj` into the **Auth** column for the subject table query.

*Source: Fields.* The fields to be used in the search. Because it will be filling in the `value=attribute` element in our authority inputting tag, the first element must be the primary key of the authority table. This is because this is the value that will be placed in the appropriate foreign key field of the linked table. If we used a descriptive primary key, we need to place only the one field name here. However, if we used an arbitrary primary key (such as `auto_number`), we should place the primary key first and then, after a comma, add the name of a field in that table that will meaningfully describe each particular record (which will identify the contents of the record to the user). In this case, because we are using an arbitrary key for `subjects`, we use two fields: `subjectno` and `subject`.

*Source: Table.* Here we enter the name of the table to be searched, in this case, `subjects`.

*Source: Where.* In case we want a subset of all of the records in the table, we could put the appropriate filtering `WHERE` clause here. However, because we don't, leave it blank.

*Source: Order.* To help the user, we enter the name of the field to sort on, in this case `subject`.

We then proceed to do the same for the other authority table queries. The resulting entries in the **Queries** grid now look like figure 6-13.

| View | Act | Auth | Source: Fields | Source: Table | Source: Where | Source: Order | Notes |
|------|-----|------|----------------|---------------|---------------|---------------|-------|
| Authority | Q | qsubj | subjectno,subject | subjects | | subject | |
| | Q | qctyp | content_typeno, content_type | content_types | | content_type | |
| | Q | qsupt | supportno, support_name | supports | | support_name | |
| | Q | qstat | status | statuses | | status | |
| | Q | qfmt | format | formats | | format | |

Figure 6-13

*Defining Tasks*

Now that we have established each of the main views, we need to define which fields are used in which task. As noted, there are three main categories of task: adding and inserting, querying and searching, and editing and updating (deleting, though conceptually separate, is often integrated into the editing and updating). We now go through each of these three tasks to indicate how they should be handled (see figure 6-12).

ADDING AND INSERTING RECORDS    The first task we work on is adding records to the database. We do so by defining how each field is handled in the adding and inserting process. There are five possible values, not including leaving the field blank:

> *X* means that the value is added to the field name indicated in the **Name** column in the table named in the **Table** column. If it is to be added to a field with a different name, that name will be indicated in the **Notes** cell.
>
> *G* indicates that it is generated, the type being indicated in the **(Value)** column. If `auto_increment`, we place **(AUTO)** there to indicate that it is automatically created and specify it as `auto_increment` in the **Notes** column.
>
> *H* indicates a hidden value recorded in the **(Value)** column will be entered in the table indicated in the **Table** column. A logged-in user's username is one example, which might be stored in a hidden field and then entered into the appropriate field of the appropriate table when the record is added to the database.
>
> *(H)* indicates that the value is a hidden one that, because it is within parentheses, is not to be added to the database. A good example of this is seen during the editing function, when the primary key for the record being edited is passed to the updating action page as a hidden value so the system will know which record to update.
>
> *(D)* indicates that the value is for display only and will not be recorded permanently in the database.
>
> *Blank* means that the value is not part of the adding and inserting process.

In entering these values, you will also need to include values for **Size** for text inputting and **Cols** and **Rows** for textarea boxes. In creating these definitions, you may find that creating mock-ups of inputting and outputting screens is a useful exercise.

Finally, because we are dealing with two fields here in the **Sites** view— `subject` and `content_type`—whose values reside in other tables, we need to define how our application can get to those fields. We therefore define the relational paths in our database that establish the connections to obtain that information in the **Links** grid. After placing an **X** in the **Link** column of the **Views** grid (to let us know we need to look elsewhere for linking information), we go to the **Links** grid and input the following information:

> *View*—name of the view with which this query is to be associated
>
> *Linking Table*—name of the table into which the link information will be placed
>
> *Primary Table.Key*—`Table.field` containing the primary key for the primary data table
>
> *PFKey Field*—(primary/foreign key) name of the field in **Linking Table** into which the **Primary Table.Key** value will be placed
>
> *SFKey Field*—(secondary/foreign key) name of the field in **Linking Table** into which the **Secondary Table.Key** value will be placed
>
> *Secondary Table.Key*—name of the secondary (authority) table field containing the primary key of records containing desired value(s)
>
> *Secondary Table.Value*—name of the field in the secondary table containing the desired values
>
> *Secondary Array*—name of the array coming from the form containing array of **SFKey Field** values
>
> *Field(=Value)*—column into which you can put other values that appear in linking tables (such as due dates in checkout records)

The result is shown in figure 6-14.

| View | Linking Table | Primary Table.Key | PFKey Field | SFKey Field | Secondary Table.Key | Secondary Table.Value | Secondary Array | Field(=Value) |
|---|---|---|---|---|---|---|---|---|
| Sites | sites_subjects | sites.siteno | ss_siteno | ss_subjectno | subjects.subjectno | subjects.subject | $subject_no[] | |
| | sites_types | sites.siteno | st_siteno | content_typeno | content_types.content_typeno | content_types.content_type | $content_type_no[] | |

Figure 6-14

**EDITING RECORDS**  Editing databases generally involves two tasks: selecting a record to edit and updating and saving changes. In general, each task involves its own pair of form and action pages. I have included columns for each pair in the **Views** grid: **Query** and **Edit** (see figure 6-15).

*Querying and searching.* For querying we have two columns in the grid. In the first—**Query**—column, we define how a field is used, if it is used at all. There are five possible values in this column:

> *X* indicates that the field is present in the query page, using the same input values (**IType**, **Size**, and so on) as in the view definition.
>
> *A* uses an authority query to select an individual record.
>
> *M* uses the field, but not as defined in the view (the character of the input being defined in the **Notes** column).
>
> *K* means use a keyword search.
>
> *Blank* means not included in searching.

The other column (**Display**) indicates whether the field should be displayed in the search output. There are four codes for this column:

> *S* means to display in short (summary) record.
>
> *L* means to display in long (full) record.
>
> *B* means to display in both.
>
> *Blank* means to not display in either.

*Editing and updating.* Once a record is retrieved, we need to define how it participates in the editing process. As with the previous tasks, there are certain codes that are used in this column:

> *X* can be edited and the results are saved to the field listed in the **Name** column in the table defined in the **Table** column.
>
> *H* is included in the form as a hidden variable, along with a value attribute—given in the **(Value)**—to be added to the database in that field.
>
> *(H)* is present as a hidden variable, but is not updated (usually the primary key to allow the action form to know which record to update).
>
> *(D)* is displayed in the editing screen but not updated in the database.
>
> *Blank* is neither displayed nor updated.

Our **Views** grid now looks like figure 6-15.

| View | Action | IType | Auth | Name | VType | Size | Max | Rows | Cols | Add | Query | Display | Edit | Link | Table | (Value) | Notes |
|---|---|---|---|---|---|---|---|---|---|---|---|---|---|---|---|---|---|
| Subjects | M | | qsubj | (subjectno) | INT | | | | | G | A | | (H) | | subjects | (AUTO) | auto_number |
| | M | T | | subject | STR | 50 | 100 | | | X | A | | X | | subjects | | |
| | M | T | | lcsh | STR | 50 | 100 | | | X | | | X | | subjects | | |
| | M | TA | | subject_scope_note | STR | | | 4 | 80 | X | | | X | | subjects | | |
| Content_Type | M | | qctyp | (content_typeno) | INT | | | | | G | A | | (H) | | content_types | (AUTO) | auto_number |
| | M | T | | content_type | STR | 50 | 100 | | | X | A | | X | | content_types | | |
| | M | TA | | content_type_scope_note | STR | | | 4 | 80 | X | | | X | | content_types | | |
| Support | M | | qsupt | (supportno) | INT | | | | | G | A | | (H) | | support | (AUTO) | auto_number |
| | M | T | | support_name | STR | 50 | 100 | | | X | A | | X | | support | | |
| | M | T | | support_email | STR | 50 | 100 | | | X | | | X | | support | | |
| | M | T | | support_phone | STR | 12 | 12 | | | X | | | X | | support | | |
| Statuses | M | T | qstat | status | STR | 50 | 50 | | | X | A | | X | | statuses | | |
| Formats | M | T | qfmt | format | STR | 50 | 50 | | | X | A | | X | | formats | | |
| Sites | M | | | (siteno) | INT | | | | | G | | X | (H) | | sites | (AUTO) | auto_number |
| | M | T | | name | STR | 50 | 125 | | | X | X | X | X | | sites | | |
| | M | T | | url | STR | 50 | 125 | | | X | | X | X | | sites | | |
| | M | TA | | description | STR | | | 4 | 80 | X | M,K | X | X | | sites | | |
| | M | T | | help_page | STR | 50 | 125 | | | X | | | X | | sites | | |
| | M | Y | | requires_proxy | Y/N | 1 | 1 | | | X | | | X | | sites | | |
| | M | TA | | restrictions_on_use | STR | | | 4 | 80 | X | | | X | | sites | | |
| | M | | | (added_date) | DATE | | | | | X | | | | | sites | $today | date("Y-m-d") |
| | M | Y | | subscription | Y/N | 1 | 1 | | | X | | | X | | sites | | |
| | M | Y | | alphabetical_list | Y/N | 1 | 1 | | | X | | | X | | sites | | |
| | M | S | qfmt | sites_format | STR | 50 | 50 | | | X | X | X | X | | sites | | |
| | M | S | qstat | sites_status | STR | 50 | 50 | | | X | X | X | X | | sites | | |
| | M | S | qsupt | sites_supportno | INT | | | | | X | | | X | X | sites | | |
| | M | C | qsubj | subjectno[] | ARY | | | | | X | X | | X | X | sites_subjects | | |
| | M | C | qctyp | content_typeno[] | ARY | | | | | X | X | | X | X | sites_types | | |

Figure 6-15

## Interface Design—Creating the Screens

While working through the **Views** grid, you will need to begin defining what fields will be used and what the interface will look like. Specifically, you need to work through how you will lay out the various inputting boxes and lists on your page. As noted, creating mock-ups is a useful exercise. There are a number of ways in which these can be created, including pencil and paper drawings, proto- typing software, and HTML forms. Of these, creating HTML forms is probably easiest and the most useful. If you choose to go this route, you'll want to bear several things in mind:

> Using an editor that supports macros allows you to create the forms much more easily.

> Naming each input element with the name of the field into which the data will eventually be placed simplifies the development process.

> Creating the forms as part of the design process moves you that much farther along the road to implementation.

> Creating just one form as a kind of application prototype (say, the Add form) and showing it to users for their comments allows you to make the inevitable layout and content changes to just one page.

In this stage you should attempt to create representative forms for each type of view (authority, searching, outputting, creating dynamic pages, and so on). Not only does this involve the users in the design of the interface they will be using, it allows you to present the project in a manner that allows them to see how the final application will work. It allows them to provide feedback on what works and does not work and permits them to add features and fields. Because the cost of making changes goes up dramatically at each stage of a project cycle, this process can cut down significantly on expenditures, misspent time, and frustration levels.

## PUTTING IT TOGETHER—PUBLIC INTERFACES

Defining data maintenance routines is only part of the job. We need to define the public-access components of the application as well. We begin by creating a view name for each interface we are going to create. The planning document itemizes requests for dynamic Web pages containing links of sites by subject, organized by type of information they provide, and for searching based on subject, type of site, or descriptions of the site. We now define each of these views, the data to be contained in those views, and the definition of the public interface screens. When we finish, our project planning phase will be over and it will be time to go on to the programming.

### Pages by Subject

The first view we consider is for outputting subject resources by content type. The idea behind this application is that it will be written in such a way that the library Webmaster can place a link into the library's Web site that will launch an action page that takes the input search term and uses it to search and to output all resources catalogued with that particular term. In this case, we will pass it a subject (the `subject` field of the record in the `subjects` table containing the subject we wish to search). The action page will then take that key, do the appropriate searches, and output a list, broken down by type of content. Given that we are not going to be doing data maintenance—or even creating a form for user input—this view will be much simpler than those we have done before. However, we still need to think through how we are going to proceed.

The steps in creating this view are fairly straightforward (see the completed grids in Views.pdf, part of the companion materials download file):

We enter the name of the new view—**Subject Pages**—into the **View** column and place an S into the **Action** column to indicate that this is a page that will SELECT records for display. Although there is no direct user input, we will pass a subject to the page via a URL so that it can create a page containing all entries in the database that have been assigned that subject. We therefore define U as the **IType** for subject. We leave the rest of the **IType** column and the **Auth** column blank.

We copy the field name of every field we want to include from the **Table Definitions** grid, both for searching and for displaying, entering the name of the table from which the field can be found in the **Table** column and placing an X in the **Query** column of those fields to include in the query form and an X in the **Display** column for those fields we want to display.

We place an X in the **Link** column indicating the linking table we will need to use to search for the value in the **Table** column. Then, when creating this page, we can refer to that grid for the linking path to our desired information.

## Public Searching Interface

The other view we look at will be to support an end-user searching application. Given that this program is essentially the same task as the query function within the **Sites** view, the definition of this view looks remarkably similar, as can be seen from the **Views** grid. The only difference is that we won't be creating links to allow editing (though we will be providing a similar link to allow display of a long record).

## TESTING PROCEDURES

It is critical that a formalized testing procedure be agreed upon before beginning a project. In designing the system, it is important to create a testing document, based on the **Views** grid definitions for each task, that ensures that all data are properly handled. Such a document ideally consists of a list of all views in the application, and within each view, a list of each field that makes up that view provides a checklist for each way in which data are used in the application. For example

> For Add, does it display? If so, can it take the required input? Are business rules being enforced properly? Does it get added properly? Do foreign keys get inserted properly?

For Query, do all input fields display properly? For authority-table created fields, do the correct values show up in the proper order? Do all possible combinations of search parameters work properly?

For Search, is the search bringing up what it is supposed to? Are there any records being retrieved that shouldn't be retrieved? Are there records that should be retrieved that are not?

For Display, does the output display properly? Are all fields being displayed? in the proper order?

For Edit, does the proper value from the record get displayed properly in the editing screen? If you change a value in a field, does it get updated properly? do business rules get enforced properly? If changing or deleting an authority record where nonarbitrary keys are used, do linking records get updated properly?

For Delete, are records removed successfully? Are any records deleted that should not have been deleted? Are the appropriate updates made to related tables/fields? Is relational integrity being maintained?

Is the application able to deal with anomalous input, such as badly formatted dates? Is the user given an understandable screen? Does it cause the system to crash? If so, you will need to check the input before it gets sent to the database and put up an appropriate message to the user.

You also need for the end-users who will work with the system to test it and make sure it works according to their expectations and will meet their needs. Within this process, there are a number of questions to be asked:

Who will do the testing?

Will users lose any work they did on the test system once it goes into production? If so, do they fully understand that?

How long will the testing period be and how do we clearly delineate the switch over into production? It is important that the testing period be clearly delineated and that it not be unduly extended. The greater the ambiguity as to when the testing phase is over, the greater the chance of the undermining of the system by users caused by their thinking they are in production before the testing period is officially concluded.

Who will define the tasks that will be used to test the application? This should probably be worked out by developers in conjunction with users.

## FORMALIZING THE PROCESS

Once the complete design and data specifications have been agreed upon, it is important to put them into writing. There are a number of reasons why this is useful:

It provides a contractual basis for the development process. In case of any disagreements, the documentation provides the answer.

It greatly facilitates the development process. As you will see in the next chapter, having it all down on paper makes the actual programming very straightforward.

It serves as documentation for the application for support by others.

Certain documents will ideally be included in this collection and updated as things change. Below is a list describing the most important of these:

*planning documents*—the initial documentation that lays out the scope, rationale, goal, and timeframe of the project

*table definitions*—a complete list of all tables, the fields they contain, and their function within the application

*relational diagram*—a graphic representation of the relationships between the various tables, showing how the tables are linked between primary and foreign keys

*program flow*—a layout of the various processes of the programs, showing the views involved in each

*views grid*—definition of the tables, views, and queries involved in each point in the program flow

*queries grid*—a list of all queries used within each view

*links grid*—a list of all many-to-many links maintained in each view

*file definitions grid*—a listing of all files used in the application, the view or views they support, and their function within the application

*testing documents*—documents and checklists of things to test to ensure that the program is working properly

We are now ready to implement the system. Undertaking this structured approach to planning makes the process of implementation easy and straightforward and helps you to avoid most (though probably not all) nasty surprises with which you might otherwise have to deal.

### Notes

1. For information on conducting such interviews, see Michael J. Hernandez, *Database Design for Mere Mortals* (Reading, MA: Addison-Wesley, 1997), 72–79.
2. See Planning_Filled.pdf in the companion materials download file for a complete description of each element.
3. Program Evaluation Review Technique was developed by the U.S. military in the 1950s to handle complex projects. It is a type of report that is available in a number of planning software programs, including Microsoft Project.
4. For more information on PERT charts, see the bibliography.
5. See Grids.pdf in the companion materials download file for a complete listing of the columns included and the values of the codes used in the grid.
6. See chapter 2 for a discussion of index types in MySQL.
7. The use of the word view here should not be confused with the RDBMS technique of views. I use the term here to describe the organization of fields from multiple tables into individual logical groups. RDBMS views provide an automated way of implementing such groupings.
8. A complete explanation of the grids is included in Grids.pdf in the companion materials download file.
9. The M in the **Action** column indicates the type of data maintenance view—in this case a **Maintenance** view.

# 7 PROGRAMMING THE APPLICATION

Now that the specifications have been developed and agreed upon, comes the easy part. Although it may seem strange to call programming easy, in many ways it really is. By taking the time to get it right in the planning phase, programming becomes a matter of filling in the blanks. Here we will use information from the grids that we created in chapter 6 to fill in those blanks. My hope is that in the process you will see how useful they can be. The steps we will follow include

- using phpMyAdmin to implement our data model in MySQL
- creating a configuration file for the application
- building the application, including all data maintenance routines

In the chapters that follow, we will look at data and application security, creating public access applications, and good program development procedures. (Throughout I will use functions included in the companion materials download file. To understand how this code works, you can refer to ala_functions.pdf, a fully annotated source code file, and Functions_Guide.pdf.)

## SETTING UP THE APPLICATION

Before we can begin programming, we need to implement the data model in the database and to create a configuration file that will contain information and parameters to be used throughout the application. We take each of these in turn.

## Implementing the Data Model

First we implement the data model we developed during the design phase using phpMyAdmin. We do this much the same way we did in chapter 3, by taking the **Table Definitions** grid we just created in chapter 6 and using it to define the database, tables, and fields, and then setting up a user account. For the latter, we define an administrative user named Web_Sites and give it a password of ws_admin. As before, we give this user account only those rights in the database that it needs on web_sites (SELECT, INSERT, UPDATE, DELETE, and LOCK TABLES).[1]

As part of this process, there are two questions we need to ask:

> Do we want to include transaction support in this application? As we discussed in chapter 2, doing so greatly increases data security and integrity in multitable apps.

> How do we want to maintain referential integrity (making sure all relations are properly set and maintained) between tables? Will we want to have the database maintain referential integrity for us via foreign key constraints? Will we need to program it in ourselves?

The difficulty is that how you answer these questions has an effect on how you configure MySQL to store your data and thereby what you will be able to do with that data. By default, MySQL uses the MyISAM file format—one that provides neither transaction nor foreign key constraint support. To get those features, you need to set up those tables for which you wish to use these features (both the primary key and the foreign key tables) as InnoDB type files.

However, one drawback to that course is that InnoDB does not support the FULLTEXT indexing we used in chapter 5 to implement keyword searching. For that, we need MyISAM files. Therefore, if you want keyword searching you will either need to forgo transactions and foreign key support or find another way of implementing it. In fact, I will show you that alternative (using functions in ala_functions.php) that will let you have your cake and eat it, too!

## Setting Up Foreign Key Support

To implement foreign key constraint support within phpMyAdmin (version 2.6.2), proceed as follows after creating the database:

First make sure that both tables (the one with the primary key and the one that will hold the related foreign keys) are the InnoDB type. To do so, you first create the tables (making sure that both the primary key and foreign key fields are of the same data type and size and that the latter is defined as NULL).

Then, for each table to be included, click on its name in the left-hand frame. After the table's definition has loaded in the right-hand frame, click on the **Operations** tab in the right-hand frame. Then go down the page to the **Table Type** drop-down list and change the option to INNO DB.[2]

Last, if you have not already done so, go into phpMyAdmin and create a primary index on the field containing the primary key and a standard index on the field that will contain the foreign key.

### Creating Constraints Manually

Next we can create the foreign key constraints in one of two ways. The first is to click on the SQL tab inside phpMyAdmin (with web_sites as the active database) and enter an SQL query to create the constraint manually for each primary key/foreign key pair we want. This query should use the following syntax (making sure that the <constraint name> is not the same as the name of either field involved in the constraint):

```
ALTER TABLE <foreign_tablename>

ADD CONSTRAINT <constraint_name>

FOREIGN KEY(<foreign_key_field>)

REFERENCES <table>(<primary_key_field>)

[ON DELETE (CASCADE | SET NULL | NO ACTION | RESTRICT) ]

[ON UPDATE (CASCADE | SET NULL | NO ACTION | RESTRICT) ][3]
```

Because we will be using the relationship between statuses and sites to illustrate this technique, we enter the following to create the constraint for our application:

```
ALTER TABLE sites ADD CONSTRAINT site_status_constraint
    FOREIGN KEY(sites_status) REFERENCES statuses(status)
    ON UPDATE CASCADE ON DELETE SET NULL;
```

### Using phpMyAdmin

You can also create the constraints using phpMyAdmin's GUI interface. Although it involves a bit more work up front, it provides you with additional tools with excellent and valuable features. This includes the ability to create data dictionaries and graphical representations of your database in PDF format (including drawing lines between tables where relations exist between those tables). To create the constraint in phpMyAdmin using the GUI, you need to follow these five steps:

1. Set up relational support in phpMyAdmin as explained in the instructions in Setup.pdf in the companion materials download file.
2. Select the name of the table containing the foreign key (in this case, `sites`) in the left-hand frame of that interface.
3. Select the **Relation** view link (currently just after **Print** view and just below the table structure grid) in the right-hand frame.
4. Find the name of the foreign key field in the left column. Then, within that row, use the drop-down list in the second column to select the **Table–>Field** that contains the primary key for this relation: `statuses–>status`. (Note that if you haven't created an index for the field, no drop-down for that field will appear.)
5. Define how to handle two conditions. The first—`ON DELETE`—stipulates what should be done if the record containing the primary key gets deleted. This should be set to `SET NULL`. The second—`ON UPDATE`—tells the database what it should do when the value of the primary key changes. Here we set it to `CASCADE` so that it will make the same changes in the foreign key field as were made to the primary key.

## Creating the Configuration File

Database applications require a number of items—such as database connection values—to be set in each page for the application to work. Although we were able to write them into each script in chapter 5, we will create quite a few more files in this application. Each file will also eventually require significantly more configuration commands. Creating a configuration file and then using PHP's `include()` function to read them into our pages will save much time and effort.[4] At minimum, this file should include

the connection definition parameters (host, username, password, and database name) for the user account you created

code to use those parameters to create a connection to the database

a line, if not included in the global auto-prepend file, that will `include()` the PHP functions library[5]

the code for localizing the `$_POST` superglobal

placing the configuration commands within a PHP block so that the PHP module will interpret the lines correctly

Example 7-1 provides a minimal configuration file that we can use in our application.

Example 7-1

```
1   <?php
2   /****************************************************************
3   * Establish database connection and select the database
4   ****************************************************************/
5   $user="Web_Sites";
6   $password="ws_admin";
7   $dbname="web_sites";
8   $db = mysql_connect("localhost",$user,$password);
9   mysql_select_db($dbname,$db);
10
11  /****************************************************************
12  * Use the php list() function to de-reference the $_POST superglobal.
13  ****************************************************************/
14  if ( isset( $_POST ) ) {
15     while (list($key, $value) = each ($_POST)) {
16        $($key)=$value;
17     }
18  }
19  ?>
```

Please note that the previous list is just the beginning of what should be placed in the configuration file. We will encounter others as we proceed through the chapter. Please consult Functions_Guide.pdf in the companion materials download file for a complete list of what should be in the file.

For this configuration information to work, we need to make sure each file in the application contains it. There are three ways to do this:

1. Use PHP's `include()` statement at the top of each page to read in the script—one possible approach, but one that requires a lot of typing, is prone to error, and needs to be changed in every file should the name of the included file change.
2. Work with the system administrator of your server to see if you can include an .htaccess file in your directory where you can type in the PHP command to automatically load it (see Setup.pdf in the companion materials download file for what this means and how it can be achieved). Doing so makes it available in that directory and every directory under it.
3. Set it up so that it can be loaded via the systemwide configuration file (in our case, prepend.php). If you follow the instructions provided in Setup.pdf, you simply create a file—named local_prepend.php—in the application directory and it will automatically be loaded each time any PHP script is accessed in that directory. (The examples in the rest of this chapter will assume that you have done one of these last two.) If you cre-

ate subdirectories using this third option, you will need to create separate local_prepend.php files for each directory.

Note that you can name your configuration file anything you want. In the examples in this book, I have chosen to call it local_prepend.php and have set up the global prepend.php to include it if it exists. As a result, that is the name that I will be using for the configuration file. However, if you want to use a different name, all you need to do is to change the appropriate line in prepend.php to use the new file name.

If you are creating an application in a directory where end-users have the ability to read and modify files, it is not a good idea to leave a file containing database connection information lying around for easy reading by anyone who happens by. Again assuming that you have followed the setup instruction in Setup .pdf, you can enhance your application security in two easy steps:

> Move this configuration file into the include file directory in the `include_path` directive in the php.ini file and give it a name such as web_sites.php (make sure that the name is unique, and ideally one based on the database or application name; see Setup.pdf for more information).[6]

> Create a local_prepend.php file in your application directory with the following three lines to read in your configuration file:

```
<?php
include( "web_sites.php" );
?>
```

> Then, when local_prepend.php gets called, it will include web_ sites.php (because the directory that contains it is in the include_ path variable in your php.ini—again, if you followed the instructions in Setup.pdf).

## PROGRAMMING THE APPLICATION

### Authority Table Maintenance

We begin by programming the authority file maintenance segment of the application (annotated source code for all scripts is available in the companion materials download file; see chapter 1). We do so for two reasons. First, we need populated authority tables for our drop-downs and checkboxes before we can begin programming the **Sites** view. Second, creating authority table maintenance apps is simpler and starting there will allow us to learn some basic techniques that we can build on later.

Although we could manually add records to the authority tables using phpMyAdmin, we might as well create the applications now. Besides, it is an extremely bad idea to maintain data in relational database applications through the database administration module rather than a programmed application. This is because it is far more tedious to do it that way and without the control and business rules built into a program, it can be quite easy to create data integrity problems.

### Subjects

We start by implementing the **Subjects** view, then proceed to the other views in turn. In creating these applications, we will follow the pattern defined in chapter 6, creating our adding/inserting, querying/searching, and editing/updating action page pairs in turn, plugging in the appropriate fields from the **Views** grid into each.

ADDING RECORDS   The first scripts we will create will be to add `subjects` records in the database. We start with the form to input new records and name it subject_add.php.[7] If we created a prototype inputting page in the design phase, we can use that as a model for our page. Otherwise, we take the fields and lay them out on the screen, making sure all fields from the **Views** grid are represented. In the case of `subjects`, we see three fields identified: `subject`, `lcsh`, and `subject_scope_note` (because `subjectno` is to be generated by the system, we don't provide an inputting element for it in the form).

In building this form (as well as the other forms in this application), we will be using HTML tables to define and organize the inputting elements. As we build the page, we go through the list of fields we have identified in the **Add** column of the **Views** grid with an **X**. We use the values we find there to decide which fields to include in the form, defining the `name` (using the field name), `size` (based on screen layout needs), and `maxlength` (based on the field size) respectively. For example, for the `subject` field, we write the following inputting tag:

```
<input type="text" name="subject" size="50" maxlength="100">
```

We then go through the rest of the form in the same manner, using the textarea type, rather than text, for `subject_scope_note`. Using the values from the **Views** grid allows us to be sure that the name of the variable will be the same as the field into which the associated value will be placed. It also helps guarantee that the `maxlength` of the inputting box will not be larger than the field into which the value will be placed. Finally, to make the form look better, we use a table within a table for the **Add Record/Clear Form** button area.

INSERTING RECORDS    The next step is to build our action page, using the name—subject_insert.php—that we defined in the `action` attribute of the <form> tag in the inputting form. Aside from the basic HTML needed to create the page and to provide response, the actual business is done in lines 46–49. As we can see in example 7-2, we take the fields identified to be added using values in the **Add** column and plug them into an SQL query and send the query to the table indicated in the grid's **Table** column.

Example 7-2

```
45  <?php
46  $query = "INSERT INTO subjects
47          ( subject, lcsh, subject_scope_note )
48          VALUES( '$subject', '$lcsh', '$subject_scope_note' )";
49  $result = mysql_query( $query, $db ) or die( mysql_error() );
50  echo "Your record has been added<p>";
51  ?>
```

After delineating the PHP block in the first line (45), we create the SQL query. The syntax for the query is

```
INSERT INTO <table> (<field_list>) VALUES(<individual_field_
    values>)
```

Although <field_list> before the **VALUES** keyword can be optional, it is optional only if you are inputting values for all of a table's fields in exactly the same order as they appear in the database. As you may recall from chapter 2, if you want to insert only some fields, you must use the preliminary field list (making sure that the values are in exactly the same order as the corresponding field name in the field list).

In the next line (49) we use the PHP `mysql_query()` function to send the query to the database. Note that I have added `or die( mysql_error() )` to the end of the line. This provides some error handling and essentially says "execute the mysql_query() successfully or die (stop all execution) and print out the error message MySQL sent when it died." Then, if the query does fail, the developer is given a message from MySQL that s/he can use to diagnose and hopefully fix the problem.

EDITING RECORDS   Once data are in the database, we need to be able to retrieve them to edit them. We accomplish this with the subject_get.php script. As we did in the multi_keyword_query.php file in chapter 5, we create a drop-down list of subject table records from which the user can select the one to edit. Also, as we did previously, we select the primary key and display name fields from the subjects table to create the drop-down list, sorting by the display name field (subject). Then, in creating the select list in example 7-3, we use the primary key as value and the display name to display.[8]

Example 7-3

```
50   <select name="subjectno">
51   <?php
52      echo "<option></option>";
53      $query = "SELECT subjectno,subject FROM subjects ORDER BY subject";
54      $result = mysql_query( $query, $db ) or die( mysql_error() );
55      while ( $row = mysql_fetch_array( $result ) ) {
56         $subjectno = $row["subjectno"];
57         $subject = $row[1];
58         echo "<option value=\"$subjectno\">$subject</option>";
59      }
60   ?>
61   </select>
```

*Editing screen.* Because we used the table's primary key—subjectno—as the value for each item, when the user selects a given subject and submits the form, that primary key is forwarded to the action page, subject_edit.php. There it can be used to retrieve the desired record, where that record's contents are used to populate the values in the editing screen.

The editing page is essentially the same as subject_add.php, with three important differences. The first is that the page includes a search to retrieve the record, which it does in lines 40–42 of example 7-4, executing a search and saving the retrieved record to an associative array named $row.

Example 7-4

```
36   <?php
37   /*************************************************************************
38    * Use primary key passed from subject_get.php to retrieve record for editing
39    *************************************************************************/
40      $query = "SELECT * FROM subjects WHERE subjectno=$subjectno";
41      $result = mysql_query( $query, $db ) or die( mysql_error() );
42      $row = mysql_fetch_array( $result );
43   ?>
```

Second, we use the record values in $row to fill in the editing screen's value attributes which we see in example 7-5. Because we are currently in an HTML area and we need to use the PHP engine to output the PHP variables, we use `<?php echo $row["<fieldname>"] ?>` to output the value into the value parameter of the tag.

Example 7-5

```
60    <tr>
61       <td>
62          Subject:</td>
63       <td>
64          <input type="text" name="subject" size="60" maxlength="100" value="<?php echo $row["subject"] ?>">
65       </td>
66    </tr>
67    <tr>
68       <td>
69          LCSH:
70          </td>
71       <td>
72          <input type="text" name="lcsh" size="60" maxlength="100" value="<?php echo $row["lcsh"] ?>">
73       </td>
74    </tr>
75    <tr>
76       <td colspan="2">
77          Scope:<br><textarea cols="60" rows="3" name="subject_scope_note" wrap="virtual"><?php echo $row["subject_scope_note"] ?>
78          </textarea>
79       </td>
80    </tr>
```

The third thing we need to do—in fact we must do—is to embed the primary key name and value as a hidden variable (as noted in the **Views** grid) so we can pass it to the action page (see example 7-6). If we don't, the update action page won't know which record to update.

Example 7-6

```
57    <input type="hidden" name="subjectno" value=<?php echo $subjectno ?>>
```

*Updating action page.* Once the user clicks on **Update Record**, the values are passed to the action page (subject_update.php), where an update query is created (lines 45–49 of example 7-7) and sent to the database (line 50).[9]

Example 7-7

```
44    <?php
45    $query = "UPDATE subjects
46             SET subject='$subject',
47             lcsh='$lcsh',
48             subject_scope_note='$subject_scope_note'
49             WHERE subjectno = $subjectno";
50    $result = mysql_query( $query, $db ) or die( mysql_error() );
51    echo "Your record has been updated";
52    ?>
```

DELETING RECORDS   Deleting records follows much the same pattern as editing, with the exception that records are deleted rather than updated. Due to the need for security for such tasks, we will postpone considering it until we have dealt with user authentication and authorization.

## Other Maintenance Apps

Next we proceed to create the other data maintenance applications for the other views, one each for the **Content_Types**, **Supports**, **Formats**, and **Statuses** views. Because the first two both use arbitrary keys in the same way as subjects, we create them in exactly the same way. I therefore won't go into any detail here. The full source code for them, however, is included in Authority_Source.pdf in the companion materials download file.

FORMATS   On the other hand, `formats` and `statuses` use descriptive (as opposed to generated) primary keys and those real values are stored in the foreign key field of `sites` records. The first point means that we need to modify our format_query.php drop-down list. Because the display value is also the primary key, we use the single value of the `format` field both for value and for display.

However, the fact that we can change the contents of the primary key presents us with a problem: if we change the primary key value as we are editing the record, we are changing the identifier by which the action page knows which record to update. If the primary key's value is changed, the action page won't be able to specify which record to update, either in the `formats` or in any table where it is used as a foreign key.

As you can see in example 7-8, we get around this problem by creating a second hidden variable in the editing form (format_edit.php) in which we store the current value of the primary key (as it is in the table before editing) to `PKeyVal`, where it can be forwarded to the action page.

Example 7-8

```
55   <input type="hidden" name="PKeyVal" value="<?php echo $row["format"] ?>">
```

*Action page.* To make this change work, we need to slightly modify our updating query, and name it format_update.php. Instead of the expected WHERE `format='$format'` we substitute the variable containing the value as it currently resides in the database (line 45 of example 7-9):

Example 7-9

```
44   <?php
45   $query = "UPDATE formats SET format='$format' WHERE format='$PKeyVal'";
46   $result = mysql_query( $query, $db ) or die( mysql_error() );
47   $link_query = "UPDATE sites SET sites_format='$format' WHERE sites_format='$PKeyVal'";
48   $link_result = mysql_query( $link_query, $db ) or die( mysql_error() );
49   echo "Your record has been updated";
50   ?>
```

Finally, to maintain referential integrity with `sites` (remember, we didn't set up foreign key constraint support for this relation), we program the updating of foreign keys in the `sites` table. The query that we use for this is shown in line 47, with `$format` containing the new value the user has placed there and `$PKeyVal` containing the old value.

STATUSES   Handling `statuses` is essentially the same as `formats`, with one exception. Because we built a foreign key constraint in the relationship between `formats` and `sites`, we don't need to create an additional query to maintain relational integrity. MySQL does it for you. Everything else is done the same way.

## EXTENDING THE APPLICATION

Now that we have examined the basics of database maintenance apps, let's look at some ways to enhance our application. I will introduce you to a few additional concepts and the ala_functions.php library to show you how those concepts can be implemented.

## Checking for Duplicates

### Fields with Duplicate Entries

One thing you will want to do—especially when populating authority tables—is to prevent users from creating duplicate entries for the same value. Not only is this mandatory when creating primary keys, it also is highly advisable when inputting the display values for authority records. Although you may not use the `subject` field as the primary key, you still want to make sure that you don't end up with two records with the same subject (otherwise, which one will catalogers use?). MySQL's `UNIQUE` index does enforce uniqueness. However, it does so by throwing out a rather cryptic (at least for most users) error message if a user attempts to enter a duplicate value. This is clearly not the most user-friendly of approaches. It would be much better—more efficient—to check for duplicates before attempting to update the database.

There is a function—`Check_For_Dup_Fields()`—in the functions library that can handle this check for you. When calling it, you provide it with three parameters: the name of the field you wish to check, the name of the table containing the field you wish to examine, and the superglobal (`$_GET` or `$_POST`) containing the set of values passed from the form. For example, to check the subject that the user entered, you would call the function as seen in line 56 of subject_insert2.php, in example 7-10. The function searches the `subjects` table to see if it contains a record that already contains a record with the `subject` value the user has entered. If so, it lets the user know that the entry would duplicate an item already in the database; the function exits before the record can actually be added.

Example 7-10

```
56   Check_For_Dup_Fields( "subject","subjects", $_POST );
```

`Check_For_Dup_Fields()` allows you to check multiple fields in a single search. However, if you do pass it multiple fields, it will check for records where the same set of fields has the same values—as a group. Thus, if even one of the fields does not have a duplicate value, the function will not find a duplication. If you want to ensure that individual fields have unique values, you need to check each one separately.

## Duplicate Records

Another type of duplication you want to avoid is creating two records with the exact same information (again we'll reference code from subject_insert2.php). One feature of the Web is that clicking on **Reload** or **Refresh** in a browser causes the server to generate the page a second time. If the page in question happens to be an action page where a record has been added to the database, reloading it will create a duplicate entry in the database for the record you just added. If you click **Reload** five times, five identical records will be added.

You can avoid this by checking to see if there is already a record in the database with the current values before adding the new one. If there is, you can then warn the user and stop execution, thus preventing the duplicate entry from being added. One of the functions in the library—Check_For_Dup_Records()— does exactly that. All you do is call it with the table name (subjects) and the superglobal containing the form input values ($_POST). It then searches for a record with all of those values already there (see example 7-11 from subject_insert2.php). If it finds one, the user is warned and the (duplicate) record won't be added.

Example 7-11

```
57   Check_For_Dup_Records( "subjects", $_POST );
```

Both this and the previous function provide built-in responses. Although this can be useful, there may be times when you want to create your own message to the user. In both cases, there is an optional additional parameter—custom— which, if set to Y, will return the number of rows retrieved by the search. You can then check to see if the number retrieved was greater than zero. If so, you can take appropriate action, such as outputting a message and exiting. On the other hand, if no record is found, you can take a different action, such as proceeding to add the record. I have provided examples of how you can do this in example 7-12.

Example 7-12

```
65   $is_there = Check_For_Dup_Fields( "subject","subjects", $_POST, "Y" );
66   if ( $is_there > 0 ) {
67     echo "Sorry - this record has already been entered";
68     exit;
69   }
70   is_there = Check_For_Dup_Records( "subjects", $_POST, "Y" );
71   if ( $is_there > 0 ) {
72     echo "Sorry - this record has already been entered";
73     exit;
74   }
```

## Query Logging

The next technique implements something we discussed in chapter 3. There we noted that it is important to maintain a transaction log of each database-modifying query that is sent to the database. Not only does it aid in debugging problems, it provides a means of backing up data between system backups. Creating a log involves opening a file for input, writing the query and current date to that file, and closing the file.

This can require some involved programming. I have therefore provided a function in the subject_insert2.php script that can add this capability to our action pages. To use it in your application involves only two steps:

Create a subdirectory (folder) under the directory containing the insert/ update application script, naming the directory dblog. If you are working in a non-Windows environment, you will also need to make sure that the dblog subdirectory is owned and writeable by the same user—usually the user nobody—as the Web server.

Invoke the Write_Log() function, passing it the query name and the file name to which to add the query (see example 7-13).

Example 7-13
```
 90    Write_Log( $query, "good.log" );
```

Invoking this function causes the contents of $query to be written to the file good.log, located in the dblog subdirectory. By consistently using the Write_Log() function from the very beginning of your development, you can save yourself much time and many headaches.[10]

If you want to use your transaction log for database recovery, it is important that you use the same file for all log writing. This means that all scripts in an application that modify the database must write to the same log file. That way, the interactions can be restored in the same order in which they were initially entered. Having them in separate files will not allow for this, thereby causing potential database integrity problems (particularly when we start working with multiple tables).

Although using a single subdirectory works for simple applications, things can get complicated once you begin developing more complex programs—particularly if you implement transactions. For that reason, the logging functions in the library provide much more flexibility than is indicated here. We will discuss some of those options later. For complete information on Write_Log(), please consult Functions_Guide.pdf in the companion materials download file.

## Input Validation

Another issue concerns whether certain fields in a record are to be filled in. In some cases, such as the display fields in your authority records, you want to make sure the user inputs a value (it is not very helpful if your display name is an empty string). There are two ways to accomplish this:

> Use client-side scripting (using tools such as Javascript) to check a designated field or fields and then, if there is no input, display a warning dialog box and not permit the user to move to the action page until the field or fields have been filled in.

> Check at the beginning of the action page before processing, but after the information has been sent, to see if there is a value in the designated fields and, if not, notify the user that a value needs to be entered in that field. We explored this approach in chapter 5 in verifying that users had entered search parameters.

There are pros and cons to each approach. The first uses less network bandwidth and allows the input to be checked before the browser goes to another page. At the same time, it poses several possible problems:

> Browser support for Javascript code is unpredictable, particularly if pop-up blocking software is installed. On the other hand, if you are dealing with a known set of browsers within an organization over which you presumably have some control (or at least knowledge), this is less of a factor.

> The developer must know or learn yet another programming language.

> PHP and Javascript are not compatible in regard to arrays. PHP uses square brackets at the end of its array variables—something Javascript cannot currently handle. Because of this, we cannot use Javascript to check checkboxes and combo lists.

On the other hand, checking the variables after they are sent is much easier to code and maintain; does not require learning a (potentially) new language; avoids interbrowser compatibilities that can make Javascript programming a nightmare; and does not depend on whether Javascript is enabled in a browser. At the same time, this method presents its own stumbling points:

- Once you click on the **Submit** button, you leave one page and load another. If, for some reason, your browser does not cache the first page, clicking on the **Back** button may return you to an empty input form.

• Network traffic increases thanks to sent transactions that "don't take."

In the interests of balance, I provide information on using both approaches.[11] Looking at the client-side approach, I have included code inside the function library, named (not surprisingly) `Validate()`, that creates Javascript validation code to add to the <head> section of your page. The syntax for this function is

```
Validate(<textfields>,<multi-option_fields>);
```

This function takes two parameters: one comma-parsed list of all text, textarea, and select fields, and a second that checks `Y/N` and radio button fields, both lists being enclosed in double quotes. Placing the following in the <head> of your form creates Javascript code to check the `format` field (line 35 from format_add2.php, in example 7-14).

Example 7-14

```
33    <head>
34       <title>Add a Format</title>
35       <?php Validate("format","") ?>
36    </head>
37    <body>
38    <center><h1>Add a Format</h1></center>
39    <hr>
40    <form name="add_format" method="post" onSubmit="return validate(add_format)" action="format_insert.php">
```

For this approach to work, you also need to create your form tag in such a way that it will invoke the Javascript when the form is submitted.[12] You do this by using the format shown in example 7-15 for the opening form tag.

Example 7-15

```
<form name=<formname> method=<method> onSubmit="return validate(<formname>)" action=<action_page>>
```

The two essential elements here are the <formname>, a unique and relatively arbitrary name that you give the form, and the attribute `onSubmit` `="return validate(<formname>)"`, which causes the Javascript to be run when the form is submitted. By including these two things (replacing <formname> and <action_page> with the names of the form and action page respectively), if any field listed in the `validate()` parameters is not filled in, an alert box will pop up to indicate the name of the field, and the user will not be able to proceed until the required information is provided (see line 40 of example 7-14).

## Providing Useful Response

After taking care of business, we need to provide the user with useful feedback, perhaps indicating where to go next. There are several approaches. The first is to create a simple HTML page with a link to add another record or to check the record that was just input before submitting it to the database.

## Output Entry

Another approach is to let the user see what was sent to the action page. This involves going through the PHP superglobal and outputting its contents as an HTML table. Although we could do this manually, I have included another function—Show_Global_Vals()—that automates the process. In doing so, it outputs the values that were submitted to be added to the main data table. Example 7-16, taken from subject_insert2.php, demonstrates this.

Example 7-16
```
79   Show_Global_Vals( $_POST );
```

A more useful approach is to let the user see everything that was entered and, if needed, to correct any problems. You can do this by creating a link to an editing screen. I will show you how you can do this below.

## Jump to a Previous Page

The user may wish to return to the record selection screen or search page to choose another entry to edit. You can do this by inserting a Javascript link at the bottom of the page that takes the browser back a defined number of pages. By clicking on the link below, the user would be taken back two pages (that is, over the editing screen back to the search screen):

```
<a href= "javascript:history.go(-2)">Return to Search
     Screen</a>
```

If you have trouble remembering exactly what the syntax for this is (as I usually do), there is a function that will create the above Javascript link automatically. By calling Go_Link() and including the number of pages you wish to go back, for example, Go_Link( -2 ), the link will be created in your output page.

## Functions for Database Maintenance

You may have noticed that HTML form parameters and database queries and searches are written so that, though the individual parameters may change, the basic structure does not. We can turn this observation to our advantage by writing functions that create the structure that allows us to fill in the blanks using appropriate parameters. Not only can this make it easier and quicker to program your applications, it results in less typing and fewer typos (aka "bugs").

To this end, I have included functions in the ala_functions.php library that support a wide variety of tasks by simply calling a function and passing it values from the grids into the appropriate parameters. Then, when the script is run, the PHP engine runs the program code and creates the HTML for you.

### Inputting Functions

For example, let's take the following HTML inputting element and replace it with a function call. In this code shown in example 7-17, we see five elements: the input type (1), the name (2), the size (3), the maxlength (4), and the value (5).

Example 7-17

```
           1            2          3            4                    5
<input type="text" name="subject size="50" maxlength="100"" value="<?php echo $row["subject"] ?>">
```

We can take those elements and plug them into a `TextBox()` function that will create the HTML code when the page is run by the PHP engine, as seen in example 7-18.

Example 7-18

```
          1         2      3    4        5
<?php TextBox("subject","50","100",$row["subject"]) ?>
```

Even though it is a bit shorter, this example is not all that impressive. However, when we look at other input types, we can see a much more dramatic difference. For example, in example 7-19, we see the code for the creation of `select` lists we have been using (I won't even try to show the difference in checkboxes or radio buttons).[13]

Example 7-19

```
<td>Subject: <br>
</td>
<td> 1              2
<select name="subjectno">
<option></option>
<?php               3              4              5
$query = "SELECT subjectno,subject FROM subjects ORDER BY subject";
$result = mysql_query( $query ) or die( mysql_error() );
while ( $row = mysql_fetch_array( $result ) ) {
  $subjectno = $row["subjectno"];
  $subject = $row["subject"];
  echo "<option value=\"$subjectno\">$subject</option>";
}
?>
</select>
</td>
```

Example 7-20 shows how you can replace all of that code with a simple function call.

Example 7-20

```
<td>
Subject: <br>
</td>
<td>   1        2         3              4          5
<?php SelectList( "subjectno", "subjectno,subject", "subjects", "subject" ) ?>
</td>
```

Although the function might look like so much gibberish, I have numbered each parameter and shown in the previous example where that parameter is used. Specifically, we use

1. `SelectList`—function call that will create a `select` list
2. `subjectno`—the primary key used in the `name=` attribute
3. `subjectno, subject`—the two fields containing the primary key and display name values to be used in the option list items
4. `subjects`—the table containing those fields
5. `subject`—the field on which to sort

All the other functions work in similar ways. We will take a look at them later.

### Database Maintenance Functions

Besides items to support inputting into forms, ala_functions.php also includes functions to maintain the database. As with inputting, manually creating these, though not rocket science, opens the door to typos and other problems. In addition, there are a number of features—such as duplicate checking and logging—that you don't want to have to type in each time you create a page. (Note that using these functions will work only if you give the value name in your form the same name—including case—as the field into which the data will be entered.) Using functions allows us to simply pass the appropriate information to the functions to let them do all of the work. `Insert_Record()` is such a function. Let's see how it works.

In example 7-21, I take the code that we saw used in example 7-2 to insert a record into the `subjects` table and modify it to use one of the ala_functions that I will show you.

Example 7-21

```
50  $fields = "subject, lcsh, subject_scope_note";
51  $table = "subjects";
52  $subjectno = Insert_Record( $fields, $table, $_POST, "Y", "good.log" );
53  echo "Your record has been added:<p>";
```

Although the latter has significantly fewer characters to be typed, the real advantages of using the function are more substantial:

1. Several other tasks are supported by the `Insert_Record()` function, such as query logging, duplicate record checking, error checking, and, as we will see a bit later, support for transactions.
2. The `$field` list is a simple comma-parsed list where each field name is typed in only once and is very easily read (which is important if you are

dealing with large tables). If you need to make a change, you do it there, rather than having to do it both in the field list and in the **VALUES** elements (making sure that you entered both of them correctly and in the same order).

3. MySQL's **mysql_id()** captures the **auto_increment** value of the newly created record and returns it to the calling script, where (in this case) it is saved to **$subjectno**. This value can then be used in adding linking records as needed.

4. The fourth parameter can be very useful, especially if you like to see your SQL queries before running them or need to debug cranky ones. It essentially tells the function whether to run the query. If it is **N**, the query won't run, but the function will print the query that would be run. If the parameter is **Y**, then the query will run. If it is **D**, then it will also run, but the function will not check for duplicates.

There is also an **Update_Record()** function that uses the similar parameters and which is available for updating data records in the database. The only difference between the two in the way that they are called is that **Update_Record()** has an additional parameter that passes the primary key to the function so it can know which record to update.

LINKS FOR EDITING A RECORD   As noted, one thing that users can find useful is to be able to check—and if necessary correct—information they have input. Given that you have the primary key available to you at the end of the insert screen, you can create this link by creating a URL similar to that shown on line 51 of example 7-22.

Example 7-22

```
49  echo "Your record has been added<p>";
50  ?>
51  <a href="ctype_add.php">Add another record</a>
```

UPDATING AUTHORITY RECORD CHANGES   One other situation needs to be addressed—how we update authority records where the primary key has changed. We need a way to handle potentially changed primary keys similar to that shown in example 7-9. Two functions address this situation. The first, **Update_Auth_Record()**, is run on line 52 of format_update.php in example 7-23, using the following parameters:

$fields—the list of fields to be updated

$table—the name of the authority table

$_POST—the superglobal array containing the values from the form

format—the name of the primary key

$PKeyVal—the old value for the primary key, used to identify the record to be updated

Y —whether to run this function for real

good.log—the name of the log file to which the query should be written

Example 7-23

```
52  Update_Auth_Record( $fields, $table, $_POST, "format", $PKeyVal, "Y", "good.log" );
53  Update_Auth_Links( "sites_format", "sites", $format, $PKeyVal, "Y", "good.log" );
```

Next, we need to propagate the changes to foreign key fields that link to this record. For this, we run **Update_Auth_Links( )**, which we can see in line 53 of example 7-23. Here, the function is passed the name of the field containing the foreign key, the name of the table containing the foreign key field, the new value, the old value, whether the query should actually be run, and the log file name.

I have given a cursory introduction to these functions. Please consult Functions_ Guide.pdf in the companion materials download file for a complete description of each, explanations on how they are used, and the parameters they include. (For a complete set of fully annotated scripts for authority file maintenance that use these functions, see Authority_Functions_Source.pdf in the companion materials download file.)

## Testing the Application

Before proceeding, I would like to discuss an important part of the development process. In programming, it is critical that you make sure that your program is working correctly, that the data at any point are what they are supposed to be, and are going to where they need to go. In testing, you should use the materials you developed as part of the design process (see the end of chapter 6). You can use these documents to create checklists that you can use to work your way through the application, testing to make sure the program is doing what it should from beginning to end.

## CREATING THE MAIN APPLICATION

## Adding Records

You have now seen the basic structure of a data maintenance application using PHP and MySQL. Next, we will program the maintenance applications for the

**Sites** view (see Sites_Source.pdf in the companion materials download file for the annotated source code of these scripts). We begin with adding records.

## Adding Form

Looking at the **Views** grid for the **Sites** view, we note that the **ITypes** for that view includes select lists, text, textareas, checkboxes, date, and yes/no. We have already seen the first three. Let's now take a look at the last three in some detail.

CHECKBOXES   Unless you place everything in one column, creating checkbox (or radio button) input lists can be very code-intensive. Each checkbox has its own complete inputting tag requiring a lot of typing if there are a large number of alternatives; even if you do use one column, it still involves a lot of typing. However, the process of automating it can be quite tricky. To produce the list in the easiest way possible—left to right, top to bottom—requires you to know how many columns you want for each row and, as you go through your results, to know when to end one row and begin the next. It becomes even more difficult if you want to produce the list the way that many people prefer them: top to bottom within a column and then left to right with as even a number of rows in each column as possible.

The `CheckBoxes()` function seeks to make this process much easier, even allowing you to select whether you want horizontal or vertical display of your options. The snippet of code shown in example 7-24 from the site_add.php form shows you how it is called. This code creates the table shown in figure 7-1.

Example 7-24

```
 99    <tr>
100      <td colspan="2">
101        <center>Subjects:</center>
102      </td>
103    </tr>
104    <tr>
105      <td colspan="2">
106        <?php CheckBoxes( "subjectno[]", "subjectno,subject", "subjects", "subject", "6", "1" ) ?>
107      </td>
108    </tr>
109    <tr>
110      <td colspan="2">
111        <center>Type of Content:</center>
112      </td>
113    </tr>
114    <tr>
115      <td colspan="2">
116        <?php CheckBoxes( "content_typeno[]", "content_typeno,content_type", "content_types", "content_type", "4", "1", "", "horizontal" ) ?>
117      </td>
118    </tr>
```

Although the first four parameters of the `CheckBoxes()` function are the same as `SelectList()`, the last two are not. The fifth (6) indicates the number of columns to include within the `checkboxes` table and the sixth (1) indicates the `border=` value for the table. You can add an eighth parameter (adding an empty string for the intervening `$default_vals` parameter) of `horizontal` if

| Subjects: | | | | | |
|---|---|---|---|---|---|
| ☐ - Agriculture | ☐ - Communications | ☐ - Ethnomusicology | ☐ - Languages | ☐ - Multidisciplinary | ☐ - Social Work |
| ☐ - Anthropology | ☐ - Computer Programming | ☐ - Geography | ☐ - Law | ☐ - Music | ☐ - Sociology |
| ☐ - Architecture | ☐ - Computer Science | ☐ - Geology | ☐ - Leisure Studies | ☐ - Musicology | ☐ - Statistics |
| ☐ - Art | ☐ - Dance | ☐ - History (American) | ☐ - Library Science | ☐ - Philosophy | ☐ - Technology |
| ☐ - Astronomy | ☐ - Economics | ☐ - History (European) | ☐ - Literature (non-Western) | ☐ - Physics | ☐ - Theater |
| ☐ - Biology | ☐ - Education | ☐ - History (non-Western) | ☐ - Literature (Western) | ☐ - Political Science | ☐ - Urban Planning |
| ☐ - Black Studies | ☐ - Engineering | ☐ - Human Ecology | ☐ - Mathematics | ☐ - Psychology | ☐ - Veterinary Medicine |
| ☐ - Business | ☐ - Ethnic Studies | ☐ - International Studies | ☐ - Medical | ☐ - Religion | ☐ - Women's Studies |
| ☐ - Chemistry | | | | | |

Figure 7-1

you want the output to read left-to-right, top-to-bottom (something I have done in line 116 of example 7-24 for the **Type of Content** options; see figure 7-2 for what the output looks like). However, if it is not there, the function will assume that you want the default value of vertical.[14]

| Type of Content: | | | |
|---|---|---|---|
| ☐ - Background Information | ☐ - Current events | ☐ - Full text | ☐ - Indexes and Abstracts |
| ☐ - Instructional | ☐ - Media | ☐ - Opinions | ☐ - Organizations |
| ☐ - People | ☐ - Quick Reference | ☐ - Research | ☐ - Statistics |
| ☐ - Web Portals | | | |

Figure 7-2

One thing slightly different about the `CheckBoxes()` function, and its sibling `RadioButtons()`, is that it creates a table within a table. That is, for them to function properly, they must be placed within a table, even if you are not using tables for your input form (using a `border=0` attribute conceals the fact that a table structure is in place).

If you are working within an established table, you can specify the number of columns within which the checkboxes (or radio buttons) are to be displayed. To do this, we use the colspan attribute inside the opening <td> tag (line 105 of example 7-24) that precedes the function call.

DATES   Dates can be entered in a database in any number of ways. There are not many formats, however, that permit searching, comparing, or sorting. If you don't wish to have the date be searchable, you can use any type of character-based entry format. If you do, you can opt for one of the following:

> If you are working with years only, you can use a four-character or -integer field and, as long as you are consistent in putting four characters or numbers into each field, you will be able to search and sort. If you make the field character-based, the function also allows you to use fuzzy dates. For example, in keyword searching on the field, you can truncate (192*) so that the function brings up anything in the 1920s. Also, if you consistently use four characters, you will be able to search on ranges of years, such as 1925–1931.

> You can expand on the fuzzy-date approach by making the field up to eight characters in the following format: YYYY-MM-DD. You can then truncate at any level of specificity. This is not, however, the most intuitive format to read and it is difficult to program searching against it. It is more advisable to create a data authority table containing the ranges of years that you can then use to create a drop-down box to use in data maintenance and searching.

> For the full range of possibilities in using dates, you can use MySQL's DATE field type. This allows you to sort, search, and fully compare (for example, before June 27, 1978). The only drawback is that you must provide an exact date—month, day of the month, and year.

This last option can be a particularly involved operation to program. First, the native MySQL format in which dates are stored is not the most intuitive format out there. Although you can obtain the data using a more user-friendly interface in a variety of ways, these can be code-intensive and are prone to typos and invalid date entry (February 29, 2003, for example, or September 31, 2005). What is needed is a method that allows users to enter dates in a familiar format that will also check that any date input is valid.

The `Display_Date()` function (example 7-25, whose output is shown in figure 7-3) has been designed to do just that. It creates select lists for month, date, and year from which the user can choose. When it is submitted, there is a corresponding function—`Build_Date()`—shown in example 7-27, that we will use to validate the input and create a properly formatted date field for entry into the database.

Example 7-25

```
96    <?php Display_Date( "added", "1", "", "today" ) ?>
```

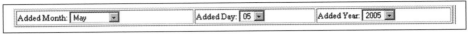

Figure 7-3

The values that are passed to the `Display_Date()` function include (see Functions_Guide.pdf in the companion materials download file for a complete description of this function):

> *added*—the prompt to be displayed in the form and the prefix to be added to _month, _day, and _year to create the variables that will be sent to the action page (to distinguish them from other possible dates in the form)

> *1*—value for the border attribute of the table tag in which the dropdowns will be displayed

> *" "*—blank string, the function will use the default value for range of the current year into 10 years in the future

> *today*—current date from the server used as default

YES/NO PROMPT    There are several ways to prompt for `Y/N` answers. Radio buttons are especially user friendly.[15] Although easily created, they can be somewhat code intensive, particularly in editing screens where you need to create code to test the value in the field so that it will know where to place the `CHECKED` in the editing screen. To make this easier, I have included a `Y_or_N()` function in ala_functions.php (available in the companion materials download file) that makes it easy to create `Y/N` input elements (example 7-26).

Example 7-26
```
88      <?php Y_or_N( "Include in Alphabetical List?", "alphabetical_list" , "N" ) ?>
```

As you can see from example 7-26, there are three pieces of information you pass to this function (the output is shown in figure 7-4).

> *Include in Alphabetical List?*—the prompt to be displayed in the form

> *alphabetical_list*—the name= variable to be passed to the action page and the name of the field into which to save the value

> *N*—default value for the field (if left blank, neither option will be checked)

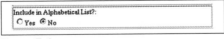

Figure 7-4

## Inserting Action Page

In creating our action page, we need to do several things. First, is to assemble the date variables created by our `Display_Date()` into a value that can be inserted into the database. We do this on line 53 of example 7-27 from site_insert.php. This function takes the name of the field into which we want to place the value (`added_date`), the three variables created by `Display_Date()` (`$added_year`, `$added_month`, and `$added_day`), and the `$_POST` superglobal. From this it builds a YYYY-MM-DD date. Then, before adding it to `$_POST`, it makes sure that the date is valid (that is, not something like February 31). Once the function has been run, `$added_date` can be added to the `sites` table.

Example 7-27

```
53  $_POST = Build_Date( "added_date", $added_year, $added_month, $added_day, $_POST );
54  $fields = "name, url, description, sites_format, sites_status, requires_proxy,
55              help_page, alphabetical_list, subscription, added_date,
56              restrictions_on_use, sites_supportno";
57  $table = "sites";
58  $siteno = Insert_Record( $fields, $table, $_POST, $prod="Y", "good.log" );
59  if ( isset ( $subjectno ) ) {
60      Insert_Links( "sites_subjects", array( "ss_site_no"=>$siteno ),
61                  array( "ss_subject_no"=>$subjectno ), $prod="Y" );
62  }
63  if ( isset ( $content_typeno ) ) {
64      Insert_Links( "sites_types", array( "st_site_no"=>$siteno ),
65                  array( "st_content_type_no"=>$content_typeno ),
66                  $prod="Y" );
67  }
```

After defining the `$fields` into which we want to insert data (lines 54–56) and defining the name of the `$table` containing those `$fields` (line 57), we call the `Insert_Record()` function to add the record to the database. Because we need to know what the primary key of the data record is so that we can use it for foreign key fields to link other table records to this new record, `Insert_Record()` is called here in such a way that the value of that record's primary key returned by the function is saved to a variable named `$siteno` (line 58).

We can now use the value in the `Insert_Links()` function to create the linking table records. After making sure that there are values for `$subjectno` coming in from the form (line 59), we call the function as follows (lines 60–61). The parameters include

> *sites_subjects*—the name of the table into which the links are to be placed
>
> *ss_siteno*—name of the foreign key field in `sites_subjects` into which the primary key of `sites` will be stored
>
> *$siteno*—name of the variable to which the primary key of the inserted `sites` record was saved by `Insert_Record()`
>
> *ss_subjectno*—name of the foreign key field in `sites_subjects` in which the primary key of `subjects` will be stored

*$subjectno*—name of the array, coming from site_add.php, containing the primary keys of the subjects that the user has selected (values then inserted as foreign key values in the linking records: note that square brackets are used only in input forms)

*Y*—whether this is a production query (in this case, it is)

*good.log*—name of the log file to which the query should be logged

After doing the same for $contentno array, we close off the page by using Display_Values() to output the data we have saved to the main data table. We provide two links: one to edit the record we just added and one to allow us to add another record.

## Editing

To begin the editing process, we need to perform a search—similar to those in chapter 5—to retrieve a list of records from which we choose one to edit. Because the values by which we will want to search are not in a single table, we will explore techniques to search multiple tables.

### *Searching*

In site_query1.php, we see an example of one possible search form. It uses the same basic principles as we saw earlier. This time, however, it uses the ala_function.php library to create select lists for four of the fields (subject, content_type, format, and status) and a simple text input box for name and description.

The major change comes in site_search1.php—the action page that implements the search. We begin (lines 40–49 of example 7-28) by defining some variables for the search:

$fields—list of fields to be retrieved (sites.*)

$tables—all tables involved with the search (either because they contain data or are used in defining the relations), beginning with the base table, sites, and adding others as required

$display_fields—array containing the names of the fields to be output in the order of output

$num_fields—number of elements in the $display_fields array (used in the for block that outputs results)

`$link_str`—in case linking statements are needed to define relations to be followed (start with it blank so that if there are no parameters it won't disrupt the eventual WHERE statement)

Example 7-28

```
40  $fields = "sites.*";
41  $tables = "sites";
42  $link_str = "";
43  $where_str = "";
44
45  /*********************************************************************
46   * Create the array of fields to display
47   *********************************************************************/
48  $display_fields = array( "siteno", "name", "url", "description", "sites_format", "sites_status" );
49  $num_fields = count( $display_fields );
```

In example 7-29, we see the code where we go through each possible field—as in chapter 5—checking to see if the user has entered a value and, if so, to add an appropriately formatted element to the `$where_ary` array of WHERE conditions. When our search involves tables other than the main `sites` table, we concatenate the new table names to `$tables`, separating them with commas. We then add the required additional linking condition or conditions (which we obtain from the **Links** grid) to the end of the `$link_str`. For example, in checking for a `subject` condition in lines 65–70 if `$subjectno` is not blank, we add the values in lines 66–67. Also, because we are using InnoDB tables, I have resorted to the use of LIKE to search the `name` and `description` fields (line 95). I will show you an alternative shortly.

Example 7-29

```
64  $x=0;
65  if ( $subjectno != "" ) {
66      $tables .= ",sites_subjects";
67      $link_str .= " AND sites.siteno=sites_subjects.ss_siteno ";
68      $where_ary[$x] = " ss_subjectno = $subjectno ";
69      $x++;
70  }
71
72  if ( $content_typeno != "" ) {
73      $tables .= ",sites_types";
74      $link_str .= " AND sites.siteno=sites_types.st_siteno ";
75      $where_ary[$x] = " st_content_typeno = $content_typeno ";
76      $x++;
77  }
78
79  if ( $sites_format != "" ) {
80      $where_ary[$x] = " sites_format = '$sites_format' ";
81      $x++;
82  }
83
84  if ( $sites_status != "" ) {
85      $where_ary[$x] = " sites_status = '$sites_status' ";
86      $x++;
87  }
88
89  if ( $name != "" ) {
90      $where_ary[$x] = " name like '%$name%' ";
91      $x++;
92  }
93
94  if ( $description != "" ) {
95      $where_ary[$x] = " description like '%$description%' ";
96      $x++;
97  }
```

We begin this section (in line 64) by setting our counter variable ($x) to 0. Each time we add a new WHERE element, we increment (add one) to $x. If we get to the end and $x is still equal to 0, it probably means that no values were input—something we check in lines 115–122 in example 7-30. If it does still equal 0, we ask the user to go back and enter a value to be searched. On the other hand, if $x is not equal to 0, it means that a value was entered and we begin constructing our where string ($where_str) by stepping through the $where_ary. We then take the $where_str variable and, along with other constants and variables we have defined, use it to build our SQL statement.

In constructing this query, I have used one little SQL trick to make life easier. Because the first WHERE condition can neither have an AND in front of it (WHERE AND <condition> will give you a syntax error), nor may the last condition have a dangling AND at the end of it, and because we don't know which element will be the first condition, I have hard-coded the beginning of the conditional part of the query with WHERE 1 (line 129 of example 7–30). In MySQL this construct means TRUE (or "everything that could be retrieved by this query").[16] Although it is a bit redundant, using it means that we can place AND in front of every condition we create and do not need to figure out which one is first beforehand because 1 will always be the first condition.

Example 7-30

```
115  if ( $x == 0 ) {
116      echo "You need to enter a search";
117      exit;
118  } else {
119      for ( $a=0; $a<$x; $a++ ) {
120          $where_str .= " AND $where_ary[$a] ";
121      }
122  }
123
124  /****************************************************************
125   * Now let's create the $query variable, do the search (saving it to $result).
126   * Next, check to see if there are any rows in the result set.  If not, let
127   * the user know that fact.
128   ****************************************************************/
129  $query = "SELECT DISTINCT $fields FROM $tables WHERE 1 $link_str $where_str";
130  $records = Do_Search( $query );
131  $num_rows = count( $records );
132  if ( $num_rows == 0 ) {
133      echo "<center>No Records Found</center>";
134      exit;
135  } else {
136      echo "<center>$num_rows Records Found</center><hr>";
137  }
```

Once we have created the query (129), we pass it to a new function—Do_Search()—to do the search and return an array of records for us to process (130).

Once we have that array, we use it to create the output (lines 142–169 of example 7-31):

Create an opening <table> tag to begin our outputting table.

Create a `for` loop that will walk through the `$results` array, storing a new record each time to `$row`.

Use a `for` loop to walk through the `$display_fields` array for each record from `$results`, reading a name from `$display_fields` into `$fld` and then using that value to output the displayed string and appropriate value.[17]

See which field is being processed using an `if` statement and take appropriate actions. (If `$fld` is `siteno`, for example, use it to create a hyperlink to site_edit.php, including the `siteno=$siteno` as a parameter. Thus, when users click on this link, they are sent to the site_edit.php form, which then uses the `$siteno` value to retrieve the appropriate record or records to populate an editing form.[18] Because the `$display_fields` array is processed in order, placing `siteno` as the first element guarantees that the link will come at the top of the record.)

Add an extra `<tr><td><br></td></tr>`, after a `$row` is completed, to separate this record's display from the next record.

Provide the closing `</table>` tag, after the loop is completed, and close off the HTML page.

Example 7-31

```
142   echo "<table border=\"0\">";
143   for ( $a=0; $a<$num_rows; $a++ ) {
144       $row = $records[$a];
145       for ( $b=0; $b<$num_fields; $b++ ) {
146           $fld = $display_fields[$b]; // save name from $display_fields array to $fld
147           $label = ucwords($fld);  // make first letter of each word in $fld upper case
148           if ( $fld == "siteno" ) { // if the $fld is "siteno", create link to edit
149               echo "<tr><td align=\"right\"><b>$label</b></TD><TD><a
150   href=\"site_edit.php?siteno=$row[$fld]\">$row[$fld]</a> (Edit this record)</td></tr>";
151           } elseif ( $fld == "url" ) {
152               $URL = $fld;
153               $value = $row[$fld];
154               if ( trim( $value ) != "" ) {
155                   echo "<tr><td align=\"right\" valign=\"top\"><b>URL</b></td><td><a
156   href=\"$row[$fld]\">$row[$fld]</a></td></tr>";
157               }
158           } else {
159               $value = $row[$fld];
160               if ( trim( $value ) != "" ) {
161                   echo "<tr><td align=\"right\"
162   valign=\"top\"><b>$label</b></td><td>$row[$fld]</td></tr>";
163               }
164           }
165       }
166       echo "<tr><td><br></td></tr>";
167   }
168   ?>
169   </table>
```

To make this searching application truly useful, we need to allow for searching multiple subjects or content types. I will also demonstrate a better alternative for keyword searching below.

## Making Changes

After clicking on the link provided in the search output, the user is taken to the editing page (in this case, site_edit.php). There, the primary key ($siteno) is used first to retrieve the appropriate record from the sites table (using the Get_Main_Record() function) and then to retrieve all linking table records that have $siteno as the foreign key field for sites (using the Get_Linked_Records() function, see example 7-32).

Example 7-32

```
52   $sites_row = Get_Main_Record( "*", "sites", "siteno" );
53   $subject_ary = Get_Linked_Records( "sites_subjects", "ss_subjectno", "ss_siteno", $siteno );
54   $ctype_ary = Get_Linked_Records( "sites_types", "st_content_typeno", "st_siteno", $siteno );
```

In line 52 of example 7-32, the fields we want to retrieve (*), the main data table (sites), and the primary key for the main data table (siteno) are passed to Get_Main_Record() and the record is returned as an associative array back to $sites_row, constructing the array name using <tablename> as a prefix to "_row" (using prefix names for your result rows can be valuable if you ever need to deal with data from multiple tables in the same form). Once this array is created, it can be used to fill in the blanks in our editing screen.

In the next two rows (53–54), we call Get_Linked_Records(), using information from the **Links** grid to pass it:

- the name of the linking table
- the name of the field containing the authority table's foreign key
- the field name containing the main data record's foreign key
- the value to search for in the main record's foreign key field

Using this information, the function returns the results, which are then stored to the appropriate array names: $subject_ary and $ctype_ary respectively. These arrays will be used to display the current values for those multivalued authority fields in the record editing screens.

Next, we create our HTML form, using Validate() to require fields and creating our form appropriately (line 72 of example 7-33). Inside the form, we place a hidden variable containing the **sites** table's primary key that will be passed to the action page so it can tell MySQL which record to update (line 73).

Example 7-33

```
72   <form name="update_form" method="POST" onSubmit="return validate(update_form)" action="site_update.php">
73   <input type="hidden" name="siteno" value="<?php echo $siteno ?>">
```

Finally, we create the editing screen input fields using the same functions we used in site_add.php. However, so that the program will know what value to place into the inputting box, we add an additional parameter to the function call—one that causes the current value for that field in the database to be placed in the **value** parameter in the inputting form (example 7-34). In the case of single-value fields where the value is coming from the main record, we use the **$sites_row** associative array, entering the field name as the array index (for example, **$sites_row["name"]** gives us the contents of the **name** field).

Example 7-34

```
88   <tr>
89     <td colspan="2">
90       Name: <br><?php TextBox( "name", "60", "125", $sites_row["name"] ) ?>
91     </td>
92   </tr>
```

As you can see in example 7-35, in the case of the linking values, we simply enter the name of the array we created at the top of the page as the seventh parameter. For example, when creating the **subjects** list, we enter the name of the array of values we retrieved (in **$subject_ary**).

Example 7-35

```
144      <?php Checkboxes( "subjectno[]", "subjectno,subject", "subjects", "subject", "4", "1", $subject_ary ) ?>
```

**UPDATING THE DATABASE** Finally, we use the following function commands shown in example 7-36, using the data we received from the input form, to update the database.

Example 7-36

```
48   $fields = "name, url, description, sites_format, sites_status, requires_proxy,
49              help_page, alphabetical_list, subscription, restrictions_on_use,
50              sites_supportno";
51   $table = "sites";
52   Update_Record( $fields, $table, $_POST, "siteno", "Y" );
53   if ( isset( $subjectno ) ) {
54       Update_Links( "sites_subjects", array("ss_siteno"=>$siteno),
55                     array("ss_subjectno"=>$subjectno), "subjects", $prod="Y" );
56   } else {
57       Delete_Links( "sites_subjects", array("ss_siteno"=>$siteno), $prod="Y" );
58   }
59   if ( isset( $content_typeno ) ) {
60       Update_Links( "sites_types", array("st_siteno"=>$siteno),
61                     array("st_content_typeno"=>$content_typeno),
62                     "content_types", $prod="Y" );
63   } else {
64       Delete_Links( "sites_types", array("st_siteno"=>$siteno), $prod="Y" );
65   }
```

As before, we check to make sure that there has been user input before running the `Update_Links()` function (example 7-36, lines 53 and 59). However, if there is not, it might mean that the user did not add any or eliminated links that had been there. To handle this situation, we assume that, in either case, the user wants no subjects or content types associated with the record. Therefore, if there was no input, we run the `Delete_Links()` function to delete any links that may be associated with the record.

Note that in our call to `Update_Links()`, we have included an additional parameter. This parameter—the name of the authority table—is included so that, if the function finds an unmatched foreign key, the error message displayed in the screen will contain the table in which the primary key should have been found. This in turn helps with tracking down the problem.

### Lost Foreign Key Values

One of the problems in using authority tables for editing is that, if there is a value in a foreign key field that does not have a corresponding entry in the primary table, a value will not be displayed in the editing screen. Although this cannot occur if foreign key constraints have been established between the two tables, in some cases you may not want to—or be able to—set those constraints, such as needing to use MyISAM file type to support FULLTEXT indexing.

There are a number of ways in which we could end up with orphan foreign keys. For example, an authority table record is deleted without taking appropriate actions in the foreign key tables. Or if the foreign key field has had data added to it outside the application process or outside authority control, then there was no way to enforce the appropriate integrity. No matter how it happened, we need to have a way to deal with it. Otherwise, when the record is updated, the anomalous field entry will be lost permanently.

Although it may seem rather drastic to discard data, it makes sense if you think about it. After all, the idea behind a controlled vocabulary is to control the vocabulary. Having a term in the database that is not in the authority list violates that control (to say nothing of referential integrity) and we should keep unauthorized terms out. On the other hand, the unauthorized term may be important. We want a way to deal with it rather than just throw it out sight unseen (and not even know that it was there).

To address this problem, the authority list keeps track of all default values that are passed to it and, if it finds that any of those values are orphans (don't have an associated authority table entry), a flag is set (at least one of the values to be sent to the database is set to `have_f_key_problem`), and an error message is displayed to the screen. In addition, it creates a hidden value named `have_f_key_problem`. Then, if the user attempts to update the record, each of the updating functions checks to see if any of the values coming in from the inputting form has this value. If they find it, an error message containing the primary key of the database and a statement telling the operator to contact the database administrator is displayed; and all processing stops. (If you want to allow this behavior to be overridden, see the Functions_Guide.pdf in the companion materials download file.)

## Multiple Values within a Field

Before proceeding, let's expand some of the searching techniques we are using. There will be times when you or your users will want to search by multiple values within a field (see figure 7-5 for an example).

Although we have provided ways of doing that for text inputting boxes, we have not done so for drop-down lists. To allow us to select multiple values, we

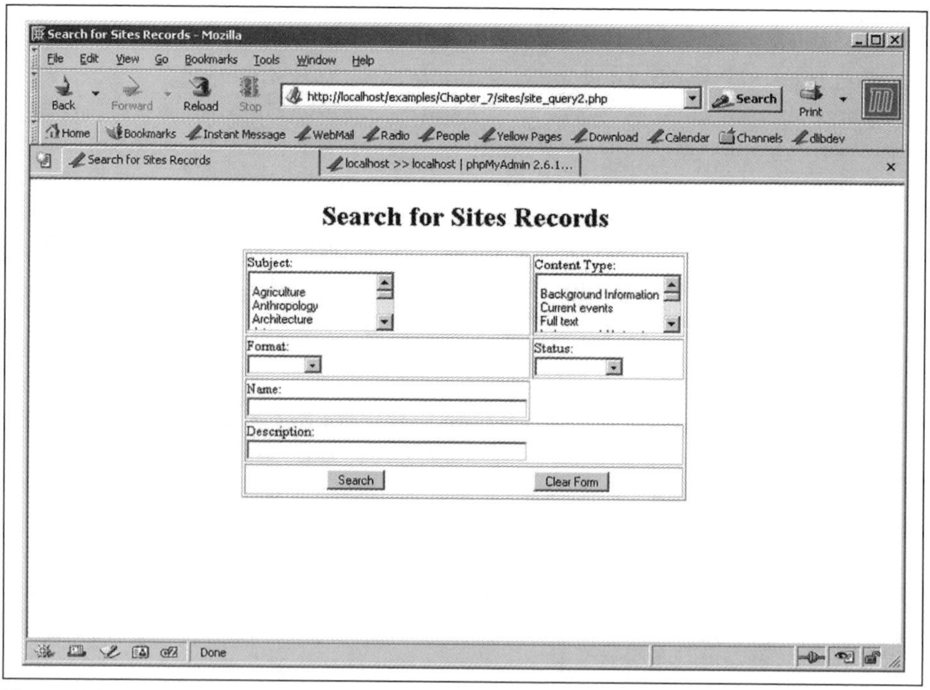

Figure 7-5

need to change the inputting functions for **subjects** and **content types** from **SelectList( )** to **ComboList( )** in site_query2.php, making sure to add square brackets ([ ]) to the end of the variable name, so that it will pass input values as an array to the action page, and defining the number of items to display—both of which we do in lines 50 and 53 of example 7-37.

Example 7-37

```
49      <td>
50          Subject: <br><?php ComboList( "subjectno[]", "subjectno,subject", "subjects", "subject", "4" ) ?>
51      </td>
52      <td>
53          Content Type: <br><?php ComboList( "content_typeno[]", "content_typeno,content_type", "content_types", "content_type", "4" ) ?>
54      </td>
```

Looking at line 50, we see that, after providing the label (**Subject**), the function is called with the following parameters (in order):

> **subjectno[ ]**—the HTML name variable
>
> **subjectno, subject**—the fields from the **Views** grid used to create the list
>
> **subjects**—the table containing the values to be placed in the list
>
> **subject**—the field to sort on
>
> **4**—the number of lines to show in the combo list

## Implementing Keyword Searching

Next we make a couple changes in the action page (site_search2.php). First, we need to turn the array elements into a **WHERE** statement that can be used in an SQL query. This involves

- breaking the array into individual elements
- building a **WHERE** element from the constituent **OR** parameters passed from the user (parentheses need to embrace strings with more than one value)

In the interests of saving time and effort, I have constructed a **Process_ Query_Array( )** that takes care of this for us. We can see an example in lines 68–76 of example 7-38 (from site_search2.php).

Example 7-38

```
68      if ( isset( $_POST["subjectno"] ) ) {
69          $tmp_str = Process_Query_Array( "ss_subjectno",$subjectno );
70          if ( $tmp_str != "" ) {
71              $tables .= ",sites_subjects";
72              $link_str = " AND sites.siteno=sites_subjects.ss_siteno ";
73              $where_ary[$x] = $tmp_str;
74              $x++;
75          }
76      }
```

We check to see if a subject was input (line 68). If so, we pass the appropriate parameters (name of the field to search and name of the array containing values to be searched) to the function. The function in turn outputs a fully formatted `WHERE` condition, which we save to `$tmp_str`. If the string is not equal to `""`, something was input. We therefore enter the loop, where we add `site_subjects` to the `$tables` list (line 71), the linking condition needed to find `sites` records associated with these values added to `$link_str` (line 72), and of course, the new condition to the `$where_ary` array (line 73), incrementing `$x` in the next line (74).[19]

As we have said, we are unable to use MySQL's `FULLTEXT` searching, due to our use of InnoDB table format for the `sites` table. Fortunately, MySQL incorporates a very powerful technique—regular expressions—that we can use to address the problem. Although we have nowhere nearly enough time to delve into a detailed examination of regular expressions (see the bibliography), this technique provides you with some very sophisticated tools that can look for and manipulate strings of characters within longer strings. In this case, we can use them to search for a string as a word (between spaces, punctuation, or other non-word characters) inside a field, thus avoiding the limitations we encounter with `LIKE`.

To provide a painless way for you to use regular expressions in your searching applications, I have created a function—`Process_Query_String()`—that creates regular expression–based MySQL `WHERE` elements that replicate MySQL's `FULLTEXT` searching capabilities. Example 7-39 (taken from site_search2.php) is an example. In this code, if the condition (`$description != ""`) is true, the script calls `Process_Query_String()`, passing it the field name (`description`) and the variable name (`$description`), and saves the result to `$tmp_str`. Then, in line 115, it adds `$tmp_str` to the `$where` array. This technique allows us full Boolean searching, including: by full words and phrases, with right-hand truncation using asterisk, and both `AND` and `OR` operators (`OR`'ing before `AND`'ing after) similar to the and_or_search.php we saw in chapter 5.

Example 7-39

```
113   if ($description != "") {
114       $tmp_str = Process_Query_String("description",$description);
115       $where_ary[$x] = " $tmp_str ";
116       $x++;
117   }
```

At this point, we have a working Web-based application, even if it's a bit simpler than we eventually might want. One component is missing, however, and it's a critical one. We need our data to be secure, beyond the reach of both external and internal hackers. In the next chapter, we address security-related techniques that we can apply to a database-backed Web-based application.

## Notes

1. See http://www.databasejournal.com/features/mysql/article.php/3311731 or http://dev.mysql.com/doc/mysql/en/privileges-provided.html for information on each of these rights.
2. Actually, in order to enable transactions (which I will be showing you later in this chapter), you need to turn on InnoDB support for all tables. You must also have set up InnoDB support in your my.cnf file. See Setup.pdf in the companion materials download file for more details.
3. See the MySQL manual for more options.
4. The `include()` function reads the contents of the file name you give it directly into the file. If the file is not there, an error message is sent out, but the application will continue as best it can. If you want to have the program stop dead in its tracks if a file is not there, use the `require()` function.
5. If you follow the setup procedures provided in Setup.pdf (in the companion materials download file), this will be unnecessary.
6. When naming any include file, it is critical that you provide PHP-related files with a .php extension. Although some systems suggest that you can use .inc, this is a bad idea—particularly for files that contain sensitive information (such as passwords). If they have .php as their extension, the Web server will automatically execute them rather than displaying them as a text document.
7. In using this name, we are following the recommended naming conventions described in appendix B.
8. Note that subject_get.php is an exception to the form and action page pairing in this application. The reason is that the script retrieves a list of records from which the user selects one to edit. It is thus both an input form and an action page.
9. I have broken up the query over multiple lines to make it easier to read.
10. Although MySQL does provide logging support, those files are stored in binary format, making them hard to read for debugging, and include queries from all databases in a single file. Creating your own log makes the information easier to access and to keep separate.
11. For another example of action-page-based validation, see lines 57–60 of site_insert2 .php.
12. If you use this formulation of the <form> tag, you must use the `Validate()` function and enter at least one field into it. Otherwise, at least the current version of Internet Explorer will complain about a missing object.
13. For an idea on `CheckBoxes()` or `RadioButtons()`, look at the two function calls in sites_add.php and then look at the actual function in ala_functions.pdf in the companion materials download file.
14. If you don't enter values, the defaults are 4 columns, border=1 and horizontal output.
15. Another technique is to use the function's `WHERE` parameter to take values from a list, thereby allowing you to use radio buttons in other types of situations. See Functions_ Guide.pdf in the companion materials download file for more information.

16. Other database engines, such as PostgreSQL, use `WHERE TRUE`.
17. For example, the first element of `$display_fields` is `siteno`. The first time through the `for` loop, `$fld` will contain `siteno` and `$row[$fld]` will be equal to `$fld["siteno"]`, which will be the contents of the `siteno` field.
18. Remember, not only is `siteno` the primary key of the `sites` table, it serves as the foreign key for all linked records. We can thus use it to retrieve associated `subjects` and `content_types` information.
19. Note that `Process_Query_Array()` automatically places a Boolean `OR` between the elements. Using `AND`, though a bit more complicated when dealing with many-to-many searches, is certainly doable. I show you a function for doing them when we talk about public searching applications.

# 8  SECURITY-RELATED TECHNIQUES

The preceding chapter outlined the basics of creating a Web-based application. In the best of all possible worlds, this is all you would need. However, Dr. Pangloss notwithstanding, this world is not such a place (at least not when it comes to computers).[1] We therefore need to build some functionality into our application to provide some security.

## APPLICATION SECURITY

There are both a number of ways your application can be compromised and techniques to deal with those threats. Here I detail a few of these to help you to begin securing your applications. Unfortunately, it is not possible to discuss them all. The "bad 'uns," as Dickens called them, are infinitely inventive and resourceful and new exploits are being created every day. You therefore need to have a source where you can get up-to-date security information. A list of places where you might look is included in the bibliography.

One major step you can take is to always give your configuration files a .php extension. Although you can include files with any extension, those with .php are automatically parsed by the mod_php engine. If you use another extension, such as .inc, a crafty user could access that file and read it. Although there are tricks that you can do in httpd.conf (Apache's configuration file) to keep that from happening, using the .php extension is the easiest approach.

## Internal Threats

If you are the only person who has rights to log into your server, then these will, for the most part, not be a problem. However, if your applications will be running on a server with other Web publishers who might view your database or other application data, you start by placing that information in a file in an area outside the Web document area. You can then `include()` it where needed (see Setup .pdf in the companion materials download file for information on how to do so).

Another approach—and one that has the further advantage of increasing external security—is to incorporate SSL into your Apache server and place database maintenance applications (as opposed to public interfaces) in your https directory.[2] Then, as long as you don't provide any users access to that area, no one will be able to view or modify your files.

One drawback of using a programming language that allows you to include files from anywhere on the server is that it potentially opens up your database connections to anyone. All a nefarious user needs to do is to `include()` your file to gain full rights to do whatever that include file allows. One way to get around that is to place code in the include file to check to see where the file that is calling it resides. If the call comes from somewhere the script has not explicitly defined (approved), the script can simply exit with a warning (or more stringent measures, if you wish).

What you do is use the `$_SERVER["SCRIPT_FILENAME"]` superglobal value, which contains the name and full path—from the root directory of the Web server—of the calling script, that is, the name of the file requesting to `include()` your configuration file. Using PHP's regular expression function `eregi()`, you can check at the top of your configuration file to see "who's calling"—that is, compare that information to what you've defined. If they match, the inclusion can proceed. If not, however, you can exit—perhaps logging the incident and taking appropriate measures. Examples 8-1a and 8-1b provide example code (for Windows and Unix/Linux respectively) that you can place at the top of your include file (making sure that the full path to the application directory is correct).

Example 8-1a

```
38  $script = $_SERVER["SCRIPT_FILENAME"];
39  if ( !eregi("^c:/webdb/apache/htdocs/examples/chapter_7/sites", $script ) ) (
40      echo "You are not allowed to use this script";
41      exit;
42  )
```

Example 8-1b

```
38  $script = $_SERVER["SCRIPT_FILENAME"];
39  if ( !eregi("^/usr/local/apache/htdocs/examples/chapter_7/sites", $script ) ) (
40      echo "You are not allowed to use this script";
41      exit;
42  )
```

Including such a function will cause any program that does not reside inside the designated path (`!eregi( "^c:…`) to shut down with an appropriate message before it can access any database connection or other parameters. The `eregi()` function checks to see if two strings match: the exclamation mark (the negation symbol in almost all programming languages) in front of the function call essentially tells the computer to determine a "not match" rather than a match.

One other internal (and to some degree external) threat is allowing end-users to access password information. One way to make the `users` table more secure is to encrypt user passwords. Encrypting passwords involves taking the information input into a form and, using an encryption algorithm, transforming it into something not readable by humans before storing it to the table. Then, when the user attempts to log into the application, the input is encrypted using the same method and compared to what is in the table to see if there is a match. Encryption is a one-way street: passwords cannot be decrypted from the files that store them, they can only be compared against what the user inputs, and either verified or rejected. Casual users would thus not be able to do anything with the information in the `users` table were they able to access it. Scripts that allow you to set encrypted passwords are included in the companion materials download file.

## External Threats

Although hackers can compromise your system in any number of ways—and there are a host of ways to deal with it if they do—you can undertake certain precautions to make things more secure from enemies from without in the first place. Assuming (as the book does) that you are running PHP using mod_php rather than the CGI version, some of these include

> First, make sure that `register_globals` is off in php.ini (or set it to that in your local .htaccess file).[3] If this cannot be changed, call input values (especially session values) by using their full superglobal array name (for example, `$_SESSION["name"]` instead of `$name`).

> Always define parameters (fields, tables, and so forth) used in modifying the database and names of include files within the script, never with values input from a form.

> If possible, enable SSL (Secure Sockets Layer) support on your server and place all database maintenance applications in that area. This

ensures that all traffic between the user's browser (including passwords) and the server is encrypted.

If SSL is enabled, do not rely on Apache's `basic_auth` (use of .htaccess files with user authentication handled by htpasswd-created user files) for sensitive information. Those browser-server communications are not fully encrypted.

Set up phpMyAdmin to use cookie-based authentication on an SSL-enabled site for database administration.[4] This allows for distributed database administration (so that people can administer their own databases) and timeouts to ensure that live connections are not left open (a danger if one is doing administration on a computer where multiple people have access to the workstation).

Avoid passing user input to an external program or process such as sendmail. If you must do so, make sure to check for potential problems so that only appropriate values are passed on.

Although setting the php.ini settings for `error_reporting` to **on** and `display_errors` to `E_ALL` (every error, including undefined variables, gets reported) is fine during the development process, these settings can provide potential hackers with information they shouldn't have. It is therefore recommended that, when placing an application in production, you set `display_errors` to **off** (to log errors to the standard Apache error log file) and `error_reporting` to `E_ALL & ~E_NOTICE & ~E_STRICT` (to keep from being inundated with error messages). Note that you can also set the `error_log` directive in php.ini to specify a different log file or to even e-mail you error messages that occur.

Always place query parameters within single quotes (for example, `name='$name'`), even if they are numeric (neither MySQL nor PostgreSQL minds) and make sure that all query elements have single quotes escaped, either via setting `gpc_magic_quotes` to **on** in php.ini or by using `addslashes()` on them. Not only will they make your queries work better, it will mean that putting something like `music'; drop db web_sites` at the end of a search parameter will cause the nefarious code to be treated as a search parameter, and not executed as a separate SQL command.

Whenever you take user's input and `echo` it to the screen, always use the `htmlspecialchars()` function to convert any code—such as Javascript functions—into HTML text.

## ACCESS CONTROL

Given that these applications allow for data in the database to be changed, you want to restrict access to only those persons authorized to do so. There are two levels of control:

> *Authentication* uses a list of those allowed into the system, checks against it when someone attempts to access the system, and ensures that the person is who the person claims to be.
>
> *Authorization* verifies that the user in question is allowed to do the task he or she is attempting to perform.

I now explain what is involved in setting up each mechanism.

## Authentication

As noted, authenticating means verifying that the person is who the person claims to be. Although there are a number of different ways in which authentication can be handled, the easiest is to use username/password pairs. There are two techniques we can use in our application: the Web server's basic access control mechanisms and an application-based authentication process.

### Web Server Authentication

Because it is easily implemented and does not get in the way of developers, we can use the Web server's access control process, at least during initial development. This does keep the curious out and allows access until the user closes the browser. Setting up server-based authentication involves two steps:

- creating a password file (or adding to an existing one) with username/password combinations for each user
- configuring the Web server to require the user to enter this information[5]

### Application Authentication

We can also use our application to check users. To do so, we create a table in our database—one that we will call `users`—that we can use to authenticate our users.[6] Although there are a number of useful elements we might include, we will limit ourselves here to five:

> *userno* (tinyint)—primary key (`auto_increment`) field for this table
>
> *full_name* (varchar(50))—full name of the user

*username* (varchar(25))—name the user will use to log in

*password* (varchar(12))—password to verify their identity

*rights* (varchar(100))—comma-parsed list of roles (rights) the person will have in the system (we will discuss this a bit later when we address authorization)[7]

Once we have created the table, we add a record for each user we want to have access to the system, filling in their `full_name`, `username`, and `password` fields (the case-sensitive username/password combination that comes with the `web_sites` database loaded with data from the companion materials download file is jsmith/abc123). We then create, first, a form in which the user is prompted for a username and password and, second, an action page that, after the user clicks the **Submit** button, checks to see if that username/password pair exists in the database. If such a record is found, the user is authenticated (if not, the user is not granted access).

If we decide that we want to encrypt our passwords—probably not a bad idea—we will need to write a `user` table maintenance application that will encrypt the password in the insert and update action pages before sending it to the database. I have included a set of such scripts (user_*.php) in the sites directory of the download file that you can use to add and edit user records (using the `users` table created as described). These scripts are similar to those we saw in the database maintenance functions earlier with the following differences:

The action pages allow you to set two variables—`$encrypt_fields` and `$encrypt_method`—to define which fields to encrypt and how they should be encrypted (sha1 or md5). If these variables are left blank, nothing will be encrypted.

If encryption values are set, they use the sixth and seventh parameters of `Insert_Record()` and the seventh and eighth parameters of `Update_Record()` to pass those two additional values to the function.

Both input forms require the data entry person to put the password in twice to verify that it was typed in correctly (and the action pages won't continue processing if the two iterations are not the same). This is particularly important with encrypted passwords because they cannot be read or edited.

The user_edit.php script does allow you to enter password information to update the password field. However, if you enter nothing, user_update.php will not update the password field with a blank value.

Example 8-2 provides an example of how you can do this. Note that if you do use encryption in storing the records, you must set the third parameter of the `Check_User()` call in your login script to use the same encryption method—sha1 or md5—that was used in entering user's information into the `users` table. Otherwise, the user will never be able to get in.

Example 8-2

```
45    if ( $_POST["password"] != $_POST["password_verify"] ) {
46        echo "The passwords do not match.";
47        exit;
48    }
49    $encrypt_fields="password";
50    $encrypt_method="sha1";
51    $table="users";
52    if ( $_POST["password"] != "" ) {
53        $fields=array( "full_name", "username", "password", "rights" );
54    } else {
55        $fields=array( "full_name", "username", "rights" );
56    }
57    Update_Record( $fields, $table, $_POST, "userno", "Y", "", $encrypt_fields, $encrypt_method );
58    echo "Your record has been updated<p>";
```

The next problem is letting each of the pages in your application know that the user is authenticated. This is made difficult by the fact that the Web is stateless: that each interaction between server and browser is a discrete event unrelated (as far as the server is concerned) to any other event. Once an interaction with the user has been completed, the server has no natural (that is, without developer programming) way of knowing anything about the user from page to page or session to session.

One way to deal with this is to set a hidden field value that contains the login ID and then pass it from page to page within the application. In addition to not being very secure and being tedious to program and test, this also suffers from the weakness that all it takes is one page where the ID doesn't get set properly and the authentication information is lost.

Another approach is to set a cookie so that the server can know who has passed muster and who hasn't. For this, you need to send the browser an authentication cookie once the user has successfully logged in. Then, within each page of your application, the system needs to check to see if a cookie has been set. If it hasn't, the application sends the user to the login screen where, once the user is authenticated, the cookie is set. We will be looking at a variation of this below.

## Authorization

Although authentication does keep unwanted people out, it does not allow us to be selective in deciding who is able to do what in the system. To do this, we need to add an authorization layer. An authorization system assigns users access levels within the system and permissions to perform certain tasks. Then, when a user attempts to do something, rights are checked to see if the user is permitted to do so.

To set up authorization (in the context of the examples in this book), you need to define a list of words defining the roles or tasks that you want your application to support. Then, when you add a user to the `users` table, you enter a comma-parsed list of the user's rights into the table's `rights` field. Thus when a user attempts to perform a certain task, credentials can be checked against appropriate permissions. Although we could create our own cookies-based mechanism to do this, it would become very cumbersome in practice. This is where sessions come in.

## Using Sessions

As of version 4.0, PHP added what is called session support to its repertoire of techniques. Sessions are a mechanism whereby PHP can remember individual users. The way it works is that, when a user initiates a session, the PHP engine tells the Web server to send the browser a special kind of cookie called a session ID named `PHPSESSID`. Once the session is set, each time the browser returns to request another page, the server checks the ID (`$_SESSION["PHPSESSID"]`) in the browser to see if it is set for the server to associate the proper information with the user.

The valuable thing about sessions is that, when PHP sets up a session, it creates an associative array of values (in the form of a `$_SESSION` superglobal array) that it stores in a file (in the directory defined in the `session.save_path` directive in php.ini), using the `$_SESSION["PHPSESSID"]` as the basis for the file name. This then helps associate that file of values to the session ID stored as a cookie in the browser. Developers can use this feature to define (register) variables within the session and then use them to set values that can be accessed from any page in the application.

To use sessions, we must begin by calling PHP's `session_start()` function. This call either sets the `PHPSESSID` and sends it to the browser (if this is the first time through the page) or renews it. Because of its role in setting the session, this function call needs to be both loaded with each page and before any other session calls are made. Otherwise, that session information will not be stored by PHP. To that end, we add the following lines to local_prepend.php that will allow us to authenticate users. We begin by starting the session and using `session_start()` (shown in example 8-3). Then, as shown in example 8-4, we define the code—again in local_prepend.php—that will require that users log in.

Example 8-3

```
69   /****************************************************************
70   * Set up sessions
71   ****************************************************************/
72   session_start();
```

Example 8-4

```
124   $page = Get_Page_Name();
125   $pos = strpos($page,"login.php");   // Check to see if page is login.php.  If
126   if ( $pos == 0 ) {                   // so, skip to avoid an infinite loop
127       if ( $_SESSION["authenticated"] != "true" ) {
128           header("Location: login.php?page=$page");
129       }
130   }
```

Although much of the code here is explained in the comments at the end of each line, one section—lines 124–125—warrants a bit of discussion. Here we call the `Get_Page_Name()` function to get the name of the file the user has requested (literally, to see what is the name of the file into which the local_ prepend.php is being included).[8] It does this so that, once the user is authenticated, the system knows which page to return to.

In line 126, if the page is not login.php (literally, if the position of `"login.php"` is not greater than 0 in the `$page` variable), then the user is redirected to a login page named login.php (if we didn't exclude login.php, we would end up with an endless loop). In redirecting the user to the login page, we append the name of the current `$page` to the URL as a GET value so that the user, after being authenticated, can be returned to the originally requested page.

Once you place these lines into your configuration file, any user who tries to access any PHP page in this directory before they have logged in will be forced to the `login.php` page. Note that this will not protect any pages without the .php extension so that .html pages would not insist that the user log in. This is because the PHP engine needs to process a page for this code to be run.

One critical security point: in looking at local_prepend.php, please note that `session_start()` comes after the lines that localize the `$_POST` or other superglobal variables. This is extremely important in that you must, for security reasons, localize those values before you start a session. The reason is that you cannot create a session variable before a session is started. However, once it has been started, you can. That means, if you start the session first and then localize the `$_POST` values, hackers can pass values from a form to your script in such a way as to create and/or modify a session variable (something that could severely compromise your security).

The login page (login.php) begins with some PHP code to see if the `$_POST["form"]` value has been set (see example 8-5). The first time through—because the page is being called from local_prepend.php—it will not be, and the `$page` value (containing the name of the page that the user originally requested that is passed from local_prepend.php) is retrieved from the `$_GET` superglobal, because that is the way in which it was passed from the configuration file. We then skip the rest of the PHP code to the inputting form.

Example 8-5

```
37  ?>
38  <?php
39  if ( !isset( $_POST["form"] ) ) {
40      $page = $_GET["page"];
41  } else {
42      if ( $_POST["form"] == "login" ) {
43          $page=$_POST["page"];
44          $test = Check_User( $username, $password );
45          if ( $test["passed"] == "Y" ) {
46              $_SESSION["authenticated"] = "true";
47              $_SESSION["username"] = $test["username"];
48              foreach ( $test as $key=>$value ){
49                  session_register('$key');
50                  $_SESSION[$key] = $value;
51              }
52              header("Location: $page");
53          } else {
54              echo "No";
55              $page = $_POST["page"];
56          }
57      } else {
58          $page = $_GET["page"];
59      }
60  }
61  ?>
```

In example 8-6 we see a pretty straightforward HTML form. However, there are three lines to note from this example (with code from the login form):

*Line 69.* We set the method to POST and the action page to login.php, the name of the current page. Thus, on clicking **Submit**, the user will be directed back to login.php.

*Line 70.* We define a hidden variable named **form** and assign it the value **login**. Thus, when we do click on **Submit** (which causes login.php to be run again), the PHP code at the top of the form will be executed.

*Line 71.* We define a second hidden variable—**page**—that passes the name of the originally requested page (as a `$_POST` value, because in line 69 the method was set to POST) to the next process.

Example 8-6

```
69  <form method="POST" action="login.php">
70  <input type="hidden" name="form" value="login">
71  <input type="hidden" name="page" value="<?php echo $page ?>">
```

Once the user enters the information in the boxes and clicks on the **Log in** button, login.php is called with the values just mentioned and the code shown in example 8-5 is run. When it hits the `if` statement in line 39, it will take the second fork in the road (because at this point, `$_POST["form"]` has been set). The first thing it will do is to call the `Check_User()` function with two parameters: `$username` and `$password`. If you are encrypting passwords, you will need to add a third parameter designating which encryption method—sha1 or md5— you used. If `Check_User()` finds a record in the authentication table that matches the information that the user has input, it creates an array of values that are returned to the calling form. Specifically, this array includes a `passed` element that indicates if a user record was found and a `username` element to store the user's login name.

It also takes the comma-parsed list of rights contained in the `rights` field and creates an associative array element for each right it finds, using the name as the element index and storing `Y` as the value for that element. Thus, if a user had "admin, staff, student" in their `rights` field, then three array elements would be created: `$test["admin"]`, `$test["staff"]`, and `$test["student"]`, with the value of each being set to `Y`.

When the array is passed back to the login page, the code checks to see if the user has passed (line 45). If so, it sets a number of session variables:

`$_SESSION["authenticated"]` = `"Y"` indicates that the user has passed muster. Then, each time through the local_prepend.php when the code checks, the user will be allowed through (line 46).

`$_SESSION["username"]` makes the user's username available for display and entry into the database, such as storing it in an `added_by` field to let you know who entered a record (line 47).

`$_SESSION[<right>]` = `"Y"` means that for each `rights` element created by `Check_User()`, a separate session variable will be created in the form of `$_SESSION[<right>]` = `"Y"` (lines 48–51).

Finally, the user is redirected to the originally requested page. From then on, as long as the session stays established (which it will until the user closes the browser or logs out) and the `$_SESSION["authenticated"]` stays set to true, the user will be authenticated for your application.[9] Now, any time you wish to restrict access to a particular task, you simply use `if` to check to see whether the `$_SESSION[<rights_name>]` variable has been set to `Y` and then, allow only those users with such a value to proceed.[10] We will see some examples of how to do this later when we deal with deleting records.

Note that the way that we have set up the `rights` field breaks one of the rules that we laid down in chapter 2: we are placing more than one value in a field rather than creating a separate table and then relating it to the `users` table. However, as we noted at the time, normalization rules should be followed unless there is a strong case not to do so. In this case, there is. Placing them in a comma-parsed list not only makes processing this information quicker, but also provides an example of how this can be done. Also, many of the problems associated with nonnormalized data, such as relational integrity and the inability to use drop-down lists, do not apply in this case.

This code assumes that the user information is in a table named `users` with fields named `username`, `password`, and `rights`. If you wish to change any of these, see the documentation for the `Check_User()` function in Functions_Guide.pdf in the companion materials download file for information on how to do so.

## APPLICATION CONTROL

Controlling access to the application is one consideration. Dealing with what happens within the application once users are interacting with records in the database is another.

### Transactions

When dealing with single database interactions, as we were doing in the authority maintenance apps, things were very simple: either the database was updated or it wasn't. However, in the **Sites** view, we are dealing with multiple queries, any one of which might "go over to the dark side." We therefore need to use transactions (described in chapter 2) to keep things from really being added to the database until we are sure all went well.[11]

I have included transaction support in the function libraries in the form of three functions: `Begin()`, `Commit()`, and `Rollback()`.[12] In addition, I have built error handling and log file maintenance into the function library. Before you use transactions, you need to have taken care of several items:

> Made sure that all tables involved in the transaction are the InnoDB type
>
> Enabled sessions (for a number of reasons, including logging, sessions are required for the function library's transaction support to work properly)

Called the `Begin()` function to start the transaction process before entering any database maintenance command

Entered the database maintenance functions

Called the `Commit()` function after the last query has run so that the results will be stored to the database (because the functions have built-in call to `Rollback()` if any database interaction fails, the assumption is that—if you have gotten this far—everything went well)

The code in example 8-7, taken from site_insert2.php, demonstrates how a transaction is handled.

Example 8-7

```
89    Begin();
90    $siteno = Insert_Record( $fields, $table, $_POST, $prod="Y" );
91    Insert_Links( "sites_subjects", array( "ss_siteno"=>$siteno ),
92                  array( "ss_subjectno"=>$subjectno ), $prod="Y" );
93    Insert_Links( "sites_types", array( "st_siteno"=>$siteno ),
94                  array( "st_content_typeno"=>$content_typeno ), $prod="Y" );
95    Commit();
```

## Logging

The approach to logging we discussed earlier works in a limited way. Once you begin using transactions, or if your application resides in multiple subdirectories (as it does here, using the different dblog directories for the authority table maintenance and sites subdirectory for the **Sites** view), it will not work. As noted, we need to have a single log file so that all interactions to the same database can be restored in the proper order.

For this to happen properly, we need to set global logging configuration that every script in the application can use. To set up this logging (as shown in example 8-8), you need to

- make sure that sessions are enabled in every application configuration file
- set the following variable in each configuration file:
  `$_SESSION["global_logging"] = "Y"` (line 79 of example 8-8)
- set your logging parameters (lines 80–81)

Example 8-8

```
79    $_SESSION["global_logging"] = "Y";
80    $_SESSION["global_log_path"] = "/export/www/lib/examples/Chapter_7/sites/dblog";
81    $_SESSION["global_log_file"] = "sql.log";
```

The two session variables that get set are: `$global_log_path`, which is the full path from the server's root directory to the directory where the log will reside, and `$global_log_file`, which is the name of the file to which log entries should be written. Then, if you use the functions, and do not enter anything in the `$log_file` parameter in your function calls (as we do not in the examples in this directory), every log will be written to this global log file. The only things you need to do are to make sure that all configuration files in your application include this function call with the same parameters, and that the path or log file names (or both) are unique for each application on the server.

If you want the complete transaction to be logged by your function calls, you will need to define how you want logging to be done. As noted, logging transactions is a major reason we need sessions. Because we have no way to rollback our logging, we must wait to write to the log file until `Commit()` is called (meaning that all queries executed correctly). We therefore need to store our queries to see if everything goes well and, if it does, we can write the queries out to our log file; if not, then we can discard them or write them to an error file for later analysis.

To allow us to do that, the `Begin()` function includes setting two session variables. The first is `$_SESSION["transaction"]`, to set a flag that a transaction is in progress. The second is `$_SESSION["transaction_log"]`, to serve as a variable to which we can save successfully executed queries. Then, if all goes well, the contents of the latter are saved to the log file as part of the `Commit()` function's work. Otherwise, the accumulated queries are discarded as part of the `Rollback()` function. See the discussion on `Write_Log()` in Functions_ Guide.pdf in the companion materials download file for more information.

## Encryption

Protecting our applications using authentication and authorization is a good start, but does not fully protect our database. The reason for this has to do with the way that the Internet works. Left to their own devices, our Web applications will send usernames and passwords in the same way they do any other text: as plain text available for anybody with the proper software and connections to read. This, of course, can expose the information to others online who can intercept the information. In sum, they would then be able to access your database.

Just as encryption scrambles a password so that it can't be read by the "wrong" people, so it can scramble all transactions between the server and the user's browser. To accomplish this, you need to implement Secure Sockets Layer (SSL) on your Web server. Any communications between the user's browser and the server are then scrambled using strong encryption methods included in SSL packages (hence their use in commercial financial transactions). Once SSL encryption is installed, you need only place your documents in the designated secure server directory (folder) and all interactions with your application will be encrypted. Please see the bibliography and Setup.pdf in the companion materials download file for more information.

## Deleting Records

Eliminating records from the database is a task that needs to be supported, but one that also needs to be undertaken with great care. Not only do you need to define who will be able to delete records, but you also need to determine where information resides and what the effect of deletion will be on overall database integrity. Keep the following guidelines in mind:

Limit the ability to delete records to highly trained and responsible individuals. One method is user authorization.

Provide the user with a list of records that would be affected by a deletion before the record is deleted when the record the user wants to delete contains a primary key to which one or more foreign tables may be linked.

Delete the record and take appropriate actions with all linked records once the user confirms the deletion. In some cases, the records from the linking table will be deleted. In others, if the foreign key resides within a data table, the value of the foreign key field should be set to NULL.

Do not use phpMyAdmin or other administrative tools to delete records within a multitable application unless you are using built-in foreign key constraints.

Example 8-9

```
76  <?php
77  echo "<center>";
78  if ( Check_Rights( "admin" ) ) {
79     Delete_Record_Check( "site_delete.php", "siteno", $siteno );
80  }
81  echo "</center>";
82  ?>
```

Verifying deletions can be handled in a number of ways. One is to provide a link inside the editing page to a confirmation page where the user can verify the deletion. This is what we do in example 8-9 from site_edit.php. First, the code uses the Check_Rights() function to see if the admin right has been set to Y. If so, the next line calls Delete_Record_Check(), passing it the name of the confirmation page (site_delete.php), the name of the primary key (siteno), and the primary key of the record to be deleted ($siteno). The function then creates a link on the page to a confirmation page (site_delete.php) with the parameter siteno=$siteno. Clicking on this link (assuming the user hasn't turned off Javascript or popups) creates another window in which the site_delete.php page will be displayed. At that point, the user will be able to verify whether to actually delete the record.

Looking at the site_delete.php page (example 8-10), we see the following:

1. This page, like login.php, uses the technique of placing hidden values in the body of the form to pass when it calls itself. In this case, there are three:

    The first sets action equal to delete (line 68) and causes the page, when reloaded, to execute the PHP code at the top of the page.

    The second parameter—siteno—is used to pass the primary key on to the deletion function (line 69).

    The third defines do_it (line 74), which is the user's decision on whether the record should be deleted.

2. Within the PHP code at the top of the page (lines 45–46, example 8-11), two things are checked to see whether the deletion code should be executed. The first is whether $action is set to delete. The second is whether the user has admin privileges.

3. If the user passes step #2, the script enters the if condition block. Then, if $do_it has been set to Y, the record is deleted. In addition to calling Delete_Record() to delete the main record (line 49), we use the Delete_Links() function to delete linking records (lines 50–51). We need to do this manually, because we didn't define foreign key constraints between the primary and foreign keys.

4. Transactions are being used, as seen by the use of Begin() (line 48) before and Commit() (line 52) after the queries.

Example 8-10

```
68   <input type="hidden" name="action" value="delete">
69   <input type="hidden" name="siteno" value="<?php echo $siteno ?>">
70   <center>
71   <table border="1">
72      <tr>
73         <td>
74            <?php Y_or_N( "Are you sure?", "do_it", "N" ) ?>
75         </td>
76      </tr>
77      <?php Submit_Reset( "Submit", "Clear", "1", "0" ) ?>
78   </table>
79   </center>
```

Example 8-11

```
45  if ( isset( $_POST["action"] ) ) {
46    if ( $action == "delete" && $_SESSION["admin"] == "Y" ) {
47      if ( $do_it == "Y" ) {
48        Begin();
49        Delete_Record( "sites", "siteno", $siteno, "Y", "admin.log" );
50        Delete_Links( "sites_subjects", array("ss_siteno"=>$siteno), $prod="Y", "admin.log" );
51        Delete_Links( "sites_types", array("st_siteno"=>$siteno), $prod="Y", "admin.log" );
52        Commit();
53        echo "Record deleted<p>";
54      }
55      echo "Please close this browser to proceed";
56      exit;
57    }
58  }
```

There are two other useful techniques you can use. The first one involves using `Display_Affected_Record()` to show records that would be affected by the deletion of an authority record. These involve adding a value for `$link_str` that will set the appropriate relations (see subject_delete.php in Authority_Functions_Source.pdf in the companion materials download file).

The other technique involves the situation where the deletion of an authority record should only set the foreign key field in the foreign record to NULL. To do this, we utilize a different function—`Blank_Links()`—to undertake the task. The file status_delete.php in Authority_Functions_Source.pdf shows you how this can be done.

## NEXT STEPS

We've gotten you started on ways to make your applications more secure. It's time to put a face on the programming. In the next chapter we run through the process of developing effective public access interfaces, undertaking user testing, and putting the application into production.

### Notes

1. Dr. Pangloss is a character in Voltaire's *Candide* who insists—in true Enlightenment fashion—that this is the "best of all possible worlds." Unfortunately, events keep proving him wrong.
2. See the bibliography for more information.
3. See Setup.pdf in the companion materials download file for more information.
4. The setup of Apache with SSL support is beyond the scope of this book. See the bibliography in the companion materials download file for more information.
5. For information on how to do this with Apache, see Setup.pdf in the companion materials download file.
6. See data/users.sql in the companion materials download file.
7. Although the table and field name information is what is used in the book, the `Check_User()` function has been written to allow you to use whatever names you wish.

8. The $_SERVER superglobal contains values that are sent to the page by the server and include such things as HTTP values (referrer, user agent, and so on). In this case the function uses $_SERVER["PHP_SELF"] to retrieve the name of the file that is including local_prepend.php.

9. To close a session, you should create a logout.php page containing the session_destroy() function. See the chapter_7/sites folder of the companion materials download file for an example. Also, if you are going to be running multiple applications on your server, you will need to use the Check_Authenticated_Path() function to lock authentication down to a single set of directories. See Functions_Guide.pdf for more details.

10. You can use the ala_function Check_Rights() to verify a particular right. For a complete set of fully annotated scripts for authority file maintenance that use these functions, see Authority_Functions_Source.pdf in the docs folder in the companion materials download file for more information.

11. Transactions can in fact be useful in single-query applications—such as the vacation allotment application noted in chapter 2.

12. Actually, if you use the function library's adding and updating functions, you never use Rollback() directly—its use is built into the functions.

# 9

Chapter

## CREATING PUBLIC
## INTERFACES

Until now, we have focused only on applications to enter and maintain data, and how to help make that data secure. Now we proceed to look at examples of outputting data for public use. Because even a representative sampling of possible approaches to creating public interfaces is beyond our scope here, we will examine instead a few useful ideas and techniques. In doing so, we will implement the two applications defined in chapter 6: dynamically generated subject pages and a search interface. Please note that this book was written using earlier versions of MySQL that did not support views. The inclusion of views in MySQL 5 (released late 2005) greatly facilitates the handling of multiple tables. See Using_Views.pdf in the companion materials download file for how this change affects the examples discussed here.

## DYNAMIC SUBJECT PAGES

In the first application, we will output pages similar to the report.php page we created in chapter 5 that implement what is essentially a report—specifically a list of resources by subject from our **web_sites** database. Although the structure is similar to those in chapter 5, there are two essential differences. First, this report brings together multiple tables to create its report via relations. Second, results are broken down by content type. This will make it easier for users to find those items that interest them.

**201**

We need to set this application up in a separate directory with a separate configuration file and separate permissions. Because public users won't need to add, edit, and delete data in the database, we make adjustments to accommodate the fact:

1. Create a new directory—pub_sites—to contain our new pages
2. Create a new account—Web_Sites_Public—which we allow only to access the database from localhost, give no global privileges and only SELECT (searching) access to web_sites, give it a password of pub_sites, and remove SELECT permissions on the users table
3. Create a pub_sites.php file containing username, password, and database connection routines for Web_Sites_Public (see example 9-1) and place in our PHP include directory (see Setup.pdf in the companion materials download file); create a local_prepend.php file in the pub_sites directory with a pointer to pub_sites.php file in it

Example 9-1

```
45  $user = "Web_Sites_Public";
46  $password = "pub_sites";
47  $dbname = "web_sites";
48  $db = mysql_connect("localhost",$user,$password);
49  mysql_select_db( $dbname, $db );
```

To remove SELECT rights for users, you need to make adjustments in phpMyAdmin:

- Log into phpMyAdmin and click on the **Privileges** link
- Go to the line containing the Web_Sites_Public user and click on the **Edit** icon in the far right column
- Under **Database-specific privileges**, find the line for web_sites and click on **Edit**
- Under **Table-specific privileges** either type the name of the users table or select it from the drop-down list next to **Add privileges on the following table**
- At the bottom of the **SELECT** column, check the **None** box and then click on the **Go** button

Now that user will no longer have access to the users table.

In the dynamic_page.php program, I have created basic script that outputs all of the pages within a subject, broken down by content type. The page is built in six sections:

1. We first get the subject number for requested subject (example 9-2). If the page is called with subject=<subject>, then that value is saved to

`$subject`. If no value (or a bad value) was passed, we redirect the user (line 9) to a selection page (subject_select.php).

Example 9-2

```
2   /*******************************************************************
3    * If $_GET["subject"] has not been set OR if Check_for_Dup_Fields() doesn't
4    * find an entry for $_GET["subject"], redirect to page to select a subject
5    *******************************************************************/
6   if ( !isset( $_GET["subject"] ) || !Check_for_Dup_Fields( "subject", "subjects", $_GET, "Y" ) ) {
7       header( "Location: subject_select.php" )  ;
8   } else {
9       $subject = $_GET["subject"];
10  }
```

2. We search, once a subject has been selected, to determine the subject's primary key (`subjectno`) (example 9-3).

Example 9-3

```
54  $subj_query = "SELECT subjectno FROM subjects WHERE subject='$subject'";
55  $subj_record = Do_Search( $subj_query );
56  $subj_row = $subj_record[0];
57  $subjectno = $subj_row["subjectno"];
```

3. We use the key to look up all content types represented within that subject (example 9-4).

Example 9-4

```
63  $ctype_query = "SELECT DISTINCT content_type, content_typeno
64                  FROM content_types, sites_types, sites, sites_subjects
65                  WHERE content_types.content_typeno = sites_types.st_content_typeno
66                  AND sites_types.st_siteno=sites.siteno
67                  AND sites_subjects.ss_siteno=sites.siteno
68                  AND sites_subjects.ss_subjectno='$subjectno'
69                  ORDER BY content_type";
70  $ctype_records = Do_Search( $ctype_query );
71  $ctype_num_rows = count( $ctype_records );
```

4. We take the results and create an array of content types (example 9-5).

Example 9-5

```
78  $ctype=0;
79  for ( $b=0; $b<$ctype_num_rows; $b++ ) {
80      $ctype_row = $ctype_records[$b];
81      $content_type[$ctype] = $ctype_row["content_type"];
82      $content_typeno[$ctype] = $ctype_row["content_typeno"];
83      $ctype++;
84  }
```

5. We use the array to build a type index at the top of the screen that will link to output for each type (example 9-6).

Example 9-6

```
94  for ( $w=0; $w<$ctype; $w++ ) {
95      if ( $w == 0 ) {
96          echo "<a href=\"#$content_typeno[$w]\">$content_type[$w]</a> ";
97      } else {
98          echo " | <a href=\"#$content_typeno[$w]\">$content_type[$w]</a> ";
99      }
100 }
```

6. We go through the `$content_typeno` array and output all records for the requested subject for each content type (example 9-7).

Example 9-7

```
110  for ( $x=0; $x<$ctype; $x++ ) {
111      $tables = " sites_types, sites, sites_subjects ";
112      $where = " sites.siteno=sites_types.st_siteno
113                  AND sites.siteno=sites_subjects.ss_siteno
114                  AND sites_subjects.ss_subjectno=$subjectno
115                  AND sites_types.st_content_typeno=$content_typeno[$x]
116                  ORDER BY name";
117      $out_query = "SELECT DISTINCT * FROM $tables WHERE $where";
118      $out_records = Do_Search( $out_query );
119      $out_num_rows = count( $out_records );
120      echo "<b><a name=$content_typeno[$x]>$content_type[$x]<a/></b><ul>";
121      for ( $b=0; $b<$out_num_rows; $b++ ) {
122          $out_row = $out_records[$b];
123          $name = $out_row["name"];          // assign the field names to
124          $url = $out_row["url"];             //    variables
125          $description = $out_row["description"];
126          echo "<li><a href=\"$url\">$name</a>"; // output a clickable URL
127          if ( trim( $description ) != "" ) {  // if there is a description
128              echo " - $description";          // output it
129          }
130      }
131      echo "</ul>";
132      echo "<a href=\"#top\">Return to top</a><p>";
133  }
```

A list of `content_types` is created at the top of the page (example 9-6) as it is output, each name being a link pointing to a target on the page where items of that content type will be output:

```
echo "<a href=\"#$content_typeno[$w]\">$content_type
    [$w]</a> ";
```

Then, as we output the records for a content type, we wrap the header in `<a name=\"$content_typeno[$x]\"></a>` (line 126 of example 9-7), which creates a hyperlink to the target destination. To make navigation easier, I have placed a link directing the browser back to the top of the page after each block.

We can thus use the same page for all of our subjects, simply by changing the subject string passed to the script. For example, the following produces our music page:

```
<a href="http://some.library.info/subjects/dynamic_page
    .php?subject=Music">Music</a>
```

If we were to change the URL to read `dynamic_page.php?subject=Anthropology`, a page would be created that would output links for anthropology, and if we were to change it to `dynamic_page.php?subject=History`, a history page would be output, and so forth.

Because this page requires input to know which subject to use, we need to have some way of handling those users or situations in which such a parameter is not given. As noted, if one is not, the user is directed to subject_select.php. This page uses `RadioButtons()` to create a page that dynamically generates a list of all possible subjects for the user to select from. Thus, as subjects get added, the page will automatically accommodate the new entries.

## PUBLIC SEARCHING

It is also a good idea to provide a search facility for your end users so that they can create their own result sets. To do this, we need to build a public searching application, building on techniques that we have learned, but adding some new features that make it more useful to the public. Such features include

> support contact information, where available
>
> a stopword list
>
> outputting values from foreign tables associated with the `sites` record
>
> links to full records, including information in linked tables
>
> option to control number of results per page returned
>
> allow Boolean AND searching of many-to-many fields
>
> full keyword searching, mimicking online search engines by enabling keyword searching, embedding phrases in double quotes, and searching multiple fields

Let's go through each of these to see how we can implement them.

### Including Support Contact Information

We need to provide the information we have been including in the `supports` table to provide our public users with a way of contacting library staff to obtain help. We are storing a numeric value in the `sites_supportno` field, but need to give the user the information to which it is pointing. Because the `supports` authority table contains e-mail addresses, one approach would be to output a mailto link for the `support` field. To do this, we use the `Auth_Vals()` function (in line 56 from public_search.php in example 9-8) to create an associative array of values.

Example 9-8

```
44  $_SESSION["dbquery"] = "";
45  $pager = "pager.php";
46  $_SESSION["pager"] = $pager;
47  $fields = "sites.*";
48  $tables = "sites";
49  $link_str = "";
50  $where_str = "";
51
52  /***************************************************************
53   * Create a $support_ary array to include support email addresses for those
54   * sites where a support person has been identified in the system.
55   ***************************************************************/
56  $support_ary = Auth_Vals( "supportno","support_email","supports" );
57
58  /***************************************************************
59   * Next, we define the fields to display ($display_fields) and count the
60   * number of fields that are in the array.  Then, we assign the contents
61   * of those variables to the session variable of the same name.
62   ***************************************************************/
63  $display_fields = array( "siteno", "name", "url", "description", "sites_format", "sites_status", "sites_supportno" );
64  $_SESSION["display_fields"] = $display_fields;
65  $display_fields_num = count( $display_fields );
66  $_SESSION["display_fields_num"] = $display_fields_num;
67  $num_to_display = $_SESSION["num_to_display"];
```

The function creates an associative array of values ($support_ary), using the primary key of supports ($supportno) as the array index (key) and the field containing the support person's e-mail address ($support_email) as the contents (value) of the array element. As we go through the search results, when we encounter the sites_supportno field, we use its value to obtain the e-mail address from the $support_ary associative array (see example 9-9, especially lines 207 and 208).

Example 9-9
```
206     ) elseif ( $fld == "sites_supportno" ) {
207         $supportno = $row[$fld];
208         if ( isset( $supportno ) ) {
209             echo "<tr><td align=\"right\"><B>Support</B></td><td>
210                 <a href=\"mailto: $support_ary[$supportno]\">$support_ary[$supportno]</a></td></tr>";
211         }
```

This may at first be difficult to understand, but you will soon see both how elegant it is and how powerful PHP can be. Say the record in supports with supportno of 1 has jsmith@isp.net in the support_email field. Calling Auth_Vals() as we did above would create an element $support_ary[1] equal to jsmith@isp.net. Thus, if the contents of a sites_supportno field were 1, plugging that value (1) as a key into $support_ary would cause jsmith@isp .net to be retrieved (and then be placed into a mailto link and output to the page).

## Stopwords

In searching a database, one problem that users have is that they sometimes attempt to enter a natural language query—such as "Who was Christopher Columbus?"—and expect an answer back. One way to assist those users is to create a list of "noise" words such as "who" or "was" and then filter out those words before the query is sent to the database. The Process_Quoted_String() function provides the ability to do just this. To make the most of it

> use the stopwords.sql file in the data directory of the companion materials download file to create and fill a stopwords table in your database (see Setup.pdf)

> populate the table with those words that you wish to filter out from user queries

> add a third parameter—Y—to your call to Process_Quoted_String()

Look at public_keyword_query.php for an example of how this can be used. If you have loaded the web_sites data that came in the download file, try running public_query.php with the query "Music." Then try another search "What is music?" You should end up with exactly the same results.

## Including Values from Foreign Tables

When doing a search, not all of the values that the user wants to see are contained in the main table. In our case, the user may want subjects or content types included in the search output. One approach to this is to use the primary key of the retrieved records and, following up the path of relationships, execute a search that will retrieve the associated values. This is what I have done in public_search.php, as shown in example 9-10.

Example 9-10

```
193  for ( $a=0; $a<$result_num_rows; $a++ ) {
194      $row = $records[$a];
195      for ( $b=0; $b<$display_fields_num; $b++ ) {
196          $fld = $display_fields[$b];
197          if ( $row[$fld] != "" ) {
198              $label = ucwords($fld); // make first letter of each word in $fld upper case
199              if ( $fld == "siteno" ) {
200                  $siteno = $row[$fld];
201                  echo "<tr><td colspan=\"2\" align=\"left\">
202                      <a href=\"public_site_display.php?siteno=$row[$fld]\">View Complete Record</a></td></tr>";
203              } elseif ( $fld == "url" ) {
204                  $URL = $fld;
205                  echo "<tr><td align=\"right\"><B>URL</B></td><td><a href=\"$row[$fld]\">$row[$fld]</a></td></tr>";
206              } elseif ( $fld == "sites_supportno" ) {
207                  $supportno = $row[$fld];
208                  if ( isset( $supportno ) ) {
209                      echo "<tr><td align=\"right\"><B>Support</B></td><td>
210                          <a href=\"mailto: $support_ary[$supportno]\">$support_ary[$supportno]</a></td></tr>";
211                  }
212              } else {
213                  echo "<tr><td align=\"right\" valign=\"top\"><B>$label</B></td><td>$row[$fld]</td></tr>";
214              }
215          }
216      }
217
218      /***************************************************************
219       * Use Output_Links to retrieve subjects from the subjects table, using
220       * the linking information to retrieve the subjects based on the $siteno.
221       * See the documentation for the Output_Links() function for details
222       * on the various parameters.  Once you have the string, you create the
223       * label and output the string.
224       ***************************************************************/
225      $subject_str = Output_Links( "subject", "subjects", "subjectno",
226                      "sites_subjects", "ss_subjectno", "ss_siteno", $siteno );
227      echo "<tr><td align=\"right\" valign=\"top\"><b>Subject:</td><td>$subject_str</td></tr>";
228      echo "<tr><td><br></td></tr>";
229      $displayed_rows++;
230      if ( $displayed_rows == $num_to_display ) {
231          echo "</table>";
232          echo "</body>";
233          echo "</html>";
234          exit;
235      }
236  }
```

After saving the primary key (`siteno`) to a variable that can be used in a function (line 200), I use the `Output_Links()` function to obtain the required values (225–226) and output them (line 227). Although this function has a lot of parameters, it is fairly straightforward and uses the following information:

>    `subject`—the name of the field that contains the value we want to output

subjects—the name of the authority table containing that field (for-eign table)

subjectno—name of that table's primary key (used to link to the link-ing table)

sites_subjects—the name of the linking table

ss_subjectno—linking table field containing the foreign key from the authority table's primary key

ss_siteno—linking table field containing foreign key from main table's primary key

$siteno—the primary table's primary key to enter in the search

## Links to Full Records

There is only so much room on the search results screen for outputting record values. As a result, many fields cannot be displayed. Many library systems have addressed this problem by displaying short (abbreviated) records to help the user identify what he or she may wish, and including a link within the display to bring up a long (complete) record.

If you look at line 202 in example 9-10 from public_search.php, we have used the $siteno value that we obtained in line 199 to create a link to a page named public_site_display.php. This latter page uses several functions to take the $siteno passed to it and then to create a page that outputs full records (example 9-11).

Example 9-11

```
60  $sites_row = Get_Main_Record( "*", "sites", "siteno", $siteno );
61  $subject_ary = Get_Linked_Records( "sites_subjects", "ss_subjectno", "ss_siteno", "$siteno" );
62  $ctype_ary = Get_Linked_Records( "sites_types", "st_content_typeno", "st_siteno", "$siteno" );
63  $subj_name_ary = Auth_Vals( "subjectno", "subject", "subjects" );
64  $ctype_name_ary = Auth_Vals( "content_typeno", "content_type", "content_types" );
65  $support_ary = Auth_Vals( "supportno", "support_email", "supports" );
66
67  $fields = array( "Name,name", "URL,url", "Description,description", "Format,sites_format",
68                   "Status,sites_status", "Proxy?,requires_proxy", "help_page",
69                   "Subscription?,subscription", "Date added,added_date",
70                   "Restrictions,restrictions_on_use", "sites_supportno" );
71  ?>
72  <table>
73  <?php
74  $supt = array( "Support", "sites_supportno", $support_ary );
75  Display_Record( $fields, $sites_row, "url,help_page", $supt );
76  Display_Links( "Subjects", $subject_ary, $subj_name_ary );
77  Display_Links( "Content Types", $ctype_ary, $ctype_name_ary );
```

This code works as follows (please see Functions_Guide.pdf in the compan-ion materials download file for complete information on each function):

Retrieves all records from data and linked tables (lines 60–62).

Uses `Auth_Vals()` to construct associative arrays that can be used in outputting foreign table values (lines 63–65).

Defines the fields to be output. Note that each array element is itself a comma-separated list. If there are two subelements, the first will be used as the label for the field in the output page and the second is the field name; if only one, then the field name will be used for both (lines 67–70).

Creates an array to output mailto links for the `supportno` value (line 74), the array containing the display label, the field name, and the array of e-mail addresses.

Calls `Display_Record()`, passing it `$fields`, main data table record, comma-parsed list of fields to make into hyperlinks, and the array to create mailto links (75).

Calls `Display_Links()` to output linked information (lines 76–77).

## Paging through Results

Until now, all our search results pages have output all the records that matched the query. This is not something that will work well if the number matched is large and/or there are a large number of fields to be displayed. One way to handle this is to break the results down into manageable chunks and allow the user to page through them. Although you could write the retrieved records to a temporary file and write an application to go through them, this approach has several drawbacks:

It is not easy to install the necessary software.

Programming it would not be easy.

It places a huge performance hit on your application because it relies on disk access, requiring significantly more time for each search to complete.

It requires a fair amount of disk space.

It is not easily transportable from machine-to-machine or platform-to-platform.

Fortunately, MySQL provides a wonderful feature called `LIMIT` you can use to limit your output to a defined range of records. For example, if you were to do a search such as:

```
SELECT * FROM web_sites LIMIT 0, 20
```

MySQL would perform the search and then, starting at the first record in the retrieved set, would return the next twenty records (actually nineteen plus the original one). Then, if you wanted to see the next twenty, you would enter another search:[1]

```
SELECT * FROM web_sites LIMIT 20, 20
```

which would start at the twenty-first record and output the next twenty.

## Setup

To make paging work, we need to use sessions to store parameters between pages, thereby allowing us to use them to redo the search with different LIMIT parameters and permitting us to page through large results sets. As we have seen with authentication, using sessions requires that the session variables be registered each time a page is loaded. To facilitate this, we add the following to the pub_sites.php file to register the variables (example 9-12).

Example 9-12

```
78  session_start();
79  session_register('dbquery');
80  session_register('result_num_rows');    // # of rows query retrieves
81  session_register('display_fields');     // list of fields to display
82  session_register('display_fields_num'); // number of fields to display
83  session_register('num_to_display');     // number of rows to display
84  $_SESSION["num_to_display"] = 10;       // Set # to display per screen
```

## Searching

Next, let's set up the search page. We begin by taking the query file (sites/site_query2.php) and saving it to a new name in a different directory (pub_sites/public_query.php). Next, we save the search file (sites/site_search2.php) in a similar way (as pub_sites/public_search.php). We then proceed to modify public_search.php to include the appropriate code (see example 9-8 for the following example references). After initializing the $SESSION["dbquery"] variable by setting it to "" to clean out any old query string that it may contain in line 44, we define the page that will handle paging through the results (pager.php) and define the base $fields, $tables, $link_str, and $where_str to be used in the search (lines 45–47).

Next, we store our values to the session variables that we will be using: line 63–64 of example 9-8 ($display_fields), line 65–66 ($display_fields_num). Then, as we can see in example 9-13, we define additional variables in line 153 ($dbquery) and line 167 ($result_num_rows) as well as localizing (making a superglobal value into a local value) $num_to_display (line 67 of example 9-8).

Example 9-13

```
152  $query = "SELECT DISTINCT $fields FROM $tables WHERE 1 $link_str $where_str ORDER BY siteno";
153  $_SESSION["dbquery"] = $query;
154  $records = Do_Search( $query );
155  $result_num_rows = count( $records );
156  /********************************************************************
157   * Next, we check to see if any records were returned by the query.  If not,
158   * the user is informed of that fact and the script exits.  If records are
159   * found, the number of records retrieved is displayed on the page and the
160   * records are output.
161   ********************************************************************/
162  if ( $result_num_rows == 0 ) {
163      echo "No Records Found";
164      exit;
165  } else {
166      echo "<center>Your query returned $result_num_rows records</center>";
167      $_SESSION["result_num_rows"] = $result_num_rows;
168  }
169
170  /********************************************************************
171   * Next, if we have retrieved more than $num_to_display number of records,
172   * we put in a navigational header.  The URL for each option invokes the
173   * pager.php file, passing it the option as a GET variable (type=<str>).
174   * When the user clicks on that link, pager.php will be invoked and it will
175   * use that parameter, along with the $_SESSION variables, to construct
176   * another query to retrieve $num_to_display records to display.
177   ********************************************************************/
178  if ( $result_num_rows >= $num_to_display ) {
179      echo "<center><a href=\"$pager?type=first\">First</a> | ";
180      echo "<a href=\"$pager?type=next&starting_record=0\">Next</a> | ";
181      echo "<a href=\"$pager?type=prev&starting_record=0\">Previous</a> | ";
182      echo "<a href=\"$pager?type=last\">Last</A></center><hr>";
183  }
```

Last, we create navigation links to place at the top of the page to allow us to look at different sets of the retrieved records (lines 178–183 of example 9-13). Because it doesn't make sense to page through results if we retrieve fewer records than our maximum-per-page number, we only put up the navigation links if the number of retrieved records is greater than our `$num_to_display` value (lines 178–183). Each of the lines invokes our `$pager` file (pager.php), passing it the parameter for **First**, **Next**, **Prev**, and **Last**. In the second and third instances, we also pass it the number the current search started at (initially 0). Those parameters are then used in pager.php to define which subset of records to retrieve. Thus, though public_search.php handles the initial search, any subsequent output will be handled by pager.php.

### Paging through the Results

In creating the paging script, we begin by taking the searching and outputting sections of public_search.php and saving them to a new file named pager.php. Then, at the top of the paging script, after creating the `$support_ary` array and localizing the session variables (storing them to local variables) to make them easier to use (lines 52–57 of example 9-14), we check to see with which record the users began the previous retrieval set and use that to define their next SQL query (lines 59–75). We then create our HTML page, using our updated starting numbers to redo the **First/Next/Previous/Last** navigation bar. We then do the search with our new parameters, using exactly the same code to output the results as was used in public_search.php.

Example 9-14

```
52  $num_to_display = $_SESSION["num_to_display"];
53  $result_num_rows = $_SESSION["result_num_rows"];
54  $display_fields = $_SESSION["display_fields"];
55  $display_fields_num = $_SESSION["display_fields_num"];
56  $dbquery = $_SESSION["dbquery"];
57  $pager = $_SESSION["pager"];
58
59  if ( $type == "first" ) {
60      $start = 0;
61  } elseif ( $type == "next" ) {
62      if ( ( $starting_record + $num_to_display ) >= $result_num_rows ) {
63          $start = $starting_record;
64      } else {
65          $start = $starting_record + $num_to_display;
66      }
67  } elseif ( $type == "prev" ) {
68      if ( $starting_record - $num_to_display < 0 ) {
69          $start = 0;
70      } else {
71          $start = $starting_record - $num_to_display;
72      }
73  } elseif ( $type == "last" ) {
74      $start = $result_num_rows - 1;
75  }
```

## AND'ing foreign keys

Until now, we have looked at using Boolean AND and OR between fields within a table and using OR between field value parameters in foreign key tables. However, there will be times that you will want to AND values that reside in the same many-to-many-related authority tables (such as being able to search for sites that use both Anthropology and Music as subjects). Although you could radically denormalize your database, store subjects as keywords in a keyword field in your main `sites` table, and then use keyword searching to retrieve them, this approach creates other problems, such as how you can maintain authority tables, enforce uniform entry of values, and create drop-down lists.

The problem is that the approach you think should work does not:

```
SELECT *

FROM sites, sites_subjects

WHERE sites.siteno=sites_subjects.ss_siteno

AND sites_subjects.ss_subjectno=3

AND sites_subjects.ss_subjectno=28
```

What this query is actually doing is requiring that the `sites_subjects` table have a single record where `ss_subjectno` is equal both to 3 and to 28 at the same time—something that obviously won't happen.

The solution is to create separate aliases (copies, if you will) of the linking table—one for each term to be searched—and then using those separate aliases in your WHERE statement. The result is that the following does work:

```
(1) SELECT sites.*
(2) FROM sites, sites_subjects AS s1, sites_subjects AS s2
(3) WHERE s1.ss_siteno=s2.ss_siteno
(4) AND sites.siteno=s1.ss_siteno
(5) AND s1.ss_subjectno=3 AND s2.ss_subjectno=28
```

Breaking this down, we can see how it is constructed:

*Line 1*—list of fields to retrieve

*Line 2*—using aliases (sites_subjects as S1, sites_subjects as S2) to create separate logical instances of the linking table—in this case the sites_subjects table—for each term to be searched

*Line 3*—make sure that all the aliases' primary key (in this case ss_siteno) field values are linked (equal to each other)

*Line 4*—make sure that one of them is equal to sites.siteno

*Line 5*—use a separate alias of sites_subjects for checking each foreign key (ss_subjectno) field value to see if it is equal to a value coming in from the searching form

If all of this is a little beyond what you want to deal with, don't worry. You can use the Process_Query_And_Array() function in the ala_functions.php library to do the job for you. Example 9-15 from public_search2.php shows one way to use it.

Example 9-15

```
92  if ( isset( $subjectno ) ) {
93    if ( isset( $Operator1 ) && $Operator1 == "AND" ) {
94      $tmp_ary = Process_Query_And_Array( "ss_subjectno", $subjectno, "sites_subjects",
95                                           "sites.siteno", "ss_siteno" );
96      if ( count( $tmp_ary ) != 0 ) {
97        $tables .= ",$tmp_ary[0]";       // define $tables the 0th (1st) element
98        $link_str .= " $tmp_ary[1] ";    // define $link_str w/2nd element
99        $where_ary[$x] = $tmp_ary[2];    // where string using the 3rd element
100       $x++;
101     }
102   } else {
103     $tmp_str = Process_Query_Array( "ss_subjectno",$subjectno );
104     if ( $tmp_str != "" ) {
105       $tables .= ",sites_subjects";
106       $link_str = " AND sites.siteno=sites_subjects.ss_siteno ";
107       $where_ary[$x] = $tmp_str;
108       $x++;
109     }
110   }
111 }
```

## Providing Links from Authority Entries

Before concluding, let me show you one more technique, which we can see at work in public_search2.php. It involves using values (in this case subject headings) to create links that we can then use to do another search. We do this by first adding two parameters to the call to `Output_Links()` on line 275 of example 9-16:

*Y* (to indicate we want to create links)

*public_search2.php* (the name of the file that will do the follow-up search).

Example 9-16
```
274    $subject_str = Output_Links( "subject", "subjects", "subjectno", "sites_subjects",
275                   "ss_subjectno", "ss_siteno", $siteno, "Y", "public_search2.php" );
276    echo "<tr><td align=\"right\" valign=\"top\"><b>Subject:</td><td>$subject_str</td></tr>";
277    echo "<tr><td><br></td></tr>";
```

Next, because the link created by `Output_Links()` creates a GET variable named $lookup_val, we place code at the top of public_search2.php, which will process the page if such a variable is passed to it. We see this done in lines 42–45 of example 9-17. If it does exist, we create a one-element array called $subjectno and save $_GET["lookup_val"] as that element. Otherwise, we save $_GET["subjectno"] to the $subjectno variable. By setting this variable, the search will be done just as if the value had come from public_query2.php.

Example 9-17
```
42    if ( isset( $_GET["lookup_val"] ) ) {
43        $subjectno = array( $_GET["lookup_val"] );
44    } else {
45        $subjectno = $_POST["subjectno"];
46    }
```

## Full Keyword Searching

Although fielded searching is something that most librarians take for granted, our users are more familiar with search engines like Google, AltaVista, and others where they simply put in keywords or phrases embedded within double quotes to do their searches. For such an approach to work in a fielded database, we need to be able to search through multiple fields at a time as well as being able to treat collections of words within double quotes as a single phrase and those that are not as simple keywords.

To address this need, we can use another function in the ala_functions.php library—`Process_Quoted_String()`, which also supports right-hand truncation. As with `Process_Query_Array()` earlier, we use this function to create WHERE elements that we can plug into a query. We can see a simple example of how it is used in example 9-18 where we pass it only two parameters: the name of the field to be searched and the variable containing the string to be processed (for an example of how it can be used to search multiple fields, see public_keyword_search.php).

Example 9-18

```
12   if ( $keywords != "" ) {
13       $tmp_str = Process_Quoted_String( "description,name", $keywords );
14       $where = " $tmp_str ";
15   } else {
16       echo "You need to enter a search";
17       exit;
18   }
```

Note that, due to the complexities involved in doing so, this function is not able to search values located in tables linked via many-to-many joins (in this case, either **subjects** or **content_types**). It does, however, provide the ability to search for terms within any field within a single table.

## PLACING YOUR APPLICATION IN PRODUCTION

Once the application has been written and tested, it's time for users to try it out. When presenting it, it is a good idea to walk them through the entire program, showing them how to use it and—in the case of searching scripts—what values they can use to search the database. Users should also be given a list of tasks for which the system was designed and then be left to work through each task in this list, looking for data entry or storage problems.

When users are happy with the application, it is time to move it into production. The process of moving an application into production involves a number of steps:

Use phpMyAdmin to execute a complete backup dump of the data structures and data, exporting the results to a file.

Clean up test data in the database.

Create a second database dump containing both structures and data.

Define a new production environment where the application will live and copy the complete source code tree from your development area to the new area. You may need to change internal paths, configuration information (such as logging directories and files), and other parameters so that the application will work in the new environment and will not conflict with the development version. If possible, set up the new production environment on a separate computer so that you can maintain the same database, configuration, and path information for each version of the database. (If you do not, moving new versions into production will be tricky and time consuming.)

Define a new database and use the second dump file to create and populate the tables.

Create or modify MySQL user accounts to allow access to the new database, adding this information to your configuration files, as needed.

Test the application fully, afterward deleting any test data that might have been added to the database and reloading the database.

Establish and implement a backup plan (if you have not already done so).

Continue to use the original area for development. If development will be substantial, create a third area for that development, maintaining this second area for bug fixes and minor feature enhancements.

Set up Web server authentication access control for your development area or areas. Then, if you want users to test the system, you can temporarily add them to the system and delete them when testing is over. Although the development area does not pose a security threat, placing password control on the area will keep users from mistakenly continuing to use it as a production area when testing has been completed.

Make appropriate links on your Web site to the new application.

## MAINTAINING AND UPGRADING YOUR APPLICATION

Once the program has been placed into production, your work doesn't end. Bugs will show up, features will need to be enhanced or added, and users' questions will need to be addressed. You need to make sure that you are set up to handle this type of maintenance. In addition to having separate support and production areas, there are several things you should do to make this process work properly.

First is to designate who will be responsible for maintenance. Make sure in doing so that you have adequately trained persons available (either on staff or outsourced) who will be able to support the application down the road, both in terms of programming and database maintenance.

Second is to develop processes for upgrading the application. Because users will find new features they would like included in the application, you need to have a process by which such upgrades can be suggested, evaluated, and implemented. This process will also need to include procedures—similar to those in chapter 6—in which functional requirements are established, data modeling done, and the application designed. Once the enhancements are agreed upon, you will need to implement them in your development area and fully test the resulting application.[2] As noted in chapter 6, because testing and debugging can be a time-consuming process, it is best to batch enhancement requests so that such activities can be done more efficiently.

Third is to document your application. This is a critical part of any development project—so important in fact that I devote much of the next chapter to it.

### Things to Watch Out For

It is important to understand that there are a number of things that can affect your application that have nothing to do with the code you have written. Changes in a number of things, including the php.ini file, Apache's configuration file, and the functions library can end up causing your application to crash. Although there is not enough time to get into all of them, there are a few rules of thumb you should consider:

> Be extremely careful of the changes you make in global function files, such as ala_functions.php. Changing how they work can introduce all sorts of hidden bugs into your apps. Think through all modifications you want to make to those files before making changes and test the resulting library with all applications that use the functions.

> Never make changes on the production version of the function library. Any syntax or other error you make there will cause every PHP application on your Web server to crash. A better idea is to edit it in the development environment, test all of your apps with the new set-up, and then propagate the changes into your production environment.

> Work with the server administrator—if you are not the one responsible for administering your Web server—so that no one changes basic configuration files without letting you know. Such changes might affect all PHP files throughout the system—something that .htaccess files can help address in multiuser systems, such as ISP-based situations.

## MOVING ON

We have now programmed our application, ensured data security, designed our user interfaces, completed testing, and placed the application in production. In the final chapter we will look at some practices and approaches that will make development easier and will help you avoid problems along the way.

### Notes

1. This is another example of how computers can do things in logical but counterintuitive ways. Humans begin counting with 1, computers with 0. Thus the fifth element in an array would be `$array[4]`.
2. This really does involve full testing. Given that parts of a program can interact in ways you may not expect (particularly if there are bugs in the code), you will need to test everything to make sure that they still function properly.

# 10 DEVELOPMENT PROCEDURES

In developing applications, you want to ensure that the process proceeds smoothly and efficiently, and that the application will be supported. We now discuss how best to do this.

## GENERAL PRACTICES

When undertaking any type of programming project, you want to follow certain practices while you're writing the code for your application. These are designed to standardize your approach, make code readable and—more important—supportable, and ensure proper functioning with a minimum of effort. They break down into the four areas: establishing a development process, implementing programming standards, establishing quality assurance procedures, and using good debugging techniques.

### Establishing a Process

It is important to define a development process to keep the project on track and to make things work as smoothly and as efficiently as possible. Although there are a number of ways you can do this, I suggest something along the following lines:

1. Define who is going to be given what tasks.
2. Build applications one step at a time.

3. Test and debug as you go—it is much easier to debug ten lines of code than two hundred and fifty.
4. Review code periodically, making sure that code is following programming standards (see below).
5. Check into CVS or other version control system periodically.[1]
6. Test the application fully using documentation developed in chapter 6.

## Implementing Standards

As with any area of automation, consistency and clarity in how programs are laid out makes them much easier to develop and support. Although it can be tempting to developers to throw themselves into the coding and not worry about being careless and/or cute in how they name things, the results of such development can be a trial to understand and to support. Above all, inconsistency in naming and practices requires developers to remember a lot more than they should need to (and more than people unfamiliar with the code will want to). Consistency, though boring, makes one's job much easier.

I provide, in appendix B, the standards I used in creating the applications and scripts in this book. Although some are somewhat arbitrary, the same is true of almost any standards one might create. What is important is that standards are consistent and make sense within the organization where they are adopted, not that they are an absolute truth.

## Quality Assurance

As you develop your application, submit each section to a quality-review process to make sure that it is being written correctly. Nothing is more unnerving to end-users than to have an application malfunction, leaving possibly their self-assurance (and certainly their confidence in the application) shaken. Taking the time to get it right the first time will make their (and certainly your) lives much easier.

There two things you can do to implement successful quality assurance procedures. First is to develop testing documents. Using the testing procedures we have talked about can be very valuable in finding errors. Second is to institute code reviews. In addition to debugging, reviewing code line-by-line can be extremely useful in producing quality applications. The ideal is to work with someone else—preferably an accomplished programmer—going through the programs and explaining what is (at least supposed to be) happening, what you are trying to do, and how you are doing it. Sometimes just having to explain the code line-by-line will reveal anomalies that you had not previously seen. Even doing this on your own can be a valuable exercise.

## Documentation

Following programming standards goes hand in hand with documenting the application. They're equally important. Documentation lets users know how to use the application and helps developers and support personnel know how to maintain it. Four levels should be developed: technical, code, user, and end-user help. We look at each one in turn.

### Technical

Technical documentation details how the application is laid out, how it works, and what each piece of the program does along with its relationship to other parts of the project. In large part, the documentation you developed in chapter 6 will provide the basis for this type of documentation. Other useful elements include

- a list of all files used in an application and their functions
- a road map of how the files interrelate
- annotated source code for all scripts
- fully documented function libraries, where appropriate
- testing documents and procedures

### Code

It is extremely important that your program code be documented to help programmers see more readily how the application works. Appendix B contains a description of the code annotation structures used in the book's applications. Programmers, being the creative people that they are, would far rather code something new than document code they've already written. This natural tendency needs to be overcome if you want supportable applications. Having a code review process in place can help provide the discipline needed to make this happen.

If developers comment the code as they go, the going is that much easier. Initially, preliminary comments at given points are generally adequate. As sections are completed, however (perhaps preparatory to a code review), developers should write concise yet complete comments. If changes are made to an application, existing comments in the code should be reexamined to make sure that they are still accurate. Nothing is more frustrating and counterproductive than comments that describe coding that is no longer in the program ("nothing is deader than yesterday's news").

## User

Particularly in more complex applications, users need to have support materials to help them to know what the application does, what the input fields mean and what they do, how to navigate the application, and how to know where certain tasks are accomplished. Having such documents available is critical to user training, particularly for staff who may not be familiar with the application.

One methodology is to take the roadmap created in the technical documentation above and proceed through the application, taking screen shots of each step. Then, for each screen shot, provide a description of each field, indicating what it does and what alternatives it provides. You can also indicate where alternate tasks are supported and where multiple branches can be taken, referring to the relevant screenshot at the appropriate point.

## Help Screens

Pairing written and online documentation is also useful. Given the hypertext basis of the Web, it is quite easy to provide context-sensitive help at any point in the program with hyperlinks embedded at appropriate places in the application pages.

## Debugging

No matter how good a programmer you are, you won't always get it right the first time. Things may not work as you expect; values don't get added to the database or, if they are, they are incorrect. A number of techniques that you can use with PHP and MySQL can help you track such problems down quickly.

For me, the most useful approach to debugging is to start at the beginning of the script and work your way through. The essential technique is to run a few lines of code, use `echo` to print out how things are doing, and immediately use `exit` to stop script processing. If everything is okay, you move the `echo/exit` pair down a little in the script to check things out. The moment you encounter something you don't expect, you know that the problem is between the place where you last got what you expected and the position where it failed. You want to be sure to check for several items:

> Is a loop being entered? Placing an `echo "HERE I AM"` may not be terribly exciting, but it does at least tell you if your loop is being entered. If it isn't, you need to check your conditions to make sure things are getting set as they should be, and that you don't have a typo or have misnamed a variable.

Are you not getting what you expect from an SQL query? Try either echoing it to the screen or using the `mysql_num_rows()` function to learn how many records are being returned by the query. If the number is 0, there aren't any matching records, meaning that you either need to add records or there is a mistake in your query.

Is an error message not appearing in the browser? Sometimes MySQL simply won't do this. One work-around technique I have found useful is to echo the `$query` to the screen and then to cut and paste it into phpMyAdmin's **SQL** box, and then to run it there.

Has a variable been set? Echoing a variable can also let you know whether it has been set. Using printable characters on either side of the variable is sometimes useful. For example, using the line `echo "*$var*";` will print out ** if the variable is empty.[2]

Are queries actually querying? One technique I have used throughout the examples in this book (and have included in the function library) has been to use `or die` (the `mysql_error()` function) each time I run a query. Doing so outputs the error the script gets from MySQL, prints it out on the screen, and then exits. This can be an extremely useful debugging technique.

## GETTING HELP

In the course of these ten chapters, we have taken a rather whirlwind tour of what is involved in creating database-backed Web applications. Space limitations in this book—or in any book—preclude it being a one-stop guide to a topic this complex and rich in possibilities. The good news is that there are many resources to draw on for your work. Consult first this book's website. In addition to downloadable files, you'll find a bibliography, answers to questions, and other resources. It will also have updated information on the book as well as on the sample applications and function library and their use.

Of particular use are those beloved Internet search engines with which we carry on such a love-hate relationship. Although I wouldn't want to base my scholarly research solely on them, they are a wonderful resource—particularly in this area. Chances are you aren't the first or even the hundredth person to encounter a difficulty. Because these tools are used by Web developers so regularly, someone is bound to have asked the question (or a similar one) and gotten more than one response. A keyword or keyphrase search in a search engine might just get you an answer, often within minutes.

## CONCLUSION

In this book, I have shared with you a number of ideas and techniques that I have found useful in putting databases up on the Web. Unfortunately, it is impossible to deal with all possible ways of doing things or every technique you might want to use. It is my hope that I have given you enough tools to get you started in this venture comfortably.

Good luck and happy coding!

### Notes

1. Although not necessary where there are only a few simple applications, version control systems can be very valuable where there are many complex programs being developed and supported.
2. Without the printable characters, it can be hard to know if the line is even being run.

# A

Appendix

## CREATING
## SHRIMP ÉTOUFFÉE

This appendix provides what the author thinks is a fairly good recipe for shrimp étouffée with the idea of using it to provide a full example of how easily such a recipe can translate into programming code.[1] The recipe is the result of combining various recipes along with some experimentation on the part of the author. The purpose is not to teach you how to cook well, just to understand programming (although I do happen to like this recipe). We will first write out the recipe in traditional style. We will then key each section to a graphic representation of the process below and then, using that structure, program the recipe.

### INGREDIENTS

| | |
|---|---|
| 4 tablespoons flour | 2 teaspoons salt |
| 6 tablespoons butter | 1 teaspoon white pepper |
| 5 cloves of minced garlic | 1 teaspoon black pepper |
| ½ cup chopped green onions | 1 teaspoon cayenne pepper |
| 2 cups chopped onions | ½ teaspoon oregano |
| 1 cup chopped celery | ½ teaspoon paprika |
| 1 cup chopped green pepper | 1½ teaspoons dried basil leaves |

225

| | |
|---|---|
| ¾ teaspoon dried thyme leaves | 2½ cups shrimp stock (see recipe below) |
| 1 bay leaf | |
| 1 cup tomatoes, peeled, seeded, and diced | 2 lbs. shrimp, peeled and deveined |
| | 6 cups cooked rice |

In a large saucepan, melt the butter and whisk in flour. Continue to cook until roux turns a rich brown color.

Add garlic and whisk for approximately 30 seconds and then add the onions, celery, green pepper, and spices, cooking until the vegetables are soft. Add stock and tomatoes, bringing mixture to a boil and then reducing heat to a simmer and stirring occasionally. Simmer for approximately 25 minutes.

Just before serving, add shrimp and green onions, cooking for about 2–3 minutes or until the shrimp turn a rich orange color.

Serve with rice.

### Shrimp Stock

| | |
|---|---|
| Shells from 2 lbs. shrimp | 2 stalks of celery |
| 1 large onion, cut into eight pieces | ½ lemon cut into four pieces |
| | Water to cover |

In a 4-quart saucepan, place the shells, onion, celery, and lemon pieces, covering with water. Bring to a boil, then lower heat. Simmer for approximately 2–3 hours, refilling water as necessary. Strain and throw away solids.

Makes 5–6 cups.

## "PROGRAM" STRUCTURE

Figure A-1 provides a graphic representation of the recipe as laid out above. Reading from left to right and top to bottom, you will see each of the steps we have defined to be part of the process of creating the finished product and to which we have therefore given a number. Those numbers designate the corresponding points in both the recipe and the program.

Now that we have taken a look at the real recipe and how it is structured, let's look at how this might be written in a very theoretical language—let's call it

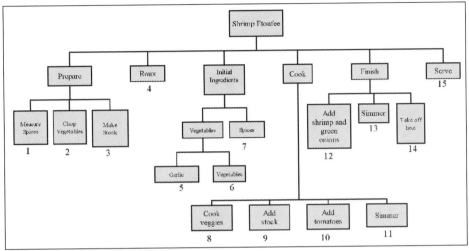

Figure A-1

WCL.[2] First of all, there are certain functions built into this language to get us started (language developers are very nice that way). Some functions from this language that we will be using include:

```
add_to_pan( $pan, $contents ) — take $contents and place them in $pan
strain_into_bowl( $pan, $contents, $bowl ) — take $contents from $pan and strain them into $bowl
heat_pan( $pan, $heat_source, $how_hot ) — heat $pan over $heat_source at $how_hot setting
observe( $pan, $parameter ) — look at contents in $pan to check the $parameter characteristic
simmer_contents( $pan ) — cook contents in $pan at reduced heat
stir_contents( $pan ) — stir the contents in $pan
remove( $pan, $heat_source ) — take $pan off of $heat_source
```

In addition to the functions that are built into the WCL language, we create three local functions (see bottom of program for function code):

```
make_roux( $pan, $fat, $thickener, $color ) — in $pan cook $thickener in $fat until $color color
make_stock( $meat, $veggies ) — make a stock using $meat and $veggies
peel_shrimp( $shrimp ) — peel $shrimp and separate into $shells and $meat
```

The code follows.

```
<?wcl
$pan = "Chef's Pan";
$heat_source = "Stove";
$how_hot = "High";
$bowl = "large mixing bowl";
```

```
$thickener = 4 * T( flour );
$fat = 6 * T( butter );
$color = "Rich Brown";
$rice = ( 6 * C( cooked white rice ) );


1
$garlic = 5 * cloves( garlic );
$garlic = minced( $garlic );
$shrimps = 6 * lb( shrimp );
$spices = array( ( 2 * t( salt ) ),
          ( 1 * t( White Pepper ) ),
          ( 1 * t( Black Pepper ) ),
          ( 1 * t( Cayenne Pepper ) ),
          ( .5 * t( Paprika ) ),
          ( .5 * t( Oregano ) ),
          ( 1.5 * t( basil leaves ) ),
          ( .75 * t( dried thyme ) ),
          ( 1 * ( bay leaf ) ) );


2
$veggies = array( ( 2 * C( chopped onion ) ),
          ( 1 * C( chopped celery ) ),
          ( 1 * C( chopped green pepper ) ) );
$tomatoes = 1 * C( tomatoes, peeled, seeded, and chopped );


3
$shrimps = peel_shrimp( $shrimps );
$stock_veggies = array( ( 1 * onion ), ( 2 * celery ), (1/2 * lemon ), ( water ) );
$stock = make_stock( $shrimps["shells"], $stock_veggies );


4
heat_pan( $pan, $heat_source, $how_hot );
$roux = make_roux( $pan, $fat, $thickener, $color );


5
add_to_pan( $pan, $garlic );
$seconds = 0;
while ( $seconds < 30 ) {
   stir_contents( $pan );
   $seconds++;
}


6
$veggie_count = count ( $veggies );
```

```
for ( $x=0; $x<$veggie_count, $x++ ) {
    add_to_pan( $pan, $veggies[$x] );
    stir_contents( $pan, "5 seconds" );
}


7
$spice_count = count( $spices );
for ( $x=0; $x<$spice_count, $x++ ) {
    add_to_pan( $pan, $spices[$x] );
    stir_contents( $pan );
}


8
$veggies_done = "False";
while ( !$veggies_done ) {
    stir_contents( $pan );
    wait( 10 );
    $done = observe( $pan, "consistency" );
    if ( $done == "soft" ) {
        $veggies_done = "True";
    }
}


9
$liquid = 2.5 * C( $stock );
add_to_pan( $pan, $liquid );


10
add_to_pan( $pan, $tomatoes ):


11
$boiling = "False";
while ( !$boiling ) {
    stir_contents( $pan );
    $is_boiling = observe( $pan, "temperature" );
    if ( $is_boiling == "True" ) {
        $boiling = "True";
    } else {
        wait( 60 );
    }
}
$how_hot = "Low";
heat_pan( $pan, $heat_source, $how_hot );
$time = 0;
```

```
while ( $time < 25 ) {³
    simmer_contents( $pan );
    if ( $time == 5 || $time == 10 || $time == 15 || $time == 20 || $time == 25 ) {
        stir_contents( $pan );
    }
    wait( 60 * seconds );
    $time++;
}


12
add_to_pan( $pan, $shrimps["meat"] );
add_to_pan( $pan, .5 * C( chopped green onions ) );


13
$time = 0;
while ( $time < 3 ) {
    stir_contents( $pan );
    wait( 30 * seconds );
}


14
remove_pan( $heat_source );


15
serve_contents( $pan, $rice );
// end make_etouffee.wcl


############################################################
# Below this line are the three local functions
############################################################
function peel_shrimp( $shrimps ) {
    foreach ( $shrimps ) {
        $shrimp = peeled( $shrimps );
        $shells .= $shrimp( "shell" );
        $meat .= $shrimp( "meat" );
    }
    $result = array( "meat"->$meat, "shells"->$shells );
    return( $result );
}
```

```
function make_stock ( $meat, $veggies ) {
    global $pan;
    global $how_hot;
    global $heat_source;
    add_to_pan( $pan, $meat );
    add_to_pan( $pan, $veggies );
    add_to_pan( $pan, $water );
    heat_pan( $pan, $heat_source, $how_hot );
    $time = 0;
    while ( $time < 180 ) {
        simmer_contents( $pan );
        wait( 1 );
        if ( $time == 30 || $time == 60 || $time == 90 || $time == 120 || $time == 150 ) {
            stir_contents( $pan );
        }
        $time = $time++;
    }
    $liquid = strain_into_bowl( $pan, $contents, $bowl );
    return( $liquid );
}

function make_roux( $pan, $fat, $thickener, $color ) {global $pan;
    add_to_pan( $pan, $fat );
    add_to_pan( $pan, $thickener );
    $roux = "not ready";
    while ( $roux != "ready" ) {
        stir_contents( $pan );
        $check = observe( $pan, "color" );
        if ( $check == $color ) {
            $roux = "ready";
        }
    }
    return( $roux );
}
?>
```

One further thing: please note certain characteristics about the way that this is coded. It is very important to observe these—or some kind of standardized—rules when programming. They make your programs easier to read and—more important—support. For an example set of standards, see appendix B.

### Notes

1. I am a Yankee, but earned a master's degree from LSU, where I became a Cajun-wannabe.
2. For Westman's Cooking Language, of course!
3. Note that, unless otherwise stated, the unit of time in this application is minutes, so this line reads "while time is less than 25 minutes."

# B PROGRAMMING STANDARDS

In developing standards for programming applications, no principle is more important than consistency. Developing a consistent approach to naming your databases, tables, fields, files, and variables as well as to how you lay out and name your programs can save you more time and frustration than you can possibly imagine. Rather than saying "what did I call that field?" and then having to go back to the database definitions to remind yourself, or having a query not work because you tried to retrieve the name field, rather than the Name field, having standards allows you to focus on what's really important: programming the application.

In this book I have developed, explained, and used a number of suggested standards that you may want to use in your programming. You may disagree with some—or even most—of the specifics, and you may or may not follow the suggestions. The important thing is to develop a consistent way of doing things.

## GENERAL OBSERVATIONS

Unless you have a sound reason for passing parameters via a URL, always use the POST method to pass values to action pages. Not only is it more secure, it also avoids limitations that some browsers have on the length of GET values they can handle. The one exception would be when passing parameters between query forms and searching action pages, where POST can require reloading the page when returning to it.

For security reasons, never rely on global variables. Always use superglobals (that is, $_GET, $_POST, and $_SESSION, and so on).

To make life easier, you can use the technique showed in example 5-20 in chapter 5 to localize $_POST variables. However, for security reasons you should not use this technique for any other type of superglobal array and always before starting any sessions.

Even if for some reason global variables are set to on, always reference any $_SESSION variable directly (for example, $_SESSION["admin"] rather than $admin). Use of the latter poses a significant security risk.

Use the shorter (and more current) form of the php superglobal arrays ($_GET, $_POST, $_SERVER, and $_SESSION) instead of the deprecated (no longer used) ones ($HTTP_GET_VARS, $HTTP_POST_VARS, and so on).

Maintain separate areas for production and production support code and databases. If you are doing serious development, create a third area (see chapter 9 for more information).

## NAMING

### General

Naming should make code self-documenting. Use names that are descriptive—that tell you what the thing is, or what is being done. For example, $number_rows rather than $no or Write_Log rather than Log. Do not make names too long—say, over twenty to twenty-five characters. Doing so makes them harder to type in and more prone to typos.

When using compound names, separate the words using the underscore (_) character (for example, $first_name) and never use a space in names. This makes them easier to read, particularly in dense program code.

Unless it makes the name too long, use full words, rather than an abbreviation (for example, $subject_row instead of $sub_row).

In general, standardize on lowercase names (with the exception of function names, for reasons to be explained below). Not only is this a standard practice in database programming, it alleviates potential problems with case sensitivity (something that can be an issue even for MySQL on the normally case-insensitive Windows platform).

Do not use reserved PHP or MySQL words (see the bibliography at this book's website for links to lists of reserved words).

## Databases, Tables, Fields

Make sure that each field name is unique within the database and application, not just the table.

Standardize on lowercase names.

In naming primary and foreign key pairs, use the full name of the concept that the key represents as a base and add a suffix to it in a consistent manner, usually including a code at the end to indicate the data type. For example, if the primary key of a `sites` table is `auto_increment`, then the name of the primary key should be concept followed by `no`. Those foreign key fields into which the primary key value to create the link is to be placed should use the primary key field name, prefixed by the name of the table in which the foreign key will be placed (adding an underscore to differentiate it from the primary key). Thus for the `supports` table, the primary key would be `supportsno` and foreign key would be `sites_supportsno`.

When names might be duplicated across different entities, prefix the field name with the name of the table (with a trailing underscore) to distinguish it (for example, `sites_format`).

## Functions

Devise a convention to differentiate local functions from PHP functions. In the case of the ala_function library, the first letter of each "word" in a function name is uppercase (all native PHP function names are all lowercase).

## Files

All file names should have a .php extension, including configuration and include files.

In naming authority tables, the name of the table should be the plural of the concept it represents (for example, format authority records go into the `formats` table).

In naming script files, use the basic format <view>_<task>.php where <view> is the name of the view whose data is being accessed or maintained and <task> is the task the particular script is to undertake (see chapter 6 for a discussion of how we mean views in this book). For example

*<view>_add.php*—name of the form used for inputting records

*<view>_insert.php*—name of action page that inserts the record into the database

*<view>_query.php*—name of file users can use to input search terms

*<view>_search.php*—name of the action page that takes the parameters from the query page, does the search, and then outputs the results, providing links to editing pages where needed

*<view>_get.php*—name of file used to select authority file record for editing

*<view>_edit.php*—name of file to which links in <view>_search.php point and that is used to edit records for this view

*<view>_update.php*—name of action page that updates the database

*<view>_delete.php*—name of action page that deletes a record and linked records

*<view>_<task>#.php*—if multiple versions, use canonic name followed by the script number (*site_add2.php*)

## Variables

Never reuse a variable name or one that has been used in a different context within the same application.

Use a consistent naming standard for variables in which you take the context or function of the variable (table name, task, concept) within the application as the base and add an underscore character followed by a standardized suffix that describes the type of value (string, array, date, number, and so on):

`$<prefix>_query`—variable for defining a query

`$<prefix>_result`—variable that will contain the result

`$<prefix>_records`—name of array in which the set of retrieved records will be stored

`$<prefix>_num_rows`—number of rows in the result query

$<prefix>_row—name of array into which individual records will be read as an associative array

$<prefix>_fields—fields to be used in this particular query

*Non-table-destined variable names:*

$<prefix>_ary—name of array to be used to store values

$<prefix>_str—name of string

$<prefix>_date—variable containing a date

$<prefix>_num—name of integer

*Other examples include:*

$tables—name for tables to be used

$fields—name of the field or fields to be included

$link_str—string that will contain the linking table information

$where_ary—array of WHERE conditions

$where_str—WHERE string for use in SQL statements

$order_by—field or fields by which to sort a query result

Use, when creating database maintenance forms, the name of the field into which a datum will be going (including case and agreement) in the name parameter in the adding/editing form. For example, if an input field is to go into the title field of a table, the inputting prompt should be: <input type="text" name="title">.

Always use associative arrays when working with values identifying names (such as database records) and named parameters (for example, $row ["title"]) rather than a numeric index (for example, $row[0]) to access values in the array.

## File Structure

Use a consistent file structure for all apps. The following provides the basic structure for the basic files mentioned above:

Always use <?php and ?> to define php blocks. Use of others, such as the ASP style (<% and %>) can cause problems, particularly in XML processing.

All HTML tags should be lowercase.

Define constants (rather than using literals in the code) at the top of the file or in the configuration file wherever possible. For example, if you want to put the Webmaster's name or e-mail address on every page, define a variable in your configuration file called `$webmaster` and assign it the Webmaster's name as its value. Then, any time you want to echo it, you just use the command `echo  $webmaster`. Doing this allows for easy changes should they need to be made.

Each time there are conditional blocks, the body of the loop should be indented one stop (that is, three spaces). The opening curly brace should come at the end of the conditional line and the closing brace should be in the same column as the first character of the opening conditional statement. For example:

```
3    if ( $a == 0 ) {
4        $b = 3;
5    }
```

If there are conditional blocks within conditional blocks, each embedded block should be indented one stop further. When setting indentation, use a setting of three spaces per level—two not being visually clear and more than three placing deeper levels of indent too far to the right. For example:

```
7    while ( $row = mysql_fetch_array( $result ) ) {
8        $name = $row["name"];
9        $department = $row["department"];
10       if ( $department == "Music" ) {
11           if ( $name == "Mahler" ) {
12               echo "Gustav is here";
13           }
14       }
15   }
```

If possible, use spaces rather than tabs (using tabs puts you at the mercy of text editors with larger tabs stops—particularly a problem with code featuring several levels of indentation). Note that though NoteTab Light uses a <tab> character, NoteTab Pro allows you the option of putting in fixed tabs, which insert the designated number of spaces.

To help ensure proper programming of blocks, you should create the closing curly brace when you open the block by typing in the opening curly brace, leaving at least one blank line between the two of them into which to write the code. This practice should be followed even if there is only one statement in a loop because there may be more down the line and placing the braces there now makes it more readable.

Separate sections of code by one blank line and place comment immediately before the new code.

Wherever a value is placed within parentheses (conditional loops, function calls, and so on), a single space should follow the opening parenthesis and another immediately precede the closing parenthesis. If there are multiple values within the parentheses, they should also have a space before them. This will make your code more readable. For example:

```
18  if ( $a == 0 ) {
19
20  }
21
22  Display_Text( $var1, $var2 );
```

There should be a space before and after all operators (=, !=, ==, ||, &&, and so forth). For example, $a = 2, not $a=2. One exception to this rule concerns those cases, such as for() loops, where adding a space would decrease legibility:

```
1  for ( $x=0; $x<$y; $x++ ) {
2          NOT
3  for ( $x = 0; $x < $y; $x++ ) {
```

## SQL Queries

Use all capital letters for SQL keywords (for example, SELECT title,name FROM books WHERE author='Dickens').

Always write your query to a variable and then use the variable when calling the mysql_query() or Do_Search() functions. This allows you to echo the query for debugging purposes, if needed.

Always surround the values you pass to the database with single quotes.

## Development Process

As noted, whenever you begin a conditional block (if, while, for, and so forth), close the block by entering the } before entering any code within the block.

Use view grids to test each application as you go.

When programming insert/update action pages, begin with filling in all of the fields in the inputting form and setting `prod=N` in the action page, making sure that all fields are filled in with the proper values before setting it to `Y`.

Always include a logging function that saves all database-changing queries to a text file that can be used to restore in case of database problems. (Although MySQL does provide a way to do this, its approach is to save all queries from all databases into a single file.)

If a section of code is used more than once, rather than typing it in again, consider moving it to a function that can be called repeatedly.

## Functions

In creating functions, be consistent with the order of parameters passed to the function (that they are sent in the same order that they will be received).

If writing similar functions, make sure that each type of parameter (for example, fields, table, and so on) is in the same order from function to function.

Always place mandatory parameters first.

If optional, give a default value so that, if there is no value passed from the form, the function will still work. If a default value is something other than a blank string, you need to set it using `_Set_Default_Value()` or some other method to ensure a value is set.

You do not need to insert a parameter for an optional value into the function call. However, if you want to pass an optional value, make sure that you insert a placeholder for any optional parameter up to the optional parameter you are changing.

## Commenting Code

All code should be commented:

Before annotating, always eliminate old debug statements or other nonfunctioning code. This will make the code much easier to read and support.

Indent comments to same column as the code the comment describes.

When a comment takes up more than one line, create a hanging indent by placing the second and subsequent lines one stop further to the right.

Differentiate style of comments:

- File
- Division
- Function
- Individual line—place at end of line, separating from code by //

Types of comments

- Function library file header:

```
 2  ####################################################################
 3  # File name: ala_functions.php
 4  # Purpose: library of basic functions that are to be used in developing
 5  #    MySQL/php/Apache database-backed applications.
 6  #
 7  # Functions in this library
 8  #     HTML Inputting - Single Values
 9  #         TextBox - inputting single lines of text
10  #         PassBox - for password and where user input should be masked
11  #
12  # ...
13  #
14  # Revision History:
15  #
16  # 4/29/2005 by SRW
17  #   Changes made:
18  #       Documented Checkbox function
19  #
20  ####################################################################
```

- Function header at the beginning of each function:

```
 8  ####################################################################
 9  # Function name: TextBox
10  # Purpose: Create a text inputting box (single line)
11  #
12  # Parameters:
13  #     $name - "name" parameter from form into which user input is stored
14  #     $size - size (in number of characters) of input box (default=20)
15  #     $maxlength - maximum number of characters that can be input (if greater
16  #         than $size, the user will have a moving window of $size number of
17  #         charaters (default=20)
18  #     $default_val - default value of field (used in editing).  Default is
19  #         a blank string
20  #
21  # Outputs:
22  #     HTML text box
23  #
24  # ALA functions called:
25  #     None
26  #
27  # php functions called:
28  #     htmlspecialchars - encode variable for HTTP transmission
29  #
30  # Called By:
31  #     HTML Forms
32  #
33  # Revision History:
34  #
35  # 9/1/2004 by SRW
36  #   Changes made:
37  #       Documented
38  #
39  ####################################################################
```

- Block comments (inside a function or program)

  Use ##### type blocks for major sections, /* */ for subsections:

```
15  ####################################################################
16  # 2. Create and send a query to the database, localizing the 4 values,
17  #    coming in from the query form. However, rather than doing each
18  #    one individually, we use php's list() function to turn the
19  #    $_POST superglobal into an array, saving the field name to $key
20  #    and the value to $value. Note the use of $($key). This is a php
21  #    trick that takes a string and creates a variable with that string's
22  #    name.
23  ####################################################################
24  while ( list( $key, $value ) = each( $_POST ) ) {
25      $($key)=$value;
26  }
27
28  /*******************************************************************
29   * Next, we go through each field coming in from the form.
30   *******************************************************************/
31  if ( trim( $Field1 ) != "" && trim( $Value1 ) != "" ) {
32      if ( $Field1 == "location" ) {
33          $temp_where_str = " MATCH (location) AGAINST ('+$Value1' in BOOLEAN MODE) ";
34      } else {
35          $temp_where_str = " $Field1 = '$Value1' ";
36      }
37  } else {
38      echo "Please enter a query";
39      exit;
40  }
```

Indent comment to the same level as the code:

```
260     /**********************************************************
261      * After initializing $html (above) and for each row retrieved by $query,
262      * we define $display_name (the field value that will be displayed in the
263      * select list output). If $field_num equals 1 (i.e. if only one field is
264      * being searched), that means that the code and display name are the
265      * same field and make $display_name equal to $row[0]). Otherwise, make
266      * $display_name equal to $row[1].
267      **********************************************************/
268     for ( $a=0; $a<$num_rows; $a++ ) {
269         $row = $records[$a];
270         $code = htmlspecialchars( $row[0] );    // give $code first array value
271         if ( $field_num == 1 ) {                // is this the first field?
272             $display_name = $row[0];            // then make $code display value
273         } else {                                // otherwise, there are two
274             $display_name = $row[1];            // thus item 2 is display value
275         }
276
277         /**********************************************************
278          * Check to see if $display_name is the same as the value passed to
279          * this function. If it is not ( $row[0] != $default_value ), then it
280          * outputs the value as an <option></option> line. If it is, the
281          * $default_code and $display_default_value are set (and will be
282          * output later.
283          **********************************************************/
284         if ( $display_name != $default_value ) {
285             if ( $row[0] != $default_value ) {
286                 $html .= "<option value=\"$code\">$display_name</option>\n";
287             } else {
288                 $default_code = $row[0];
289                 $display_default_value = $row[1];
290                 $f_key_found = 1;
291             }
```

- File header:

```
1  ###########################################################################
2  # File Name: subject_add.php
3  # Author: Stephen R. Westman
4  # View: Subjects
5  # Version: 1.0
6  # Creation date: 4/30/2004
7  #
8  # Task(s) Performed:
9  #    Creates inputting form for Subjects view
10 #
11 # Scripts called by:
12 #    None
13 #
14 # Scripts this file calls:
15 #    subject_insert.php
16 #
17 # Functions used:
18 #    None
19 #
20 # Session variables:
21 #    None
22 #
23 # Special techniques:
24 #    None
25 #
26 # Revision History
27 #
28 # 4/30/2004 by SRW
29 #  Changes made:
30 #    Created
31 #
32 ###########################################################################
```

- Inline comments—used for defining a particular line:

```
114 $page=$_SERVER["PHP_SELF"];          // Name of page loading the prepend file
115 $pos = strpos($page,"login.php");    // Check to see if page is login.php.  If so, skip
116 if ( $pos == 0 ) {                   // to avoid an infinte loop
117    if ( $_SESSION["authenticated"] != "true" ) {
118       header("Location: login.php?page=$page");
119    }
120 }
```

# Glossary

**\*nix**   shorthand way of saying Linux and various flavors of Unix, such as Solaris, HP-Unix, and AIX.

**action page**   a page that takes input, either passed to it from a form or URL or embedded in the page itself, and then acts on that input (performs a search, adds/updates a record, and the like).

**administration**   *See* database administration.

**Apache**   an open source Web server and the most popular Web server software currently available on the Internet (see http://httpd.apache.org/ABOUT_APACHE.html for more information).

**Apache module**   modules that can be built into an Apache Web server that then become integral to it. Several act as application servers, allowing developers to build HTML pages where programming instructions are included in specially marked sections of the page, and then executed by the module, with the results embedded in the HTML page and returned to the user. Scripts that use modules are much easier to code than CGI programs and run much faster. *See also* CGI.

**API**   *See* Application Program Interface.

**Application Program Interface (API)**   a set of hooks (routines) built into applications that programmers can use to write external programs that access that application. APIs provide an easy way for outside programs to send information or requests to the application and/or to access information from inside the application.

**arbitrary key**   a primary key of a table that does not reflect any content within the record in which it is contained, usually automatically assigned as a number by the computer (for example, the bibliographic record number in online catalog records). *See also* auto_increment, descriptive key.

**arrays**   a set of variables grouped based on a common characteristic or use. Whereas many programming languages require that arrays contain data of the same data type (integer, character, and so on), PHP does not. Individual items within the array are called elements and are accessed using an index, the element's "address" within the array. Indices may either be numeric (position within the array) or descriptive (associative arrays). Although some languages, such as Perl, use a different symbol to create an array, PHP uses the $ as the prefix as it does for variables. *See also* associative array; element.

**associative array**   in PHP, an array in which the individual elements within the array have a name associated with them (as an index) rather than a number indicating the element's position in the array. Associative arrays can be very useful, particularly in outputting database searches where you can use the field name to access the value for that field. For example, if we have a variable $record that contains a bibliographic record, we could access the title by looking at $record["title"] rather than having to know the number of the element within the array that has that value. *See also* arrays; index (arrays).

**authentication**   making sure that a user is who the user claims to be. Normally done through login screens that check username and password against a database containing authorized users of a system. *See also* authorization.

**authority table**   table that contains the "authorized form of entry" for a given term, concept, or person and is used to create links to other records (by placing its primary key in the appropriate foreign key field). In the Web environment, this can be achieved by creating drop-down lists, checkboxes, or radio buttons containing the authority table's primary key as the value of the inputting element, which is then sent to the action page when the form is submitted.

**authorization**   process in which an authenticated user is given rights to do the requested action. See chapter 8 for a discussion. *See also* authentication.

**auto_increment**   a technique used by MySQL that automatically assigns the next available number (from an internally maintained ordered sequence of numbers) to serve as the primary key field of a record.

**binary distribution**   a software package in which the source code has already been compiled (transformed from human-readable code to code that the computer can understand and process) for a particular platform. Although this is the more familiar way for Windows users to obtain a program, open source products often come with source code only, so that the user can, if desired, make changes to the code or to the base configuration and then compile it. *See also* RPM.

**case sensitivity**   whether a difference in the capitalization of characters within a word or phrase has an effect on the processing of that data (for example, eXist, an open source XML database, is not the same thing as exist, a state of being). A case insensitive search for eXist would retrieve records with both forms, but a case sensitive search should bring back only records about the database. By default, MySQL searching is case insensitive. *See also* SELECT... WHERE BINARY.

**CGI (Common Gateway Interface)** a protocol built into Internet Web servers by which requests can be passed from the Web server to an external program that is in turn run by the host operating system and the results returned to the Web server. Unlike Web server–based scripting, CGI scripts run outside the control of the server. The server merely passes data to the external program and then takes the output of that program and passes it back to the user. Because an external process is called, CGI tends to be significantly slower than Web server–based scripting alternatives to it. Although PHP can be used as a CGI language, the most commonly used language for CGI programs is Perl. *See also* Apache modules, Web server–based scripting.

**comma-parsed string** a single string enclosed in double quotation marks and containing a number of data elements with commas between them (for example, `"author,title,copyright"`). *See also* comma-separated values.

**comma-separated values (CSV)** a format used by applications for transferring data from one program to another or to create an array of values within an application. It usually puts quotation marks around each data element and places a comma between the values (for example, `"name"`, `"address"`, `"phone"`). This is in contrast to a comma-parsed string, in which a list of elements are separated by commas and encased in a single set of double quotation marks (`"name,address,phone"`). *See also* comma-parsed string, delimited text files.

**concatenate** to append a number of different elements to each other to create a single entity. An example of concatenation, using the PHP concatenation operator ('.'), is the following statement:

```
$person = "John";
$phrase = "Hello, " . "World." . " This is " . $person;
results in $phrase having the value "Hello, World. This is
    John".
```

**CPAN (Comprehensive Perl Archive Network)** a large repository of Perl modules that users can download and use in their own applications. A similar initiative—PEAR—is being undertaken for PHP. *See also* PEAR.

**CSV** *See* comma-separated values.

**data modeling** the process of taking all of the pieces of information to be included in a database and creating a map of where each item should be placed. The goal is to optimize efficiency of storage and retrieval of the data. *See also* database design.

**data record** record containing the data for a given set of transactions. Other types of records include authority records and linking records. *See also* authority table, linking table.

**data structures** ways in which data is structured. In the case of RDBMS databases, this can include both the logical elements (tables, fields, and so on) and the ways in which those elements were set up to support the application (indexes, foreign key constraints, and so on).

**database** the basic container where data is stored in a database management system. *See also* relational database management systems.

**database administration** a set of tasks that must be undertaken to ensure that the database continues to work efficiently and correctly. These tasks include doing backups, creating databases and implementing data models, building indexes, maintaining data and database security, and ensuring referential integrity in all database applications. See chapter 2 for more details.

**database design** the process of taking a data model and creating the database to implement that model. *See also* data modeling.

**delimited text files** text files that contain values with each value being separated from the other by a delimiter or special character. For example:

```
Dickens|Charles|Tale of Two Cities
Kazantzakis|Nikos|Report to Greco
```

*See also* delimiter, comma-separated values.

**delimiter** character within a delimited file that separates one piece of information (field) from another within a given line (record). To avoid confusing the computer, the delimiter character must not be used anywhere within the data to be stored in the file. One good character to use is the pipe symbol (|) because that value is rarely found in data fields. *See also* pipe.

**descriptive key** a value, based on the content of the record, used as the primary key for a table. Although using a descriptive key does make it much easier for humans to follow relationships when looking at the data in the database, it can create problems should the values within the record change. If you change the key to keep the key descriptive of the record's contents, you have to ensure that all foreign keys linked to the primary key are changed appropriately as well. *See also* arbitrary key, foreign key constraint, primary key.

**dynamic pages**    Web pages created when the page is accessed, usually by a database query that retrieves and presents information. *See also* static pages.

**element (arrays)**   an individual entity, similar to a field, within an array where values are stored.

**entity**   a unique concept or subject to be stored in a database. In relational databases, individual entities are usually represented by individual tables.

**error handler**   programming routines or code called in the event of a problem in application execution.

**field**   structure within a record to store specific pieces of information on the entity being described in a record. *See also* record, table.

**file type**   physical format of the digital file in which database data is stored. Although MySQL includes support for several types, we discuss only two in this book—MyISAM (MySQL default) and InnoDB (supports more advanced database techniques).

**foreign key**   value within records that points back to a primary key to create a link between the two records. Unlike primary keys, which must be unique, foreign keys values may appear multiple times within a table. *See also* arbitrary key, descriptive key, foreign key, foreign key constraints, key.

**foreign key constraint**   feature built into RDBMS products that enforces relational integrity between primary and foreign keys. Setting a constraint between a primary and a secondary key ensures that

> no foreign key field will have a value not already in the primary key field

> if the primary key field is changed or deleted, certain actions will be taken on the foreign key—such as automatically making the same changes in the foreign key fields

See chapter 2 for more information. *See also* foreign key, primary key, relational integrity.

**function**   individual section of programming code, usually designed to do one task, set apart so that it can then be called by other routines to perform that task. *See also* function library.

**function library**   files in which a number of functions have been grouped to make them easier to manage. *See also* function.

**GNU**   a recursive acronym for "GNUs Not UNIX," the GNU project started in 1984 with the goal of developing a free and complete UNIX-style operating system. GNU software is a major part of the Linux operating system.

**Graphical User Interface (GUI)**   a program interface based on graphical elements and pointing devices, rather than keystrokes, to make programs easier to use. Windows and Web browsers are two examples.

**GUI**   *See* Graphical User Interface.

**handle**   in PHP, a particular type of variable to which a database connection is assigned so that it can then be used by an application to send data to, and receive data from, that database. Although an application may have multiple handles, each handle can access only one database at a time. For example:

```
                          handle

($db)= mysql_connect( "localhost", "Phones", "Fone_Usr" );
mysql_select_db( "web_info", ($db));
$query = "SELECT * FROM phones ORDER BY last_name,first_name";
$result = mysql_query( $query, ($db)) or die( mysql_error() );
```

**increment**   increase a value by one. Useful in programming blocks to know how many times the block has executed.

**index (arrays)**   the address of a particular value within an array. The most common types of indices are numeric and associative. *See also* arrays, associative arrays, elements.

**index (databases)**   files used to quickly find and access records containing requested values within a database.

**InnoDB**   table type, created by Innobase Öy, used by MySQL to implement record-level locking as well as transaction and foreign key integrity support. *See also* table type, MyISAM.

**joins**   technique used in SQL queries to link tables, based on their primary-foreign key relationships, to access information in a relational database.

**key**   a field within a record that contains information linking it to records in other tables within the database. Keys can either be primary or foreign. *See also* primary key, foreign key, setting a relation, foreign key constraint.

**LAMP**   acronym for the very popular combination of open source tools: Linux, Apache, MySQL, and PHP. *See also* WAMP.

**legacy system**   system, usually long-standing, containing data of current, historical, or archival importance to an organization.

**linking**   *See* setting a relation.

**linking table**   tables used to relate one or more records in one table to one or more records in a second table. This is achieved by creating a table with two foreign key fields: one to contain the foreign key for each of the two records from the tables to be linked. There may be situations, such as in circulation systems, in which linking tables can also be a data table (such as checkout records that contain due dates). See chapter 2 for more details.

**localhost**    name for the loopback interface on a computer (IP address 127.0.0.1) that exists so that a computer can talk to itself. An Internet connection is not needed for this address to work.

**localizing**    taking a value from a superglobal and making it into a local variable for use. *See also* superglobals.

**locking**    temporarily restricting access to specific database resources. This may either be a WRITE lock (in which users can neither read a record or table nor write to it while the lock is in place) or a READ lock (in which everyone can read but no one can write to the resource). Most modern RDBMSs (including MySQL, if one uses InnoDB tables) support locking at the record level.

**logging**    writing computer activities—such as database interactions—to a file. Logs can be used for debugging as well as for restoring a system.

**lookup table**    *See* authority table.

**maintaining state**    the ability to remember a user from one Web interaction to the next. Because the Web is "stateless" (once a Web server is through with a task, it closes the connection and has no way of remembering anything about that task), some technique is needed to allow the server to have a way to recall things about the user from transaction to transaction. Techniques that implement this capability are said to be maintaining state.

**many-to-many relationship**    multiple records in one table are related to multiple records in another table by a linking table. See chapter 2 for more information. *See also* relations, one-to-one relationship, one-to-many relationship, linking table.

**MyISAM**    MySQL's version of Indexed Sequential Access Method (ISAM) files, which defines how database information is stored on disk and then accessed. Although the data is stored sequentially, its use of integral indexes allows for quick retrieval of information. It also allows for the creation of FULLTEXT indexes to support keyword searching.

**MySQL**    an open source relational database management system (see http://www.mysql.com/ for more information).

**normalization**    the processes involved in removing data redundancy (unnecessary data duplication); standardizing format, spelling, and case of data entered into the database; and ensuring efficient storage and use of the database. When dealing with individual data elements, it includes the process—similar to authority control in libraries—of taking variant forms of a value and mapping them to a single authorized form of the value.

**object**    within the context of object-oriented programming, an object is programming code that is self-contained and includes both data and code used in processing that data.

**object-oriented programming**    type of programming that combines data structures with programming code to create self-contained and reusable objects. This allows for the development of modules that do not need to be changed if one wants to do something slightly different. Instead, the developer creates an offspring module that can inherit features (methods, data, and so on) from the parent module, changing only those aspects that differ. *See also* procedural programming, object.

**ODBC (Open Database Connectivity)**    a protocol, developed in 1992 by Microsoft, based on recommendations from the SQL Access Group, that allows retrieval of data from any compliant database management system using a standardized command set. ODBC utilizes an intermediate entity (driver) between an application and the database system that translates the application's data queries into commands that the system understands and then returns the results back to the calling application.

**offload**    to download or extract data from a system, often for use in another system.

**one-to-many relationship**    one record in one table is linked to multiple records in another table by a primary key placed in those records' foreign key field. See chapter 2 for more details. *See also* relations, one-to-one relationship, many-to-many relationship.

**one-to-one relationship**    where one record in one table is linked to only one record in another table. See chapter 2 for more information. *See also* relations, one-to-many relationship, many-to-many relationship.

**Open Database Connectivity**    See ODBC.

**open source**    a new paradigm of software development that is community-based, rather than a product of a single—usually commercial—company. In open source projects, users of the software (along with other interested parties) are free to contribute to software development.

**operator precedence**    in a Boolean context, which operator (AND, OR, NOT) should be invoked first. The issue is one of meaning. For example, does "This summer, I'm going to Paris AND London OR Vienna" mean "I'm going to Paris and London or I'm going to Vienna" or "I'm going to Paris and then I'm either going to London or to Vienna"? If AND has precedence, then the statement has the first meaning; if OR, then the second one is true.

**parameter**   a value that gets passed to a function as a part the call to that function. The function then uses the parameter to do its assigned task. There may be multiple parameters in a single function call.

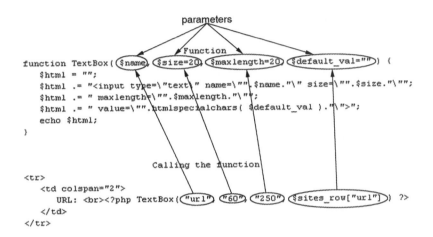

**PEAR (PHP Extension and Application Repository)**   a repository—similar to CPAN—for PHP code. *See also* CPAN.

**personal bibliography software**   software, such as EndNote and ProCite, that enables the user to create bibliographies of books, articles, and so on.

**personal information managers**   software that enables users to enter a wide variety of types of information—usually in an unstructured format (that is, no tables, fields, and so on)—and that then allows for searching and retrieval of that information.

**PHP**   an open source Web programming language that can be used both as an Apache module and via CGI (see http://www.php.net for more information).

**pipe**   the | character. Often used as a delimiter because it is rarely found in data to be included in delimited files. *See also* delimited text files, delimiter, pipe-delimited file.

**pipe-delimited file**   a delimited text file that uses the pipe symbol (|) as the delimiter. *See also* comma-parsed file, comma-separated file, delimited text file, delimiter, pipe.

**primary key**   field within a record that uniquely identifies a record within the table and is used as a foreign key in other tables to link back to that record. *See also* foreign key.

**procedural programming**   a more-or-less linear approach to programming—as described in this book—in which you essentially provide step-by-step instructions to the computer in the order you want them processed. *See also* object-oriented programming.

**programming language**   language used to write commands to tell computers what to do. Although programmers write using relatively recognizable words, for the computer to understand them, they need to be put in machine language. This can be done either by compiling it (as in C) or interpreting it (as in Perl and PHP).

**query**   command sent to a database system, telling it to do something, such as add, update, or delete records or to retrieve records matching certain criteria.

**RDBMS**   *See* Relational Database Management System.

**record**   the structure within tables containing descriptions of individual instances of the entity that the table represents. Individual elements of those entities are stored in fields. *See also* field, table.

**referential integrity**   process by which the links between primary keys and foreign keys are maintained properly. *See also* setting a relation, primary key, foreign key.

**regular expression**   a sophisticated programming technique that permits matching and/or changing strings within other strings using certain parameters.

**Relational Database Management System**   a system that incorporates relational databases; SQL support for database querying, maintenance, and administration; user and data access security; and other techniques to support the creation of sophisticated database-based applications. *See also* relational database.

**relational database**   a database in which tables are linked via setting relations using primary key and foreign key pairs. *See also* primary key, foreign key, Relational Database Management System, setting a relation.

**reserved variables**   the official PHP term for superglobals. *See also* superglobals.

**reserved words**   in databases or programming languages, certain words that have a specific use in the application which, if they are used by the user for other purposes, can create confusion within the application. See the online bibliography for sites containing lists of MySQL and PHP reserved words.

**return value**   value returned by a function after it has done its work. You capture this value by calling the function and assigning the return value to a variable. For example:

```
                        Function
function Auth_Vals( $p_key, $display_name, $table ) {
    $vals_query = "SELECT $p_key,$display_name FROM $table";
    $records = _Execute_Query( $vals_query, "S" );
    $num_rows = count( $records );
    for ( $a=0; $a<$num_rows; $a++ ) {
        $vals_row = $records[$a];
        $return_pkey = $vals_row[$p_key];
        $return_value = $vals_row[$display_name];
        $return_array[$return_pkey] = $return_value;
    }
    return $return_array
}

           return value

                        Calling the function
$subj_name_ary = Auth_Vals( "subjectno", "subject", "subjects" );
```

**RPM**   a type of package, usually for the Linux platform, that is ready to be installed directly into the system. RPM packages can come compiled or as source code. *See also* binary distribution.

**scalability**   ability to meet present needs as well as to support demands that might be placed in the future.

**SELECT... WHERE BINARY**   MySQL method for a case-sensitive search. For example, to search for eXist but not exist, you would enter:

```
SELECT * FROM <table> WHERE BINARY <field> LIKE 'eXist';
```

**setting a relation**   the process of using a shared value, placed in primary and secondary key fields in two tables, to link two records. *See also* relations.

**SQL**   *See* Structured Query Language.

**static pages**   traditional Web page content that is changed manually rather than by server programming. *See also* dynamic pages.

**stored procedure**   function or element of user-created code stored inside a database that can be run by the RDBMS for certain tasks. *See also* trigger.

**string**   an entity containing a contiguous collection of characters (including spaces).

**Structured Query Language**   standardized language for interacting with relational database management systems. *See* Relational Database Management Systems.

**superglobals**   associative arrays, built into PHP, used to pass information between pages. The most important ones are

$_POST—contains the name/value pairs in a POST transaction

$_GET—contains GET name/value pairs

$_SESSION—contains session variables, linked to a particular session ID

$_SERVER—holds the information about the server and/or server environment variables such as HTTP_REFERRER, REMOTE_HOST, and so forth

**table**   the group unit within databases in which data is stored. Within tables, data are stored in records. Information within a record is broken into fields. *See also* field, setting a relation, entity, record.

**trigger**   a stored procedure that is executed when certain conditions within the RDBMS system are met. *See also* stored procedure.

**variable**   a symbolic container that stores a value that the computer can process. Programming languages differ in how variables are named. PHP requires that all variables are preceded by the $ character (for example, $name).

**WAMP**   acronym for popular combination of tools for database-backed Web development: Windows, Apache, MySQL, and PHP. *See also* LAMP.

**Web server–based scripting**   technique by which HTML pages can contain programming code that can be run by a module and the results output as part of the page. This differs from CGI scripts in that the processing is done by modules built into Web servers rather than passing the request to an external process. Server-based scripting runs more quickly and makes development much quicker and less error-prone. PHP as used in this book is an example. *See also* Apache modules.

**Web-aware**   a database has an API or other techniques that allow Web-based programs to be written to dynamically access data contained in the database.

# Index